Post-structuralism and the question of history

Post-structuralism and the question of history

EDITED BY
Derek Attridge, Geoff Bennington
and Robert Young

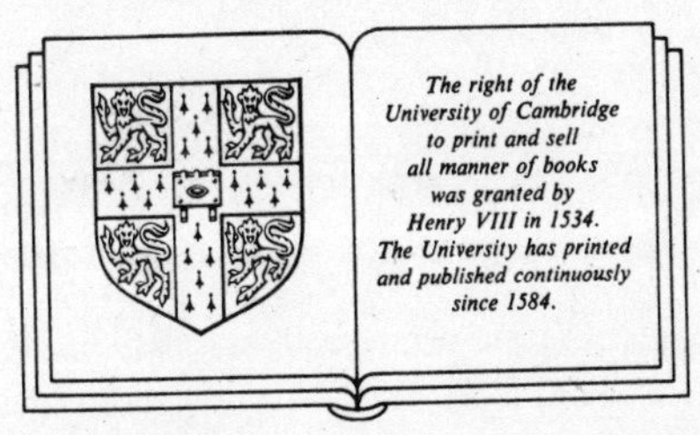

Cambridge University Press

CAMBRIDGE
NEW YORK PORT CHESTER
MELBOURNE SYDNEY

Published by the Press Syndicate of the University of Cambridge
The Pitt Building, Trumpington Street, Cambridge CB2 1RP
32 East 57th Street, New York, NY 10022, USA
10 Stamford Road, Oakleigh, Melbourne 3166, Australia

First published 1987
First paperback edition 1989

Printed in Great Britain at the University Press, Cambridge

British Library cataloguing in publication data

Post-structuralism and the question of
history.
1. Structuralism (Literary analysis)
I. Attridge, Derek II. Bennington,
Geoffrey III. Young, Robert, *1950–*
801'.95 PN98.S7

Library of Congress cataloguing in publication data

Post-structuralism and the question of history.
Includes index.
1. History – Philosophy. 2. Structuralism.
I. Attridge, Derek. II. Bennington, Geoffrey.
III. Young, Robert, 1950–
D16.9.P755 1987 901 86–12972

ISBN 0 521 32759 8 hard covers
ISBN 0 521 36780 8 paperback

FOR
ALLON WHITE

Contents

HISTORY AS TEXT

Introduction: posing the question

GEOFF BENNINGTON and ROBERT YOUNG

Every mere 'ism' is a misunderstanding and the death of history –
Heidegger, *What is a Thing?*

It could be argued that the only common factor in the various attempts that have been made to define structuralism and post-structuralism and their difference lies in the admission of the difficulty of any such definition and the questionableness of any such difference. A provisional description might, however, state that structuralism involves a method of analysis in which individual elements are considered not in terms of any intrinsic identity but in terms of their relationship within the system in which they function. A system is regarded as constituted by the differences between the elements that operate within it: structuralism attempts to examine the structure of such systems from a more 'impersonal' or 'scientific' perspective than that of the perceiving or intending subject. Post-structuralism might be said to be suspicious of the apparent ease with which this 'decentering' of the subject is carried out, and to submit that operation to more rigorous consequences of difference: the first casualty of this being the very possibility of the closed system on which structuralism is predicated.

One crucial difference between structuralism and post-structuralism involves the question of history. At first sight, the structuralist use of Saussure's distinction between the synchronic and the diachronic appears to allow for the effacement of history altogether. It is no accident that the essentially spatial model of structure seems to work well for a phenomenon such as myth, where the usual historical perspective is unavailable. But if the analysis of myth, a universal 'grammar' of narrative, and even perhaps Foucault's famous *epistemes*, can avoid the question of their own historicity, it could be said that the 'post' of post-structuralism contrives to reintroduce it. Thus Derrida, for instance, calls attention to the process by which difference operates temporally as well as spatially, introducing his well-known neologism 'différance' with the comment that:

if the word 'history' did not carry with it the theme of a final repression of differance, we could say that differences alone could be 'historical' through and through and from the start.[1]

But as this quotation indicates, if post-structuralism reintroduces history into structuralism (or, more accurately, shows that effects of history have been reduced) it also poses questions to the concept of history as such.

The question of the relations between structuralism, post-structuralism and history is therefore an extremely complex one, and the purpose of this volume is to begin to situate and untangle its complexities by engaging with it in a number of interrelated ways : by considering the claims made, especially within Marxism, for the historical determination of all literary and other discourses; by following through the operation of difference upon historical absolutes; by re-reading the aesthetic tradition within which post-structuralism (and its alleged anti- or a-historicism) is often located; and by presenting examples of close textual criticism which demonstrate the subtler interpretation of history (whether literary or extra-literary) made possible by post-structuralism. By way of introduction, it will be helpful both to examine afresh the question of history as it arises in classic structuralism and to consider a currently influential argument which, in contrast to the brief account we have just given, *opposes* post-structuralism to history.

I

Even though structuralism might at first sight appear to be very much more vulnerable to the charge of eliding the historical dimension, it has been against post-structuralism that 'history' has most insistently been paraded as if it were a definitive objection or a compelling answer to all possible questions. Structuralists, following Saussure's distinction between synchronic and diachronic modes of analysis and his emphasis on the importance of the former, often seemed quite content to ignore the existence of history, yet were less subject to attack than post-structuralists on these grounds. The reason for the reluctance to pose the question of history to structuralism may have been simple: it was in many cases Marxist thinkers, such as Goldmann, Althusser, Macherey, or Jameson, who were most actively involved in exploring structuralism's potential. Indeed, Barthes's seminal *Mythologies*, which could be read as broadly Marxist in orientation, combined structural analysis of bourgeois myth with a constant invocation of history as the repressed of naturalising mythical discourse. According to the title of a well-known anthology, Marx himself was the first structuralist,[2] while Lévi-Strauss, the anthropologist whose work was instrumental in introducing structuralism as a method of analysis in the social sciences, claimed that that work constituted nothing other than a reintegration of anthropological knowledge into the Marxian tradition.[3]

On the other hand, although we shall go on to suggest that a fundamental complicity allowed structuralism to cohabit with the history it apparently ignored (see also Derek Attridge's essay on Saussure in this volume), it would be an over-simplification to assume simple mutual tolerance. We might say that structuralism addressed questions *to* history even as it tended to repress the question *of* history. We might take as an example Barthes's 1967 essay, 'The Discourse of History', which attacks that discourse's pretension to deliver 'the facts' guaranteed by 'the real'.[4] Barthes's essay argues that the discourse of history performs a sleight of hand whereby a discursive operator, the referent, is projected into a realm supposedly beyond signification, from which position it can be thought to precede and determine the discourse which posits it *as* referent. Barthes claims that this 'paradox' 'governs the entire question of the distinctiveness of historical discourse' : 'the fact can only have a linguistic existence, as a term in a discourse, and yet it is exactly as if this existence were merely the "copy", purely and simply, of another existence situated in the extra-structural domain of the "real". This type of discourse is doubtless the only type in which the referent is aimed for as something external to the discourse without it ever being possible to attain it outside this discourse' (17). Barthes goes on to propose an eminently structuralist account of this operation: the discourse of history is guilty of reducing the three-term structure of signification (signifier-signified-referent) to a two-term structure (signifier-referent), or rather of smuggling into this ostensibly two-term structure an illicit signified, 'the real in itself, surreptitiously transformed into a sheepish signified. Historical discourse does not follow the real, it can do no more than signify the real, constantly repeating that *it happened*, without this assertion amounting to anything but the signified "other side" of the whole process of historical narration' (17–18).

This apparently powerful questioning in fact proves either too little or too much: too little if it simply points to problems in a certain way of writing history as *narrative*; too much in that such a critique of the operation of reference applies well beyond the confines of history. Moreover, although Barthes's essay opens up promising avenues of analysis (which can lead, for example, to the refined rhetorical studies of Hayden White),[5] it still necessarily presupposes a history 'in' which such discursive formations take place: Barthes's essay ends with the claim that the decline of narration in 'current historical science' implies a 'real ideological transformation: historical narration is dying because the sign of History is henceforth less the real than the intelligible' (18, translation modified). This change, says Barthes, is marked by a concern with structures rather than with chronologies. Whatever the empirical truth of such an observation, it is clear that it defers the question of history and cannot resolve it: the 'current' and 'henceforth' and the 'transformation' mark very precisely a historical *opening* in the structure of Barthes's essay, and this is an opening it can never understand. A similar point might be made about Foucault's 'archaeologies', which may, in principle at least, be able to explicate everything within the *epistemes*, but can say nothing more powerful than 'it happened' about the shift from one to the next. Any attempt to write a history of the transition from structuralism to post-structuralism would be subject to the same difficulty.

II

In view of these complications, it is surprising to find that the attack mounted on post-structuralism in the name of history should be so confident in its reliance on precisely what is in question. Undoubtedly the most influential critique in the field of literary theory has been that of Frank Lentricchia, who first raised the problem of post-structuralism and the question of history by organising his entire history of modern criticism around the premise of a 'repeated and often extremely subtle denial of history by a variety of contemporary theorists'.[6] Lentricchia's argument was quickly endorsed by Terry Eagleton, who claimed first that post-structuralism represented a 'hedonist withdrawal from history' and, a year later, that it amounted to a more menacing holocaust-like 'liquidation of history'.[7] Similarly, though moving beyond the confines of the literary, Perry Anderson has recently dismissed all post-structuralism on the grounds that it represents '*the randomization of history*'.[8]

One reason for this mobilisation of hostility against post-structuralism by writers claiming to speak in the name of history, when structuralism had escaped relatively lightly, could lie in the fact that 'difference', as understood by post-structuralism, is incompatible with orthodox formulations of the dialectic as much as it is with traditional absolutes, and therefore necessarily comes into conflict with classical Marxism in a way in which structuralism did not. As Mark Cousins argues in this volume by means of a comparison between the historian's use of evidence and that of the law-court, history cannot provide an unquestionable ground once the working of difference is appreciated: and both non-Marxist and Marxist history are subject to this critique. Such a critique, however, also suggests that post-structuralism, with its description of history as difference, should now enter into dialogue with Marxism and show how such a concept of difference would affect it from within. Some of the consequences of that reworking can be seen in a number of essays in this volume, such as Tony Bennett's 'Texts in History', or Gayatri Chakravorty Spivak's essay on Marx's texts on political economy.

Unlike later commentators such as Perry Anderson who wish to dismiss post-structuralism *tout court* in the name of Marxism and history, Lentricchia's account remains a more powerful critique precisely because it raises many of the key questions about post-structuralism and history without proposing a simple rejection of the former in favour of the 'reality' of the latter: instead *After the New Criticism* constitutes a subtle attempt to hold on to some of the most fundamental aspects of the Marxist position without rejecting Derrida or Foucault out of hand. The questions that it raises are taken up and extended or redefined by the contributors to this volume who demonstrate that Lentricchia's formulations are not always themselves unproblematical. Lentricchia contends that in the course of transportation to the USA the historical and political dimensions of European theory have disappeared, dissolving in the face of the continuing strength of the neo-Kantian aesthetics of the New Criticism. His argument, which has since been widely echoed, is that it is only American post-structuralism that denies history: to make this claim he contrasts it to the work of Derrida and Foucault. Persuasive though this thesis has been, it involves serious difficulties. The assertion that Derrida and Foucault are 'broadly' (191) or 'roughly' (209) compatible, that the agreement between the two on the subject of history is 'extensive' (192), and that they show a common 'understanding of history' (208), elides very substantial differences between the two articulated in Derrida's 1963 discussion of Foucault's *Madness and Civilisation* (1961). That that disagreement should take place over the question of history suggests an incompatibility of some moment for Lentricchia's thesis, as Ann Wordsworth shows in her detailed examination of the debate in this volume.

A further move in Lentricchia's attempted assimilation of Derrida and Foucault is a silent metamorphosis of the former's *écriture* into the latter's 'discourse'. He substantiates this by arguing that, unlike the Yale critics, both acknowledge 'some form of the principle of determinacy' (190). Accordingly, in his description of Derrida, Lentricchia turns the 'trace' into a form of determination. But as Marian Hobson's essay in this volume shows, the 'trace' in Derrida is introduced explicitly to account for the production of the effects of difference without positing a determining cause which escapes its play. Lentricchia's history, formulated in terms of the social, the ethical and the political, is always, by contrast, posited as existing outside writing and determining it.

His criticism of the Yale critics takes the form of a repeated accusation of 'aestheticism': Lentricchia argues that post-structuralist 'solipsism' (141) and 'hedonism' (145) are the logical conclusion of the Kantian aesthetics of disinterestedness. This charge has subsequently been disputed by Paul de Man, who points out that, for Kant, aesthetics, far from being 'free from cognitive and ethical consequences', functions as the articulation of the entire Kantian philosophical system. De Man contends that 'the treatment of the aesthetic in Kant is certainly far from conclusive, but one thing is clear: it is epistemological as well as political through and through'.[9] The Kant invoked by Lentricchia, he suggests, is that of a traditional misreading, and by bringing this to our attention de Man implies the need for a re-examination of the category of aesthetics itself, inaugurated in this volume by Rodolphe Gasché's account of the complicity of aesthetics and history in the texts of the founder of what has come to be thought of as the Kantian tradition, A. E. Baumgarten.

It is, finally, in the historical and institutional perspectives of Foucault that Lentricchia locates what he considers to be the necessary corrective to American post-structuralism. His use of Foucault takes the form of outlining a genealogical model of literary history extrapolated from the essay 'Nietzsche, Genealogy, History'. Setting aside the question of whether such a Foucauldian model can be, as Lentricchia claims, 'resolutely dialectical',[10] any appropriation of Foucault for literary criticism ought also to encounter the problem that it is possible to distinguish two almost antithetical positions in his writings on literature. In the early essays Foucault celebrated certain kinds of literary texts as a transgressive force comparable to madness itself. Here literature is the space in which the articulation of the other has had 'no other law than that of affirming – in opposition to all other forms of discourse – its own precipitous existence':[11] as such it does indeed escape history's manacles. As Foucault's position changed, however, towards that outlined in *The History of Sexuality* (*La Volonté de Savoir*, 1976) in which madness no longer exists outside history but, like sexuality, becomes a focus for the exercise of social control, his attention in the literary sphere was increasingly directed to the way in which both the production and consumption of literature show it to be a writing practice constituted within the terms of a restrictive discursive formation.[12] While this argument directly contradicts Foucault's earlier position, its claims have far-reaching implications. As Jonathan Culler demonstrates in his essay 'Criticism and Institutions', one effect must be that any analysis of the conventions of reading and writing has to be extended to include the history and operation of the literary institution that enforces such discursive rules.

Perhaps an indication of such restraints operating within Lentricchia's own discourse can be detected in his suggestion that American post-structuralist criticism retreats from 'a social landscape of fragmentation' to become 'something like an ultimate mode of interior decoration' (186). 'Fragmentation' is here still totalised as a 'landscape', and the dismissal of what Lentricchia calls the 'interior' in fact works as an exclusion of all that such a totalisation marginalises (e.g. the domestic). That post-structuralism facilitates the examination of differentiated and customarily marginalised histories – of phallogocentricism, of the fantasmic structures of colonialism and of fascism – is a measure by which its interrogation of a dialectical history's transcendence can be assessed. The essays here by Mary Nyquist, William Pietz, and Maud Ellmann exemplify its capacity to engage with such 'marginal' histories by means of textual analysis.

III

Post-structuralism and the question of history then, far from being a matter of the absence of history, involves nothing less than what Fredric Jameson has called 'the crisis of historicity itself'.[13] It is precisely this problem which is already picked out in some of Derrida's earliest essays, especially 'Force and Signification', dating from 1963, but already in the 1959 paper, '"Genesis and Structure" and Phenomenology', where the affirmation that:

> it is always something like an *opening* which will frustrate the structuralist project. What I can never understand, in a structure, is that by means of which it is not closed[14]

opens the question of history and adds the 'post' to structuralism before many of its major works were written. To this extent it is already a historical simplification to assume that post-structuralism simply comes *after* structuralism.

For Derrida's arguments in these essays are not *simply* historical: he begins 'Force and Signification' with the observation that structuralism would or will be (and perhaps now we could say has been or is) a problem for any historian of ideas, insofar as it involves, beyond any empirical difficulties of periodisation, 'a conversion of the way of putting questions to any object posed before us, to historical objects . . . in particular'. This implies that 'the structuralist stance, as well as our own attitudes assumed before or within language, are not only moments of history. They are an astonishment, rather, by language as the origin of history. By historicity itself'.[15]

The *question* of history is, in this description, *excessive* with respect to history: this worrying excess no doubt accounts for the repeated calls to 'get *back* to history', and for the accusations that history is what post-structuralism *lacks.* Such attacks invoke history, or History (the capital letter transforming a problem into a magic word) as a given which post-structuralism has somehow, culpably, managed to ignore. 'Language as the origin of history' (implying, as all of Derrida's analyses in *Of Grammatology* and elsewhere show, that this is no 'origin' at all), and no longer as discourse 'in' history, exceeds the History invoked by all Marxisms and historicisms. Structuralism, read in this way, not only emphasises that history is constructed as a discourse that will inevitably be contaminated by the operations of language that can no longer be historical in any simple sense, but also draws attention to a historicity inhabiting the very presupposition that history is the fundamental mode of being. Derrida's stress on structuralism's 'conversion of the way of putting questions to any object posed before us, to historical objects . . . in particular' can be compared to Heidegger's comment that 'every report of the past . . . is concerned with something that is static. This kind of historical reporting is an explicit shutting down of history, whereas it is, after all, a happening. We question historically if we ask what is still happening even if it seems to be past. We ask what is still happening and whether we remain equal to this happening so that it can really develop.'[16] Against this shutting down of history, then, we 'question historically' only from the opening or the historicity which is Derrida's concern.

Once this question is opened, it is possible to discern the fundamental complicity which allowed structuralism to cohabit with history: for just as the identification and description of structures require the operator of closure, so history is organised only by a certain closure, a 'shutting down', of historicity. This can be illustrated by the differing arguments of Jameson and Lyotard. The former passionately advocates the need to historicise, but grounds his call in a transcendental notion of History as ultimate closure on relativising and perspectival analysis.[17] This History turns out to be that provided by the Marxist 'Grand Narrative' of the modes of production, the privileged status of which cannot be non-dogmatically demonstrated. Lyotard's interrogation of the notion of the Grand Narrative[18] allows him to avoid such dogmatism (which is probably implicit in any recognisable *philosophy* of history) and to rephrase the historical in terms of names and signs (in a Kantian rather than a Saussurean sense, as explained in his essay in this volume). This takes seriously 'language as the origin of history', and opens post-structuralist perspectives on ethics and politics which the closing of the question of history had tended to reduce to unargued polemic.

Such resistance to totalisation and synthesis is perhaps the major difficulty posed by post-structuralism, understood in this sense, to both traditional and dialectical accounts of history. The logic of the 'always already', the notions of 'originary repetition' and of 'strategy without finality', which occur in Derrida's work are sufficient to unsettle *archè* and/or *telos* which all such accounts of history presuppose. Insofar as Derrida's *différance* names the historicity of history, then any attempt to explain *différance* historically (in terms of the recent political and intellectual history of France, for example) is condemned to misunderstand the question opened by post-structuralism. It is the effects of that difficult opening that the essays collected in this volume attempt to address.

NOTES

1 Jacques Derrida, *Speech and Phenomena, and Other Essays on Husserl's Theory of Signs,* trans. Newton Garver (Evanston: Northwestern University Press, 1973), p. 141.

2 *The Structuralists: From Marx to Lévi-Strauss,* eds. Richard and Fernande De George (New York: Anchor Books, 1972).

3 Claude Lévi-Strauss, *Structural Anthropology*, trans. Claire Jacobson and Brooke Grundfest Schoepf (London: Allen Lane, 1968), p. 343.

4 Roland Barthes, 'The Discourse of History', trans. Stephen Bann, *Comparative Criticism: A Yearbook 3*, ed. E. S. Shaffer (Cambridge: Cambridge University Press, 1981), pp. 7–20. Further references will be cited in the text. An earlier translation is available in *Structuralism: A Reader*, ed. Michael Lane (London: Cape, 1970), pp. 145–55.

5 Hayden V. White, *Metahistory: The Historical Imagination in Nineteenth-Century Europe* (Baltimore: Johns Hopkins University Press, 1973); *Tropics of Discourse: Essays in Cultural Criticism* (Baltimore: Johns Hopkins University Press, 1978).

6 Frank Lentricchia, *After the New Criticism* (Chicago: University of Chicago Press, 1980), p. xiii. Further references will be cited in the text. The two most significant reviews of *After the New Criticism* are those by Gregory S. Jay, 'Going After New Critics: Literature, History, Deconstruction', *New Orleans Review* 8:3 (1982), 251–64, and Andrew Parker, ' "Taking Sides" (On History): Derrida Re-Marx', *Diacritics* 11:3 (Fall 1981), 57–73. In his subsequent *Criticism and Social Change* (Chicago: Chicago University Press, 1983) Lentricchia continues his attack on deconstruction, specifically the work of Paul de Man, for its 'political defusion of writing and the intellectual life' (p. 39).

7 Terry Eagleton, *Literary Theory: An Introduction* (Oxford: Blackwell, 1983), p. 150; and *The Function of Criticism: From 'The Spectator' to Post-Structuralism* (London: Verso, 1984), p. 96.

8 Perry Anderson, *In the Tracks of Historical Materialism* (London: Verso, 1983), p. 48.

9 Paul de Man, 'Hegel on the Sublime', in *Displacement: Derrida and After*, ed. Mark Krupnick (Bloomington: Indiana University Press, 1983), p. 140.

10 *After the New Criticism*, p. 201. For an analysis of the complex relation of Foucault to Marxism see Barry Smart, *Foucault, Marxism and Critique* (London: Routledge and Kegan Paul, 1983).

11 Michel Foucault, *The Order of Things* (London: Tavistock, 1970), p. 300. For Foucault's early writings on literature see his *Raymond Roussel* (Paris: Gallimard, 1963), and the essays 'A Preface to Transgression' and 'Language to Infinity' in Michel Foucault, *Language, Counter-Memory, Practice*, trans. Donald F. Bouchard and Sherry Simon (Ithaca: Cornell University Press, 1977), pp. 29–67. The best discussion of the status of literature in Foucault's early work remains that of Shoshana Felman, 'Madness and Philosophy, or Literature's Reason', in *Yale French Studies* 52 (1975), 206–28.

12 Michel Foucault, *The History of Sexuality: Volume One: An Introduction*, trans. Robert Hurley (London: Allen Lane, 1979); 'The Order of Discourse', in Robert Young, ed., *Untying the Text: A Post-Structuralist Reader* (London: Routledge and Kegan Paul,

1981), pp. 48–77; 'What is an Author', in *Language, Counter-Memory, Practice*, pp. 113–38.

13 Fredric Jameson, 'Reflections in Conclusion', in E. Bloch *et al.*, *Aesthetics and Politics* (London: NLB, 1977), p. 198. For British Marxists that crisis was initiated by the conclusion to Barry Hindess and Paul Q. Hirst's *Pre-Capitalist Modes of Production* (London: Routledge and Kegan Paul, 1975). For Hirst's more recent views on the subject of Marxism and historiography see his *Marxism and Historical Writing* (London: Routledge and Kegan Paul, 1985).

14 Jacques Derrida, '"Genesis and Structure" and Phenomenology', in *Writing and Difference*, trans. Alan Bass (London: Routledge and Kegan Paul, 1978), p. 160.

15 Jacques Derrida, 'Force and Signification', *ibid.*, pp. 3–4.

16 Martin Heidegger, *What is a Thing?* (1935–6), trans. W. B. Barton, Jr and Vera Deutsch (South Bend, Indiana: Regnery/Gateway, 1967), p. 43. For the argument that post-structuralism dehistoricises Heidegger's thinking in the very process of appropriating it see Gillian Rose, *Dialectic of Nihilism: Post-Structuralism and Law* (Oxford: Blackwell, 1984).

17 Fredric Jameson, *The Political Unconscious: Narrative as a Socially Symbolic Act* (London: Methuen, 1981).

18 Especially in *The Postmodern Condition*, trans. Geoff Bennington and Brian Massumi (Manchester UP, 1984): any traces the body of the book may retain of linear or dialectical history are corrected in the essay published as an appendix to it, 'Answering the Question: What is Postmodernism?', trans. Régis Durand.

History, Marxism, and the institution

Demanding history

GEOFF BENNINGTON

History is demanding.

It is difficult, it makes demands. Saying that it 'makes demands' implies that history can be positioned as the sender, the *destinateur*, of prescriptive sentences, sentences the addressee and referent of which can vary.

History is also demanded.

Here history is no longer the sender of prescriptions, but their referent: this time sender and addressee are variable. A third possibility would make of history the addressee of a demand, that, for example, it deliver up its meaning or its secrets, leaving sender and referent unspecified.

Of these three possibilities, the first, in which history makes the demands, could be used to explain the writing and delivery of this paper: if I gave this type of justification, I would position myself (or, more accurately, would be positioned by the text) as history's addressee, and my 'subject' would be positioned as the referent of the demand. Anecdotally, this would mean that history prescribed, or seemed to prescribe, that in the current 'conjuncture', I, or whoever else heard the demand, should consider something like 'history and deconstruction'. This scene is immediately complicated, however, in that 'history', which in this hypothesis or story is the sender of the prescription, reappears in the position of referent. History said, 'Talk about me'. And if one accepted, with Jean-François Lyotard, that the meaning, the *sens*, of a sentence constitutes a fourth pragmatic 'pole' or 'post',[1] and if it were decided that the *sens* could also be named as 'history', then the complication would have spread.

Further, if the simplicity or propriety of the name 'history' were to be questioned, in other words if it were to be positioned as addressee and referent of a new demand (a demand as to its meaning in these pragmatic scenes), and it were to be shown that neither that addressee nor that referent were stable, but divided (at least into the standard ambiguity according to which 'history' names both a specific discourse and the referent of that discourse); and if then the word were itself 'historicised' and the specificity of that 'specific' discourse were shown to be problematic (with respect to the division between 'truth' and 'fiction', for example), then the reapplication of these divisions to each occurrence of the word 'history' in all the possible permutations of the pragmatic scene would generate a proliferation of possibilities, each of which would in some sense inhabit all the others, and all further sentences, such as these, which attempted to position as their referent one or more of the pragmatic possibilities thus generated.

The specific pragmatic 'scene' I want to consider is extracted more or less violently from this set of possibilities. A variation on the second of the three 'primal' scenes with which I began is what I shall discuss at greatest length. Here history is not the sender of the demand, but only its referent: an unspecified sender says, 'Talk about history', to an unspecified addressee. The scenario I want to look at is one in which the sender of that prescription is something that might be called 'the Left', or possibly 'Marxism' (as for example in Jameson's *Political Unconscious*, the first two words of which are simply, 'Always historicize!'),[2] and the addressee something that might be called 'post-structuralism', and especially 'deconstruction'. So I'm inflecting and condensing the title of the book a little: *Post-Structuralism and the Question of History* becomes something like 'The Left puts the question of History to Deconstruction', or 'The Left demands History of Deconstruction'. The working hypothesis is that the sender of the prescription would like post-structuralism and especially deconstruction to 'come clean' about history: and that this would also involve coming clean about historical materialism, about Marxism, and thereby about the sender of the prescription.

This still involves a certain number of worrying presuppositions, notably that the proper names occupying the two poles of the pragmatic scene not occupied by 'history' (i.e. the poles of sender and addressee), are any more stable than it. 'Deconstruction' may seem to have a more precisely locatable referent than 'post-structuralism', but is nonetheless not an unequivocal name for a unified movement. Even if (as is largely the case here) that name is used as a metonym for 'Derrida's work', the unity presupposed is only guaranteed by the fragile promise of a signature. But if the scenario I have set up is not entirely fictitious, then my excuse comes from the demand for history itself, insofar as 'the Left' or 'Marxism' tends to presuppose some such unity, and indeed to hypostatise it in the name 'deconstruction*ism*'. The last of the three names involved in the scenario is no less unstable, as my hesitation between 'the Left', 'Marxism' and 'historical materialism' suggests. Here again the justification is given less by my foisting a false unity on what is clearly a heterogeneous and conflictual movement, than by the desire of most of the identifiable atoms in that movement to represent the whole, to secure the unity of a body or the rights over a legacy.

The scenario is not entirely a fiction, and might therefore be described as itself 'historical'. Terry Eagleton's recent book on literary theory chides Derrida's work for being 'grossly unhistorical',[3] and elsewhere, in an often-repeated joke, of making history seem the same all the way from 'Plato to Nato'. This, along with the charge of 'idealism' (as for example in Coward and Ellis's *Language and Materialism*),[4] is fairly standard of Left reactions, and I'm not going to provide any detailed documentation of it here. Nor am I going to attempt to make out a case for the inaccuracy of this type of charge, although it would not be difficult to construct an argument showing that deconstruction, insofar as it insists on the necessary non-coincidence of the present with itself, is in fact in some senses the most historical of discourses imaginable. Nor would it be difficult to argue that deconstruction escapes the hold of the idealism/materialism opposition. I shall also try to resist the temptation of denouncing a very general tendency to present the operation of deconstruction as a 'critique' (of Western Metaphysics, say), of assuming that 'logocentrism' is just another word for 'idealism' (this in attempts to 'save' Derrida, or some of him, for or by materialism), and of thinking that, in Derrida's usage, 'writing' and 'text' mean the same as what others call 'discourse'.[5] Instead, I shall narrow down the scenario still further and consider something like the (hi)story of the 'Left's' engagement with deconstruction, especially with respect to its own representations of history. This restriction will seem only the more excessive in that I shall appeal to only a very small part of the available evidence, ignoring notably almost all the recent American work on the subject (and particularly Michael Ryan's recent book *Marxism and Deconstruction*),[6] and concentrate on recent work by Terry Eagleton, whom I take to be the British Marxist who has most clearly *taken on* deconstruction, in both senses of the expression 'to take on'.

But even if these simplifying assumptions reintroduce a fictive element into the historical scenario, they are not entirely unmotivated : for if the demand for history is made along the lines of this scenario, and if the Left would indeed like 'deconstruction' to 'come clean', this is motivated by a concern for its own unity and propriety. The assumption of, or desire for, a unity of 'Marxism' or 'the Left' is quite constant in the most incompatible elements which would locate themselves as 'Left' or 'Marxist'. If 'the Left', or that shifting and unstable consensus called 'Marxism', wants an answer to its question or obedience to its demand, then this is in the interests of its own constitution (or institution) *as* 'the Left' or 'Marxism'. It seems necessary to be able to *locate* deconstruction in terms of the polarities of 'Right' and 'Left', or 'Idealism' and 'Materialism', or, more precisely, to be able to 'appropriate' it (it seems to be characteristic of Marxism to assume at least the *possibility* of an 'appropriation' of a type of discourse which has expended not inconsiderable energy undermining the notion of 'appropriation'), to incorporate it, or else, if the question remains unanswered or the demand unmet, to reject or expel it. If deconstruction were to come clean (which would already imply some notion of appropriation) then it would be easier to decide, from a given position in the topological space of 'the Left', whether the apparently radical and subversive nature of deconstruction is truly or only apparently radical and subversive (the nature of the truly radical and subversive being largely precomprehended), to see which bits might be taken on board and used, and which denounced or ignored.

The metaphorics of 'coming clean' and of 'appropriation' here are in themselves paradoxical, given a pervasive and contrary metaphorics of dirt and baseness in Left discussions of history. Jameson talks about the 'ash-can' of history, for example, to which non-recuperable remains of non-dialectical theories will at some point have to be consigned.[7] Or in one of the best essays in the recent *Re-Reading English* volume, Tony Bennett wants to disrupt E. M. Forster's ideal and timeless reading room with 'the muddied boots of history'.[8] Eagleton, in the book on Benjamin,[9] talks about materialists' 'grubby hands', and of prising open ideological encirclement 'in order to allow a whiff of history to enter and contaminate the aesthetic purity of its premisses' (pp. 109 and 89). And again, in the recent *Literary Theory* book, he refers to Northrop Frye's desire to keep literature 'untainted by history' (p. 92), away from the 'sordid "externalities" of referential language' (p. 93).

Of course the use of language such as this is a rhetorical ploy, involving a strategic use of a certain representation, which I think is largely justified, of the language of the other, the 'enemy', the idealist. But the link it suggests between history and what is low (which should probably have to be referred to Marx's claim to have 'inverted' Hegel's dialectic, to have pulled the claims of the spirit down to their material conditions; and referred too, of course, to the metaphorics of base and superstructure) is complicated if it is reapplied to the history of Marxism (materialism, the Left), not necessarily in the extreme and non-specific language of the 'purge', but in the image which might be constructed of Marxism as a body. In Eagleton's *Benjamin* book there is the following characterisation of Eliot's 'tradition':

> Eliot's tradition is a self-equilibrating organism extended in space and time, eternally replete but constantly absorptive, like a grazing cow or the Hegelian Idea. Perhaps it is most usefully visualized as a large, bulbous amoeba, whose pulsating body inflates and deflates, changes colours, relations and proportions, as it digests. (p. 54)

What such a description leaves out (and in leaving it out it is doubtless true to the discourse it describes) is any notion that a body not only absorbs but also excretes: add that function, and the characterisation will do as a description of the 'body' of 'Marxism', which both secures and compromises its unity and integrity as a body by ingesting and expelling or excreting, leaving behind it a trail of what it was in the form of the waste-product, the *déchet*, the dropping. The history of what Marxism itself expels as its own 'deviations' (due to absorption of foreign bodies) or its own 'vulgar' versions (generated by internal or intestinal malfunctions), could persuasively be read, in eminently materialist terms, as a history of digestion and eventually of shit. Marxism as a history of digestion would of course have to begin with the digestion of Hegel, which is probably not yet complete: remember a famous letter from Engels on this.[10] Deconstruction has not yet been digested by the Left, I think, although there is a certain amount of rumbling in the intestines as the useful and nourishing is separated from the rubbish or roughage: but take as an example of what could be its fate a comment Althusser made on his own 'structuralist' deviation from the line, in his *Eléments d'Autocritique*: 'Et c'est sans doute à cette occasion que le sous-produit circonstantiel de ma tendance théoriciste, le jeune chiot du structuralisme, nous a filé entre les jambes'.[11] The history of 'Marxism', which is of course not necessarily identical with the history demanded by Marxism, can be read in these terms: and the link with what it denounces and rejects as 'vulgar' versions of itself is not far away.

There are many forms of ingestion and appropriation, and they all imply a concomitant expulsion. They range from what may seem to be 'merely verbal' borrowings of the term 'deconstruction' (used by, for example, Raymond Williams, to mean simply 'decoding' or 'decipherment' in an attack on some forms of semiology),[12] elsewhere to refer to any form of radical questioning or analysis (as in Peter Widdowson's presentation of the *Re-Reading English* volume),[13] sometimes explicitly connected with questionable accounts of what Derrida is reputed to say and with what's right or wrong with it (as in Catherine Belsey's *Critical Practice*[14] or Peter Brooker's essay in *Re-Reading English*[15]).

Let me return from this brief detour (which will have left its own remains) to the pragmatic scenario I sketched out a moment ago. The motivation for this scenario can, as I said, be found or constructed in the two words which open Jameson's *The Political Unconscious*, and which are, simply enough, 'Always historicize !'. This is the demand. Jameson goes on to qualify it with a sentence which is no longer prescriptive but descriptive or constative, describing this primary prescription as 'the one absolute and we may even say "transhistorical" imperative of all dialectical thought'.[16] This description again complicates the pragmatic scene : the descriptive qualification of the prescription precludes that prescription's subsequent reappearance as the referent of a repeated version of itself. You can't historicise the prescription which demands that you *always* historicise. This limitation seems to be a necessary qualification of any apparently radical historicising position, if infinite regress is to be avoided.[17] It is a version of this limitation that allows Althusser to claim that the concept of history is not itself historical (although his reasoning in support of that claim is more than dubious).[18] It also seems reasonable to suppose that this primary prescription requires its transcendental or 'transhistorical' status if it is to ground anything like a *theory*. This is also, broadly speaking, the position of Eagleton's *Criticism and Ideology*,[19] where it becomes clear that the demand for history and its transhistorical rider describe the strategy of appealing to a 'last instance' and a 'last analysis' : in *Criticism and Ideology* this demand is also the claim for science, and what science finds in the last instance is history, the 'ultimate object' of the text (p. 74), the 'source and referent' of signifying practices (p. 75), literature's 'ultimate signifier' and 'ultimate signified' (p. 72). This transcendental position for history is confirmed when Eagleton writes, 'ideological space is curved like space itself, and history lies beyond it as only God could lie beyond the universe' (p. 95). History has to be saved against 'the notion that the text is simply a ceaselessly self-signifying practice', which 'stands four square with the bourgeois mythology of individual freedom' (p. 73).

It is clear that since *Criticism and Ideology*, Eagleton has been retreating from its general scientism. In the *Walter Benjamin* book, for example, he describes historical materialism as a 'rhetoric' (p. 112). But that same book retains the desire to save history, in some form, from deconstruction and textuality, still seen as homologous with bourgeois liberalism (p. 138). However, if the chapter in which this denunciation of deconstruction is made can be read as a gesture of expulsion, there is plenty of evidence in the rest of the book of ingestion and appropriation, and this is nowhere clearer than in Eagleton's reflections on the relationship of history to narrative and textuality, within which the double gesture of ingestion and expulsion is repeated.

This discussion is preceded by a warning, based on a consideration of Benjamin's essay 'The Story-Teller' : Eagleton sees this essay as 'something of an embarrassment to those who would press [Benjamin] unequivocally into the service of an anti-narrational "textuality", enlist him in the ranks of those modernists or post-modernists for whom narrativity is no more than the suspension and recuperation of an imaginary unity' (p. 60). The important word here is probably 'unequivocally', and if 'equivocality' is treated as a first step towards dissemination and textuality, then Eagleton might be said to dramatise such a move in his writing, for the pages that follow are indeed far from unequivocal. A first step here links the storyteller to the figure of the collector (the link being established through a play on the notion that the story is a *collective* genre), and the collector is already a textualiser : 'The collector is a modernist in so far as he or she breaks with the suave schemas of the museum catalogue in the name of a fiercely idiosyncratic passion that fastens on the contingent and unregarded. Collecting is in this sense a kind of creative digression from classical narrative, a "textualising" of history that reclaims repressed and unmapped areas' (p. 61). A brief consideration of quotation, in which signifiers are 'torn from their signified and then flexibly recomposed to weave fresh correspondences across language' (p. 65), leads to the direct discussion of history and of the narrative/textuality alternative.

The ambivalence of the approach is further complicated in that it is not always clear what exactly the referent of the argument is here; whether it is 'Marxism', 'historical materialism' or 'history (itself)' which is to be described as either narrative or text. Eagleton begins the discussion by allowing that Marxism appears at first 'to take up its rank among the great narrative constructs of history' (pp. 63–4), where the duplicity of the genitive already leaves open the possibility of seeing Marxism as a way of constructing history as a narrative, or else as a more or less local narrative construct within history. Eagleton's mildly parodic sketch of this version of history (or Marxism, or historical materialism) as 'the mighty world-historical plot of humankind's primordial unity, subsequent alienation, revolutionary redemption and ultimate self-recovery in the realm of communism' (p. 64) could well be read as a pastiche of Jameson. Here Eagleton consigns the authority for this type of reading to Marx's 'early writings', and will draw firstly on the *Grundrisse* and subsequently on the *18th Brumaire* to counter it (the latter said to contain 'the seeds of a theory of historical textuality' (p. 68) : no reference is made here to Mehlman's *Revolution and Repetition*,[20] but, characteristically of the strategy of ingestion and expulsion, the book is later roundly criticised by Eagleton (p. 162)). The text cited from the *Grundrisse* pushes towards an apparently 'genealogical' account of history, although Eagleton finds in the text 'a symptomatic maladjustment here between figure and discourse, a shadowy fault-line along which Marx's text might be deconstructed' (p. 65). This possibility of deconstruction (and there is no reason to think that the word is not used in a Derridean way) *already* opts for the 'text' rather than the narrative : but what is so far recognised as text is Marx's text, not history 'itself'. On the other hand, it is not easy to see how that referent could still reasonably be described as other than textual if the writing which 'theorises' it (in fact to the extent that it is a text this theory cannot *simply* be a 'theory' in a strong sense of that word) is described as textual. But there are tensions in Eagleton's account, in that he is wary of any such generalised textuality, and wants to reconcile what textuality he concedes with a certain narrativity, which he cannot do without, as we shall see : this limited acceptance of textuality enables Eagleton to avoid the 'great human adventure' naiveties of a Jameson,[21] but the retention of narrativity generates a number of political problems.

But before this restitution of a measured narrativity, Eagleton looks more closely at the notion of textuality. Now there is an inversion, in that it is history 'itself' which becomes a sort of full-blown text in the form of a heterogeneous excess over the now only *limited* textuality of the Marxist discourse which is nonetheless seen as 'producing' that text of history in its heterogeneity. The 'heterogeneity' of history is adduced (and again this could be read against Jameson) against 'those who draw on the past for their utopias' (p. 68), and who thereby '[subdue] the heterogeneous movement of history to the enthralment of an *eschaton*' (p. 68). This type of teleological or eschatalogical construction of history allows the text describing or theorising the text of history to be in excess of the text of history it describes or theorises: in Marx's words, which Eagleton quotes, it allows 'the phrase to go beyond the content'. Against this, Eagleton writes that 'for Marxism, however, [note how Eagleton carries out the operation of appropriation on Marxism too: what he is going to claim is of course not true of all Marxism or of all Marxisms] the "text" of revolutionary history is not foreclosed in this way: it lacks the symmetrical shape of narrative, dispersed as it is into a textual heterogeneity ("the content goes beyond the phrase") by the absence around which it turns – the absence of an *eschaton* present in each of its moments' (pp. 68–9). This provokes what seems to me to be an important conclusion, namely that 'The authority of socialist revolution . . . is not to be located in the past, least of all in the texts of Marx himself, but in the intentionality of its transformative practice, its ceaseless "beginning" ' (p. 69).[22] This non-narrative but multiple and heterogeneous history is supported a little later by the observation that 'it is of crucial importance that the founding economic document of Marxism [meaning of course *Capital*], unlike that of Christianity, is not a narrative' (p. 69: it is not clear how this antithesis works in view of the fact that the Bible is not an 'economic document', or at least not in the restricted sense of 'economic' used here).

So 'revolutionary history' is a text. But what is 'revolutionary' about it is *not* the textuality of history, but, oddly enough, a reinstated version of narrative. By writing history as text, Eagleton has moved towards a position which he has consistently linked to bourgeois liberal pluralism (see in this book p. 138). At this point he seems to be claiming that history is not a narrative but a text, and that Marxism too is not a narrative but a text. This is clearly too much text, and narrative now starts to reclaim some of its rights. In fact this reclaiming has already begun to the extent that the history which is described as a text is 'revolutionary history', insofar as the notion of 'revolution' presupposes narrative. So between the text quoted above on 'ceaseless beginning' and the odd antithesis of *Capital* and the Bible, Eagleton draws back from the textual position:

> This is not to reduce socialist revolution to a form of liberal pluralism. The aim of such politics is to abolish commodity production by the institution of workers' self-government, an aim involving the planned, exclusive 'narratives' of revolutionary organisation. (p. 69)

So Marxism now becomes a text of limited plurality (rather like the 'parsimonious plural' of classical narrative as described by Barthes in *S/Z*), which has what Eagleton calls an 'ironic' relationship with the historical 'text', insofar as the Marxist narrative inevitably forecloses the now excessive (and in itself not foreclosed) 'textual' heterogeneity of history. The problem with this positioning is that the historical text is in fact projected as a *telos* (or an *eschaton*, to use Eagleton's term) by a narrative of revolution. History will only really be a text once it has been a narrative. Or, history is really a text but we pretend that it is a narrative. Or, the textuality of history exceeds narratives (even those of socialist revolution), and as that cannot be allowed to happen, then narratives must be restored.

Eagleton negotiates this nexus by marking a return to Jameson. Firstly he quotes *The Prison-House of Language* to equate the 'always already' of Derrida's text with the quite different question of the priority of material conditions over consciousness in Marxism. Eagleton himself finds this parallel a little too 'symmetrical' but lets it pass. Then he shifts to Althusser's own account of different historical times (referring to this as a 'deconstructed image of history') which he invokes as a sort of textuality. He does not recall that this particular 'textuality' is limited by the horizon of the social 'totality' in Althusser, and that it is heavily dependent on the science versus ideology distinction which the notion of textuality calls into question. Finally he returns to the later Jameson to reinstate narrative as the unavoidable feature of ideology (ideology here in an Althusserian sense from which Eagleton again takes a purely gestural distance in a note), as an 'indispensable fantasy'. And here, perhaps unavoidably, the bad old political side of Althusser resurfaces, for it turns out that this 'indispensable fantasy' is indispensable to the proletariat's identity as a revolutionary class, and something that the 'we' who know better (who have somehow got science and can write the theory of their naive narratives) do well not to disturb. Here is the argument:

> The insertion of the subject into an ideological formation is, simultaneously, its access to a repertoire of narrative devices and conventions

that help to provide it with a stable self-identity through time. We know ['we' the privileged subjects of knowledge and science] that the 'truth' of the subject has no such stable self-identity; the unconscious knows no narratives, even though it may instigate them. But this is not to argue that narrative is merely 'illusory', any more that we ['we' again] should chide the working-class movement for nurturing its mighty dramas of universal solidarity overcoming the evils of capitalism [the construction of this subject called 'the working-class movement' and of the 'mighty dramas of universal solidarity' are perhaps themselves fantasies of the other subject, the subject of knowledge and science]. And just as the individual subject is permitted [permitted, presumably, by 'us'] to construct for itself a coherent biography, so a revolutionary or potentially revolutionary class [the notion of the 'revolutionary class' *presupposes* the type of narrative fantasy which it is here supposed to account for] creates, across the structurally discontinuous social formations identified by Marxism, that 'fiction' of a coherent, continuous struggle which is Benjamin's 'tradition'. (p. 73)

It seems likely that the slightly sinister political implications of this position are a source of some worry to Eagleton, as he immediately needs to underline that this fiction 'is not a *lie*', and to argue that there are *some* continuities in real history, that they are not all simply 'mapping fantasies'. On the one hand it is not at all clear what relevance this claim for a partial truth (as *adequatio*) for narratives can have, and on the other the claim that there are 'real' continuities could only ever be substantiated by writing more narratives and telling more stories : the politically most favourable logic to be drawn would seem to be that what counts is the *effectiveness* of such little stories, which are in any case no longer anything like 'mighty dramas' – but then 'we' would have no job left to do, as the pretence of science and the subsequent indulgence for proletarian fantasies would be meaningless. The claim to be able to discern the real continuities and thus to ground those fantasies at least partially in 'truth' depends simply on the illusion of an intelligentsia as subject of science to stand outside and above that reality and those fantasies. This is on its own terms not at all a historical or historicising position : to rehistoricise *this* fantasy would be to see in it a story on the same level as others in the text, and to abandon any transcendental horizon, and with it, any notion of *telos*, *eschaton*, guarantees and dialectics.

Eagleton's strategy with respect to history and textuality seems no more satisfactory in his two most recent books. In *The Rape of Clarissa*[23] the double gesture returns : deconstruction is expelled along with the character Lovelace, who becomes a 'post-structuralist precursor', writing 'post-structuralist fictions' in a 'deconstructive style' (pp. 46, 61, 83), and although Richardson himself is an 'engagingly modern deconstructionist' (p. 22), Clarissa has to be saved from modern deconstruction, in the name of history. Eagleton warns that no reading which ignores the 'historical necessity' of the bourgeoisie's 'moral closure' (against the 'deathly dissemination' of the 'profligate force of the aristocratic pen and penis' (p. 84)) can 'fail to be moralistic' (ibid.). The success of Eagleton's own avoidance of this trap can perhaps be judged by his reference to Lovelace as 'this pathetic character' with a 'crippling incapacity for adult sexual relationship' (p. 63), or, in an aside on modern popular romantic fiction, references to 'such degraded fiction', its 'monstrously debased form' and its 'diseased impulse to transcendence' (p. 37).

Eagleton again takes on deconstruction in the most recent book, that on Literary Theory, and marks a double movement in this field of tension. On the one hand, there is a move back to simple narratives : Eagleton is concerned to write the narrative history of the rise of English studies in this country, to write 'the narrative of post-structuralism' (p. 148), here simplistically seen as 'born of' May 1968 (p. 142),[24] and even to write the narrative history of literary theory in general : 'The story of modern literary theory . . . is the narrative of a flight' from the realities of experience, and so on (p. 196). But against this move, a newly stressed notion of discourse as a question of power and strategy moves against the narrativising tendency displayed by the book as a whole, and suggests that the narratives be read neither as the materialist truth of the matter, nor as a 'mapping fantasy' allowing Eagleton to live out his position with respect to the real conditions of his existence, but simply as a pragmatically-determined move designed to obtain certain effects. This shift (already in fact anticipated in the *Benjamin* book's remarks on rhetoric) moves us far from any claim for science and last instances : 'It all depends on what you are trying to do, in what situation' (p. 211). This is perhaps why Eagleton now talks of 'political' and no longer 'revolutionary' criticism. The new emphasis seems to be on local situations and interventions nowhere subordinated to a centralising agency or a master-narrative : 'There are many goals to be achieved, and many ways of achieving them' (p. 212). And although liberal pluralism is still liberally denounced, he asserts that 'radical' critics are also 'liberal' with respect to what texts or cultural practices should be looked at, and 'pluralists' about questions of theory and method (pp. 210–11). 'Structuralism, semiotics, psychoanalysis, deconstruction, reception theory and so on: all of these approaches, and others, have their valuable insights which may be put to use' (p. 211). Feminism and Marxism are privileged with respect to this series, but only by their absence: this absence is still worrying because it could easily become transcendence, a position beyond the game in which the moves constituted by other theories are played. And in a sense this type of transcendence is *already* implied by the (violent) serialisation of those other theories, the suggestion of their ideal equivalence as instruments, or rhetorical strategies.[25] That this is all still ultimately subordinated to a great narrative of history is made clear in the book's closing paragraph, an allegory which runs as follows: '*We* know that the lion is stronger than the lion-tamer, and so does the lion-tamer. The problem is that the lion does not know it. It is not out of the question that the death of literature may help the lion to awaken' (p. 217). Here 'we' are again, outside the scene, all-seeing and knowing. We try to tell the lion that it is strong, that it should leap, roar, bite and devour: it opens one eye and yawns, recognising another tamer when it sees one.

NOTES

1 Lyotard's most rigorous formulation of these four 'posts' is to be found in *Le Différend* (Paris: Minuit, 1984), partially translated in *Diacritics*, 14:4 (1984), 4–14. This paper was written for the *OLR*/Southampton conference in 1983 – I have not attempted to modify the text to take account of more recent work, which would not, however, lead me to make substantial changes to the argument.
2 Fredric Jameson, *The Political Unconscious* (London: Methuen, 1981), p. 9.
3 Terry Eagleton, *Literary Theory: an Introduction* (Oxford: Basil Blackwell, 1983), p. 148.
4 Rosalind Coward and John Ellis, *Language and Materialism* (London: Routledge and Kegan Paul, 1977), p. 126.
5 For a generous sample of this sort of nonsense, see Michael Sprinker, 'Textual Politics: Foucault and Derrida', *Boundary* 2, 8 (1980), 75–98.
6 Michael Ryan, *Marxism and Deconstruction: A Critical Articulation* (Baltimore and London: The Johns Hopkins University Press, 1982). I have discussed this book in a review article, 'Outside story', *LTP* 3 (1984), 117–28.
7 Jameson, *The Political Unconscious*, p. 10, and see too 'Marxism and Historicism', *NLH* XI, 1 (1979), 41–73 (p. 48). For some criticisms of Jameson's positioning of rival theories with respect to Marxism, see my 'Not Yet', *Diacritics*, Vol. 12 (1982), 23–32, especially pp. 24–5.

8 Tony Bennett, 'Text and History', in *Re-Reading English*, ed. Peter Widdowson (London: Methuen, 1982), pp. 223–36 (p. 223).

9 Terry Eagleton, *Walter Benjamin, or Towards a Revolutionary Criticism* (London: NLB, 1981).

10 Engels, letter to Conrad Schmidt: 1/11/1891: 'Ohne Hegel geht's natürlich nicht, und der Mann will auch Zeit haben, bis er verdaut ist'.

11 Louis Althusser, *Eléments d'Autocritique* (Paris: Hachette, 1974), p. 53.

12 Raymond Williams, *Marxism and Literature* (OUP, 1977), pp. 167–8.

13 'Introduction: The Crisis in English Studies', *Re-Reading English*, pp. 1–14: 'deconstruction' is used on pp. 7 and 8.

14 Catherine Belsey, *Critical Practice* (London: Methuen, 1980). Belsey describes deconstruction as simply 'the analysis of the process and conditions of [the text's] construction out of the available discourses' (p. 104), suggests that 'the object of deconstructing the text is to examine the *process of its production*' (ibid.), and finally says that 'to deconstruct the text . . . is to open it, to release the possible positions of intelligibility, including those which reveal the partiality (in both senses) of the ideology inscribed in the text' (p. 109).

15 Peter Brooker, 'Post-Structuralism, Reading and the Crisis in English,' *Re-Reading English*, pp. 61–76. This essay is explicitly concerned to 'appropriate' bits of post-structuralism for a collective subject pre-comprehended as made up of good historical materialists (p. 72). Brooker finds Derrida's thinking 'patently unmaterialist', his 'conception of history . . . confined to the history of western philosophy', his 'deconstructive procedure . . . imperfectly dialectical, offering no guarantee of progressive acceleration and transformation'. Etc. It would be worth following the desire for *guarantees*, but not much else.

16 Jameson, *The Political Unconscious*, p. 9.

17 For a classic *reductio ad absurdum* of radical historicism, see Leo Stauss, *Natural Right and History* (Chicago UP, 1953), pp. 9–34.

18 See for example Louis Althusser, *Lire le Capital*, 2 vols. (Paris: Maspéro, 1966); republished in Petite Collection Maspéro, 4 vols., I, pp. 46 and 132. For some criticism of the validity of the reasoning, see E. P. Thompson, 'The Poverty of Theory', in *The Poverty of Theory and Other Essays* (London: Merlin Press, 1978), pp. 193–397 (pp. 223–5): this reference should not be taken to imply general agreement with Thompson's attack on Althusser.

19 Terry Eagleton, *Criticism and Ideology* (London: New Left Books, 1976).

20 Jeffrey Mehlman, *Revolution and Repetition* (Berkeley and Los Angeles: University of California Press, 1977), which makes brilliant use of the same text by Marx to put forward just such a reading of history.

21 See 'Not Yet' for some rather bad-tempered comments on this aspect of Jameson.

22 The reference here is to Edward Said, *Beginnings: Intention and Method* (Baltimore and London: The Johns Hopkins University Press, 1975), and is acknowledged by Eagleton (p. 68, n. 144).

23 Terry Eagleton, *The Rape of Clarissa* (Oxford: Basil Blackwell, 1982).

24 In a later piece in the *TLS*, Eagleton no longer sees post-structuralism as the child of 1968, but suggests that 'structuralism and the student movement were the prodigal children of the same distraught father' ('The Critic's New Clothes', *TLS* 27/5/83, p. 546). These explanations are really equivalent in their weakness.

25 The situation recalls Jameson's equally 'liberal' picture of a 'market-place' in which theories compete and where Marxism wins because it is *also* the transcendent measure of value. See 'Not Yet', p. 24.

Speculations on reading Marx: after reading Derrida[1]

GAYATRI CHAKRAVORTY SPIVAK

The present essay occupies itself not with the articulation between Marxism and deconstruction considered as proper names – a legitimising move that I remain obliged to question, but with annotating what it means, in the life of an academic, to turn to a cherished set of texts after having read a new set. To indicate the sets by the names of their authors commemorates a convention which is discussed below through a consideration of reading as sublation or *Aufhebung*. My turn from one set to the other remains inconclusive, halted by the suspicion that to create a con-versation, a turning-together, between Marx and Derrida, might merely emphasise what is minimally true: that they both belong to the dialectical tradition. My move cannot represent itself as a political programme, for it cannot consider 'deconstruction', named as such, as *realia* or assume that the political – or ethico-personal – narrateme can adequately represent the philosopheme.

To go via Derrida toward Marx can be called a 'literary' or 'rhetorical' reading of a 'philosophical' text. Yet such a gesture – even as the 'political' remains heterogeneous to it – also questions disciplinary nomenclatures and boundaries such as 'literature' and 'philosophy'. The reading is 'literary' only in so far as it recognises that what Marx produces is written in language. Such a reading discloses that Marx questions mere 'philosophical' justice and elegance by prying them open with the lever of practice. The strategies of a radically 'literary' approach do not reduce Marx to 'mere' literature in one of its most powerful disciplinary definitions an ultimately self-reflexive verbal text that irreducibly narrates its own constitution.

The constitution of the Marxian text remains untotalisable because its task is to articulate more than its verbal textuality. This is the implicit case of all texts. Marx's text differs in its motivated explicitation. It is here that a word must be said about the early Derridean suggestion – 'there is no absolute extra-text'. While a somewhat narrowly conceived 'literary' criticism might welcome and develop the Derridean intervention in the field of 'philosophy' as a literary reductionism (and therefore 'deconstruction' cannot be 'exculpated' from the possibility of such a supplementation), Derrida's argument implies a rather different position as well : that the so-called 'outside' of the verbal text is articulated with it in a web or network (that is 'socio-cultural', or 'politico-economic', or yet 'psycho-sexual', depending on our practical/theoretical focus) : 'it was never our wish to extend the reassuring notion of the text to a whole extra-textual realm and to transform the world into a library by doing away with all boundaries, . . . but . . . we sought rather to work out the theoretical and practical system of these margins, these borders, once more, from the ground up'.[2]

It is obvious that Derrida's work remains alterable by critical practice. A statement such as the following : 'Each time that the question of the proper emerges in the fields of economics (in the restricted sense), linguistics, rhetoric, psychoanalysis, politics, etc., the onto-hermeneutic form of interrogation shows its limit'[3] would remain contingent upon its critical situation. (Here, for example, the statement takes on a particular focus as soon as it is grasped that the context is the question of woman as limit of the 'proper'.)

I

In a long footnote to 'White Mythology' Derrida praises and criticises Marx for at once opening and abandoning 'the questions of "reality", of "the proper", of "the abstraction" and the concept (the name of reality in general) of the proper'.[4] In a certain passage in *The German Ideology*, as Derrida points out, Marx and Engels take Max Stirner to task for suggesting that property (*Eigentum*) is irreducible on the grounds that man must be defined in terms of his properties (*Eigenschaften*). If, they suggest, one remained content to say no more than this, one would not need to study the economic heterogeneity of the development of private property in the production of different forms of society. Property in idealist etymological speculation and in materialist social production 'are not the same thing.'

A deconstructive analysis would both agree with the point being made by Marx and call it into question.

Marx seems too restricted when he emphasises nothing but the binary opposition between the 'social' fact of private property on the one hand, and the 'natural' fact of 'having' (possessing, therefore, as property) a stomachache, as well as the 'metaphysical' fact of predication or definition by property, on the other. He seems not to accept that what seems the pure, natural or metaphysical origin or goal of un-alienated 'property' – the body's self-proximity in its pain or the concept's self-possession in its definition – is worked and undermined by a version of the same self-differentiation as the so-called social alienation of possessing a thing outside of oneself. The latter is not an accident that befalls the former. This is how Derrida argues, for example, against Lévi-Strauss's differentiation between societies with and without writing. It is our longing for transcendence that makes us posit a proper situation of self-proximity or self-possession against which to measure our own fallen state – to posit, in the language of the early Derrida, speech against writing.

Marx's consideration of money, as he circles that theme in the collection of notebooks posthumously published as the *Grundrisse*, can be read in terms of these general polemics of speech against writing.[5] (I am not, of course, launching an analysis of money in its various forms of appearance, or in its transformation into capital, but merely remarking upon how Marx represents the concept–metaphor, money.)

The emergence of the specific materiality of money, like, for instance 'the signs [*Zeichen*] for words, have a history, the alphabet etc.' (*Gr.* 145). Until the encroachment of money in its specific historical–material support – the fixing of value is *ad hoc* and inconvenient. Although value in exchange always conceals a social relation (who makes what why and how and who needs or is made to need what why when), and thus already shares the rusing character of a sign that conceals the presence of the thing it means, in the situation of *mere* exchange and the circulation of commodities *before* the emergence of the money-form as such, the concealment is always precarious. Once the emergence of the material appropriate to the money form permits its transformation into pure (ideal) conventionality, money is form without content, difference rather than identity: 'Money as medium of circulation becomes coin, mere vanishing moment, mere *symbol* of the values it exchanges . . . As the most superficial (in the sense of driven out onto the surface) and the most abstract form of the entire production process, [money circulation] is in itself quite without content' (*Gr.* 790). Money, like writing, is thus the sign of a sign, the possibility of the exchange of signs, not merely language but a *foreign* language (*Gr.* 163).

Money is the mark of the principle of alienation already immanent in property. 'Because money is the *general equivalent* . . . everything therefore is alienable, or indifferent for the individual, external to him [*sic*]. Thus the so-called *inalienable, eternal* possessions, and the immovable, solid property relations corresponding to them, break down in the face of money' (*Gr.* 838; italics Marx's). It is precisely this necessary and immanent alienation, the ever-recuperable chain of the negation implicit in immanent contradiction, that Derrida approaches with the open-ended graphic of supplementarity.[6] Thus when Marx writes: 'The sphere of circulation has a gap in it, through which gold (or silver, or the money material in general) enters as a commodity with a given value,'[7] Derrida would add: if circulation necessarily carries this gap, it is already complicit with, and welcomes, the money-material in general, which might seem an unwelcome interloper. Because sublation is not openly carried through into supplementarity in Marx's text, the idea, not merely of contingency, but of the interloping or usurpation associated with the received definition of writing is applied to money. 'The first form of appearance' of exchange value – the origin of money – 'arises by chance . . . and is determined by accidental needs, whims, etc. But if it should happen to continue . . . then little by little, from the outside, and likewise by chance, regulation of reciprocal exchange arises' (*Gr.* 204–5). 'From its servant-shape, in which it appears as mere medium of circulation, it suddenly becomes the lord and god in the world of commodities' (*Gr.* 221). The proper place of money is necessarily displaced (*Gr.* 234).

Derrida's name for the supplement that is (mis)represented as an accident is writing. And once money is seen as an unrecognised supplement in Marx, it shows all the marks of writing. Its work is the convenience of abbreviation, through it 'one can secure and stockpile a great value in a small space' (*Gr.* 237). The constitutive temporality of value – labour-time – is occluded as the material of money becomes its own measure, even as, in the received account, the constitutive temporality of speech is occluded by the proliferation of writing. 'Gold is therefore nominally undecipherable, not because it alone expresses an *authentic value*, but because as money it expresses *no value at all*, but merely expresses – carries on its forehead [as writing 'mediates' immediate and 'living' expression into dead inscription or impression] – a determined quantum of its own matter, its own quantitative determination' (*Gr.* 133–4; italics Marx's).

It is the story of the oppression of a living temporality by the monstrous work of spacing – 'the despotism of the eye' – that Derrida has abundantly described as the traditional account of the historiography of writing in *Of Grammatology.* Marx's story further recounts a violent mis-naming, a situation where the circuit of the names becomes more important than the presentation of the things signified. Money corrupts what is natural and turns it, *in its natural form*, into a mere visible sign for the social relation of exchange: 'The special difficulty in grasping money in its full determination as money . . . is here determined as a metal, a stone, as a pure corporeal thing outside them which is to be encountered as such, in nature, and which cannot, in addition, be differentiated in its formal determination, from its natural existence' (*Gr.* 239). Such a confounding of nature and sign is the result of historical processes for which the money-form is the determining condition of possibility. 'Centuries of the falsification of money [*Geldfalschung*] by kings and princes have in fact left nothing behind of the original weights of gold coins but their names' (*C.* 194). Money is the functionary of the improper, splitting 'the real content from the nominal content' (*C.* 222–3) through legitimised misrepresentation: 'In fact no longer 1/4 but merely 1/5 of an ounce of gold was called pound, represented money, had that name' (*Gr.* 800). The next step in the service of the improper is another step in the advancement of the technology of writing: the printing of paper money. 'The printing press . . . is inexhaustible and works like magic' (*Gr.* 121). 'The purely symbolic character is still somewhat disguised in the metallic moneymark [*Geldmark*]. In paper money it stands out visibly. One sees: *Ce n'est que le premier pas qui coûte.*'

Marx scrupulously introduces yet another topos in the thematic of writing. Money's work of usurpation is an agency of civilisation. Comparing the 'imagined' money standard of the Barbary Coast with the developed money forms of Western Europe Marx writes: 'It is the same as if, in mythology, one were to consider as the higher religions those whose god-figures were not worked out in visible form but remain stuck in the imagination, i.e., where they obtain at most an oral, but not a graphic presence' (*Gr.* 795).

Yet one cannot stop simply by showing that, in Marx, the money form is structured like writing. One cannot side with Saint Max (Marx's contender in the passage quoted by Derrida) and make an end by declaring 'impure' theories unfeasible. Here a look at the rest of Derrida's footnote might be useful.

In the second half of the passage that Derrida quotes in his footnote, Marx chastises Stirner for equating so-called synonyms – words like 'value', 'exchange', 'commerce' – that can be used to describe individual as well as commercial relationships. One could of course speculate upon the irreducibly economic metaphors of any metapsychology. I want rather to emphasise that the first moves of Derridean deconstruction were made by noticing what happened when the synonymity/identity of the 'same' word allowed contradictory or asymmetric messages to be disguised as a unified argument.

Derrida has consolidated that move by pointing at how the exigencies of *theory* lead to a suppression of irreducible heterogeneity. And it is the inevitable suppression of the heterogeneity of individual and social transactions which is Marx's count against money. Let me indicate a well-known apparent contradiction in Marx in a general way. There is, on the one hand, the 'humanist' Marx, who marks the desire to recover this heterogeneity through the archaeo-teleological idiom of 'the fulfilment of individual potential'. There is, seemingly on the other hand, the Marx of scientific socialism. The complicity of the two poles of the contradiction may be grasped if we notice that, as a scientific socialist, Marx recommends the substituting of 'spacing' – *reduction* into the regular measure of the average law of general exchange – by *constitutive* temporality, money by time: 'The economy of time, along with the planned distribution of labour time among the various branches of production, remains the first economic law on the basis of communal production. Indeed it becomes the law to a much higher degree. However, this is essentially different from a measurement of value . . . by labour time' (*Gr.* 175). To pursue this complicit contradiction is beyond the scope of this essay.

My anthology of quotations about the concept–metaphor of money in the *Grundrisse* might lead to the following generalisation: Money conceals the heterogeneity of social relations irretrievably by substituting the category of substitution for an exchange which is necessarily asymmetrical. 'In it [Money] they [exchange-values] are all equinominal or same-named [*gleich-namig*]' (*Gr.* 189). It is along this line that Marx develops that analysis of money that Nietzsche's analysis of the language of truth so uncannily resembles (in reverse): two things can be pronounced equal, identical, or substitutible by first, a making equal of different things, next, a forgetting of that move, and, finally, a metaleptically created memory that conceals this genealogy. 'It does not appear on its face that its determination of being money [*Bestimmung Geld zu sein*] is merely the result of social processes; it is money. This is all the more difficult since its immediate use value for the living individual stands in no relation whatever to this role, and because, in general, the memory of use value, as distinct from exchange value has become entirely extinguished in this incarnation of pure exchange value' (*Gr.* 239–40). Here are two passages that point at the two ends of the analysis; first, the making equal: 'the equation of the heterogeneous [*das Gleichsetzen des Ungleichartigen*], as Shakespeare nicely defines money'; and, secondly, the metalepsis: 'after money is posited really as commodity, will the commodity be posited ideally as money' (*Gr.* 163; 80).

Derrida radicalises the Nietzschean position described above in 'White Mythology', deconstructing the opposition between metaphor and concept, showing that neither is originary, that each depends on the other for its functioning and that they are therefore complicit. The general form of that critique of Nietzsche can be used to deconstruct the opposition between use- and exchange-value in the same way. This would enhance Marx's seemingly contradictory impulse toward heterogeneity, even as it does Nietzsche's for plurality.

Let us pursue the issue of metalepsis in the money-form a step further: 'From its servant-shape, in which [money] appears as mere circulation, it suddenly becomes the lord and god in the world of commodities.' We had read this as part of a *historical* narrative of the usurping sovereignty of money (p. 33). It is also, of course, a *philosophical* account of the elusive ontology of money, which can be thematised as follows:

Position: The money commodity – the precious metal as medium of universal exchange – is posited through a process of separation from its own being as a commodity exchangeable for itself: 'From the outset they represent superfluity, the form in which wealth originally appears [*ursprünglich erscheint*]' (*Gr.* 166; translation modified). As it facilitates commodity exchange 'the simple fact that the commodity exists doubly, in one aspect as a specific product whose natural form of existence ideally contains (latently contains) its exchange value, and in the other aspect as manifest exchange value (money), in which all connection with the natural form of the product is stripped away again – this double, *differentiated* existence must develop into a *difference*' (*Gr.* 147). When the traffic of exchange is in labour-power as commodity, the model leads not only to difference but to indifference: 'In the developed system of exchange . . . the ties of personal dependence, of distinctions, of education, etc. are in fact exploded, ripped up . . .; and individuals *seem* independent (this is an independence which is at bottom merely an illusion, and it is more correctly called indifference) [*Gleichgültigkeit – im Sinne der Indifferenz* – Marx emphasizes the philosophical quality of indifference]' (*Gr.* 163).

Negation: Within circulation seen as a constantly repeated circle or totality, money is a vanishing moment facilitating the exchange of two commodities. Here its independent positing is seen as 'a *negative* relation to circulation', for, 'cut off from all relation to [circulation], it would not be money, but merely a simple natural object' (*Gr.* 217). In *this* moment of appearance its positive identity is negated in a more subtle way as well: 'If a fake £ were to circulate in the place of a real one, it would render absolutely the same service in circulation as a whole as if it were genuine' (*Gr.* 210). In philosophical language: the self-adequation of the idea, itself contingent upon a negative relationship, here between the idea of money and circulation as totality, works in the service of a functional *in*-adequation (fake=real).

Negation of negation: Realisation, where the actual quantity of money matters and capital accumulation starts. Yet here too the substantive specificity is contradicted (as it is not in unproductive hoarding). For, 'to dissolve the things accumulated in individual gratifications is to realize them' (*Gr.* 234). In other words, logical progression to accumulation can only be operated by its own rupture, releasing the commodity from the circuit of capital production into consumption in a simulacrum of use-value.[8]

The idea that money is a servant who suddenly becomes lord might thus indicate a shift in the moment of appearance – position, negation, or negation of negation – in which it is considered, rather than merely rehearse a narrative. Yet Marx's political (rather than philosophical) point is anchored in the suggestion that the best example of the philosophical morphology *is* history. And a deconstructive reading would be obliged to point out that, in the arrangement of the sentence about the usurping lord, it is the first moment (positing) that is represented as the second. The political prerogative, in other words, depends on a strategic *mis*representation of the philosophical account, calling into question Hegel's insistence that 'what is first in the *science* [of logic] had of necessity to show itself *historically* as the first'.[9]

I emphasise this here because the intellectual Left in the First World today is beginning to engage in a disavowal of the economic text, basing itself on the 'discovery' that money, far from being a determinant, is a vanishing moment, 'the minor premise of the syllogism' (*Gr.* 202). It seems incapable of shifting the philosophical perspective to make room for a historical distribution of emphasis. What is sometimes represented as the ideological justification for a disavowal at once of the economic and the 'humanistic' text is a school of thought that, by cleaning the historical or empirical element out of the philosophical or theoretical, seems to offer nothing but a privileging of abstraction as such. Questioning both moves, a deconstructive reading here makes us glimpse the limits of utopianism and of the constant search for strict philosophical descriptions of the historical justification for resistance.

Marx's critique and analysis of money as a philosophical moment would define it as a species of writing or foreign language whose curious predication is 'constant appearance as disappearance' (*Gr.* 209). If the discourse of immanence in the *Grundrisse* is given its full acknowledgement (I give it minimal recognition on page 33), it must be admitted that in Marx 'the dangerous supplement' is capital; when money apparently 'closes the circle with itself by way of [money- as distinct from commodity-] circulation, this aspect already latently contains its [accumulative and supplementing] quality as capital' (*Gr* 216). I comment on the relationship between the velocity of money-circulation and the speed of concept-formation at the end of this essay. Let us notice here the necessary connection that Marx establishes between the supplementarity of capital and the supplementary or marginal play of the latent principle of exchange-value as simply the mark of an 'accidental' super-adequation – being in excess of itself – within the sphere of production–consumption : 'This character [of exchange] does not yet dominate production as a whole, but concerns only its superfluity and is hence itself more or less *superfluous* . . .; an accidental enlargement of the sphere of satisfactions, enjoyments (relations to new object). It therefore takes place only at a few points (originally at the borders of the natural communities, in their contact with strangers) . . .' (*Gr.* 204). These notions of the accidental rather than the native are rendered problematic by the necessary and essential super-adequation of labour-power to itself: it is in the nature of labour-power to create more value than it consumes.

It is the existential requirement of this definition of labour-power which makes it politically necessary to reverse moments one and two of the philosophical account in the sentence about the usurping servant that opened our recapitulation. If we remember that the 'Chapter on Money' in the *Grundrisse* is an anti-nostalgic critique of the plans of the Utopian socialists to *bypass* money, we will appreciate that Marx's outline for *combatting* the power of money uses the scenario strategically (with the power of generating an opposition) rather than 'purely' philosophically (with the capacity to articulate a contradiction).

The vignette of exchange-value 'catching on' so that the dialectic can begin to play[10] puts us in mind of the fable of the beginning of the Platonic dialectic at the end of Derrida's 'Plato's Pharmacy'. (I hasten to add that Derrida himself would undoubtedly find this association far-fetched.) There Derrida fancifully represents the preoriginary dis-semes – ante-semantic random bits – buzzing around as a result of something that came *from the inside*, from Plato's own monologue. Gradually some bits clot together – positive and negative differentiate themselves as if *from the outside* – the dialectic catches and begins its dance step:

> Plato mutters as he transcribes the play of formulas. In the enclosed space of the pharmacy, the reverberations of the monologue are immeasurably amplified. The walled-in voice strikes against the rafters, the words come apart, bits and pieces of sentences are separated, disarticulated parts begin to circulate through the corridors, become fixed for a round or two, translate each other, become rejoined, bounce off each other, contradict each other, make trouble, tell on each other, come back like answers, organize their exchanges, protect each other, institute an internal commerce, take themselves for a dialogue. Full of meaning. A whole story. An entire history. All of philosophy.
>
> '*hē ēkhē toutōn tōn logōn* . . . the sound of these arguments rings so loudly in my head that I cannot hear the other side.'
>
> In this stammering buzz of voices, as some philological sequence or other floats by, one can sort of make this out, but it is hard to hear: as *logos* loves itself, it sows [*le logos s'aime lui-même*]. [A detailed 'example' of this buzz follows in the text.]
>
> As Plato stops up his ears, he makes mouths for himself [*Platon se bouche les oreilles*] . . .
>
> He listens, means to distinguish, between two repetitions.
>
> He is searching for gold. *Pollakis de logomena kai aei akoumena* . . . 'Often repeated and constantly attended to for many years, it is at last with great effort freed from all alloy, like gold . . .' and the philosopher's stone. The 'golden rule'.[11]

Marx offers us the following etiology seriously, in the best tradition of eighteenth-century proto-sociological discourses of origin, but the elements Derrida picks out seem clear. Derrida emphasises the apparent 'outside' provenance of what is 'superfluously' produced from the 'inside' as a problem besetting questions of origin. Marx offers the outside correspondence to the inside possibility as an unquestioned dialectical given. But the metaphor of the search for the universal symbol to stabilise commerce is, I think, unmistakable. (Derrida's parataxis gives the 'fable' as the origin story of both history *and* philosophy, history *as* philosophy. I continue to suggest that, for Marx, to undermine the fit of the two is the political moment.) Here is Marx: '[The] first phenomenal form [of exchange value] . . . dies out just as much by chance as it arises. The form of barter in which the overflow of one's own production is exchanged *by chance* . . . is determined by accidental needs, whims, etc. *But if it should happen to continue*, to become a continuing act which *contains within itself* the means of its renewal, then little by little, *from the outside* and likewise by chance, regulation of reciprocal exchange arises by means of regulation of reciprocal production . . .' (*Gr.* 204–5; italics mine).

Is such an originary account, like the role of the 'primary process' in Freud, a methodologically irreducible theoretical fiction?[12] For once the account is given, the bold suggestion can be made that (exchange) value itself is a text in the sense of a representation and a differential. Thus, as in Freud's manifest dream-text, the manifest text of money, the price-structure, displaces the latent *text* of value; to consolidate my point, I will move out of the *Grundrisse* for a moment, and consider the definitive passage in the canon, the passage in *Capital I* which gives value as a differential and a representation: 'In the exchange-relation of commodities their exchange-value appears to us as totally independent of their use-value. But if we abstract their use-value from the product of labour, we obtain their value, as it has just been defined. The common element that represents itself [*sich darstellt*] in the exchange-relation or exchange-value of the commodity, is thus value' (*C.* 128). Here use-value, implicitly as that which sublates the commodity-form through unmediated consumption, is itself operating as a theoretical fiction, as that positive thing which is to be subtracted from the undifferentiated product before the origin of value.[13] It is thus that value is here a differential and a representation. It is an abstraction that is represented in exchange-value. Exchange-value, at the same time, is a representation that is produced by value as its presupposition. This play of difference and representation inhabits the simplest act of exchange, the most primitive appropriation of surplus, as well as the most spectacular orchestration of superstructural economics. Marx is here presenting the fundamental conditions of operation of the economic sphere: difference (what is left when use-values are subtracted) and representation (of Value as the product of a differentiation).

We enter a further set of dialectical inter-determinations of difference and representation if we consider the relationships between value and price – 'real' value and 'nominal' value: 'Value *itself* – independently of its rule over the oscillations of the market price ... – negates itself and constantly posits the *real* value of commodities in contradiction with its own character ... [Value] appears as the law of motions which the former runs through. But the two are constantly different and never balance out or balance *only coincidentally*' (*Gr.* 137; italics mine).

We must not identify the potential overdeterminations of the dialectic, where adequation itself is a moment within definitive inadequation, with the general economy of deconstruction. Yet it is this inter-determining operation constitutive of the economic that allows us to call it a text, in the extended sense of textuality invoked on page 31. It is the implications of this notion that are closed off when the economic is dismissed or disavowed as pre-critical determinant, the lurking reductionist last instance even in its relatively autonomous form.

Money in its function of representing this product of a differentiation, is, then, equivalent to the sign of a sign in yet another way. The unified essence of the representamen is, in other words, further contradicted: 'as money as such ... it also contradicts itself because it must represent value as such; but represents in fact only a constant amount of fluctuating value' (*Gr.* 234). The economic text is operated by difference even before representation can arise. If, as we have suggested, the analysis of money in Marx gives it the structure of writing, we might quote Derrida to good purpose here: 'Arche-writing ... cannot occur *as such* within the phenomenological experience of a *presence*. It marks *the dead time* within the presence of the living present, within the general form of all presence. The dead time is at work.'[14] The labour theory of value, where living, working time is the hypothetical measure, is never accessible except through the dead time of difference as such ('difference between magnitudes and average magnitudes is not overcome merely by suppressing the *difference in name*' (*Gr.* 138)). Marx is careful to control it within the restricted economy of the dialectic by assigning the task of such an overcoming to money: '[Money] therefore sublates itself as completed ["conceptually adequate" (*Gr.* 167)] exchange-value' (*Gr.* 234).

Just as it is the efficiency and permanence of *writing – verba volent, scripta manent* – that seals its distance from the origin – so also is it this sublated conceptual adequation of money that ensures that it will never represent labour time directly.

I have opened up my earlier reading of money in the *Grundrisse* and further emphasised the textuality of the economic (made available to us by a deconstructive reading) because the disavowal of the economic is a much graver problem on the academic Left today, in 1985, than it was in 1978, when this essay began to take shape. The new humanist Left can perhaps be compared to those :

> modern economists [who] naturally make merry at the expense of this sort of notion [the cult of money] in the general section of books on economics. But when one considers the anxiety involved in the doctrine of money in particular, and the feverish fear with which, in practice, the inflow and outflow of gold and silver are watched in times of crisis, then it is evident that the aspect of money which the followers of the Monetary and Mercantilist system conceived in an artless one-sidedness is still to be taken seriously, not only in the mind, but as a real economic category. (*Gr.* 132)

Crisis theory explicitly and the world market implicitly are the prime movers of Marx's speculations on money in the *Grundrisse*. It is the insistently managed threat of recession in the West and the sustained effort to recompose society for investment rather than consumption, and the repercussions of this effort upon the international division of labour, that make Marx's warnings in a sense timely. They lay bare, even if only for a moment, the complicity of the academic and the political.

In the 'first' phase of industrial imperialism, it was possible for the colonising liberal bourgeoisie to be in principle anti-imperialist. In the 'second' phase – following the dissolution of the old territorial empires in the wake of the Second World War – it is no longer possible for the liberal leftist to ignore his complicity in crisis management through the manipulation of the international division of labour. 'In the real development of money [we know now how 'textualised' and non-'reductionist' such a phrase can be] there are contradictions which are unpleasant for the apologetics of bourgeois common sense, and must hence be covered up' (*Gr.* 198). The anti-economist Left is thus obliged to perform the classic gesture of welcoming victimisation as privilege : celebrate 'their separation from the dominant relations of production' as the necessary poverty of economic interpretations,[15] see a reckoning with the irreducible as mere reductionism. I have elsewhere extended this argument to include micro-electronic or post-modern capitalism.[16]

To force a reading of Marx through Derrida, then, opens up the textuality of the economic. It is true that Marx, in seeing the work of money as a usurping writing-work, uses an interpretable thematic. But the steps of his analysis resemble Derrida's analysis of the exclusivist and homogenising construction of the language of theory that is the medium of metaphysics. If we recall that Marx's description of money is not merely that it is the work of convenience of an abbreviating technology of the written sign; but also that it is the *ideal* homogenisation of a heterogeneous exchange, we can see the connection more clearly by way of a common critique of idealism.[17]

As Derrida argued in 'Force and Signification', reading is constituted by its forcing. He would argue that there is no free uncoerced reading against which a 'forced reading' can be defined. The following pages note the gap or displacement between Marx and Derrida which the force of a reading that wants to read both must uncover and work at without hope of articulation.

II

> The paradoxical logic of the apotropaic: to castrate oneself *already*, always already, in order to be able to castrate and repress the menace of castration, to renounce life and mastery in order to assure oneself of them; to put into play, by ruse, simulacrum, and violence, the very thing that one wishes to conserve; to lose in advance that which one wishes to erect; to suspend that which one raises: *aufheben*.[18]

Sublation or *Aufhebung* is the name of the force-gesture of the dialectic. There may be questions about the force that moves the dialectic; but about this force-gesture, which produces a new residue – the sublate, the *Aufgehoben* – there can be no disagreement. The trace of a contradiction within a thing makes it split asunder through the generation of a negation which then produces a third thing which raises, denies, suspends, and preserves the first. Force and play are the issue here. It is fitting that the English cognate (though not 'the correct meaning') of *Aufhebung* is 'upheaval'.

(In the passage cited above, Derrida is playing on the structural similarities between *Aufhebung* and the manipulation of castration-anxiety which, according to a certain psychoanalysis, is the insertion of the subject into social discursivity itself. If, in the passage cited on page 39, philosophical discourse is presented as the auto-eroticism of the logos, here socio-psychic discourse is given as a somewhat similar male-model force-gesture. To develop this argument is beyond the scope of the present essay.)[19]

Every reading is an upheaval of that which is read, not in the same way but unevenly. The slogan of 'the correct reading' would deny this, or, at best, attempt deliberately to minimise the upheaval, demonstrably to produce a reading that is as closely identical as possible with the transcendent intention of the author. By contrast, and no doubt through an accident of historical polemics (I should hold such 'accidents' irreducible), Marx publicised the upheaval that was his reading of Hegel, and claimed that the scientific truth of Hegel was in Marx's forced reading, the sublate that at once denied and preserved the Hegelian dialectic. The most famous of these is of course in the Postface to the second edition of *Capital I:* 'The Hegelian dialectic must be turned upside down [*umstülpen*], in order to uncover [*entdecken*] the rational kernel in the mystical shell' (*C.* 103).

In *Glas* Derrida presents his credentials as an upheaver of Hegel. He cannot claim that his upheft (sublate) of Hegel is the rational kernel of Hegel. The difference between his and Marx's readings of Hegel can be plotted along the lines I have marked in the last section. For what Derrida finally does with Hegel in *Glas* is called 'a setting wild [*dérèglement*] of the *seminarium* [the seed-bed of a nursery]'. I have mentioned earlier that Derrida urges a deconstruction of the binary opposition between concept and metaphor (page 36). If the conceptuality of certain metaphors in the text of Hegel are honoured, the seasonality of time is seen to be crucial. Nowhere is this more important that in the metaphor of the *seminarium*. Paying closer attention to the apparent idiosyncrasy of metaphor, Derrida attempts to follow here a method that is not identical with that of capital. 'The sickness of seasons' – located in the metaphoricity of the phenomenology of mind and the science of logic – 'does not absolutely destroy or paralyse the infinite concept . . . The nasty trick [bad turn; *mauvais tour*] of the seasons having come to unhinge [*détraquer*] the history of the spirit, the saturnalia of the *Sa* [*Savoir absolu*; absolute knowledge] would be in league with a setting wild of the *seminarium*' (*Gl.* 260a). Like Marx, although via Hegel, Derrida's metaphor of reading involves the seed or germ.[20] The metaphoric logic, however, has been changed. For Marx to uncover the kernel, a procedure contingent upon the season of the fruit's plucking. For Derrida to set wild the seed-bed – to make the semes susceptible to dissemination.

Althusser suggests that Derrida's relationship to Marx is along the lines of the 'erasure' and 'the category of process without subject':

> (To affirm and, in the same moment, to *deny* the origin), Hegel assumed this consciously in his theory of the *Beginning* in the Logic: Being is immediately non-Being . . . Hegel's logic is of the affirmed-denied Origin: the first form of a concept that Derrida has introduced into philosophical reflection, the *erasure*.
>
> But the Hegelian 'erasure', which the logic is from its very first word, is the negation of the negation, dialectical, therefore teleological. It is in the teleology that the true Hegelian Subject arises. Take away the teleology, and what remains is that philosophical category which Marx inherited: the category of *process without subject*.[21]

I have written at length of the Derridean erasure elsewhere. The 'Process without Subject' relates to the thought of textuality in general to which I refer in the opening of this essay. I need not repeat the obvious point that to equate 'subject' with individual agent is a mistake. My focus is slightly different. It is in the area where Marx and Derrida force the reading of a philosopher who provided a description of the forcing that I force a reading and a displaced consistency. Although this is not the explicit topic of my essay, it should by now be clear that it is its point of reference.

Any extended consideration of this Hegel–Marx–Derrida conjuncture would analyse the relationship between a Derridean and a Marxian suggestion. Here is Derrida :

> All that Hegel thought within [the] horizon [of absolute knowledge], all, that is, except eschatology, may be read as a meditation on writing. Hegel is *also* the thinker of irreducible difference. He rehabilitated thought as the *memory productive* of signs. And he reintroduced . . . the essential necessity of the written trace in a philosophical . . . discourse that had always believed it possible to do without it; the last philosopher of the book and the first thinker of writing;[22]

and here is Marx : 'In its mystified form, the dialectic . . . seemed to transfigure and glorify what exists. In its rational form . . . it includes in its positive understanding of what exists a simultaneous recognition of its negation, its inevitable destruction' (*C.* 103). The type of analysis I am proposing would hinge on the deconstruction of the opposition between the rational and the mystified. I shall go on to suggest that there is room for this deconstruction in Marx's own text.

III

In *Limited Inc abc*, Derrida provides an analogy between his thought and Marx's. To catch that analogy, I shall make a summary of Derrida on the 'proper'. Marx's analysis of the irreducible impropriety of money is tied up with a critique of the impropriety of private property. I suggested in Section I that this could be 'made consistent with' Derrida's analysis of the language of theory. The analogy that Derrida himself suggests is in the service of a critique of the impropriety of the proper as such.

The investigation and critique of the 'proper' has been a very large part of Derrida's work. His speculations have circled about the implications of *proprius* and *propre*. Property as distinguishing predication and as self-possession; the proper as that which is so self-proximate that it is self-adequate or self-identical; the proper name, a genealogical mark, as the most intimate legal sign of this adequate predication, this self-proximity of self-possession. Why can we not do without these conceptual practices, these hierarchical judgements? What do they conceal, reveal, make (im)possible?

(Since *Spurs*, Derrida's critique of the proper, more specifically 'propriation', has become imbricated with the question of woman. To open that complex issue here would be beyond the scope of this essay. Since I have thus put out of play two arguments seemingly involved with feminism [here and on page 44], I should perhaps add that, in my view (a) the project of Western Marxism, indeed of much Western Marxist feminism, is discontinuous with feminism in general; my current work is almost fully devoted to this; and (b) that one does not need Derrida to realise that Marx wrote within the homo-erotic tradition of philosophy, and that he was not, *specifically*, feminist.)

In French the *propre* is not merely proper but also clean. Derrida has written on the strange kinship between *propriété* (property, propriety) and *propreté* (cleanliness). In *Signéponge* all these concerns are woven together. 'Ponge' is the poet Francis Ponge's patronymic or proper name as property-holder. The title of Derrida's essay, if broken up according to the accepted rules of word-play, would yield : *Signe et Ponge* (sign and Ponge); *Signé Ponge* (signed Ponge), and *signe-éponge* (sign-sponge; the sign as the instrument and agent of erasure and cleanliness).[23] How do cleanliness and the sign 'connect'? If one is not attending to Derrida, the connection does not spring immediately to the eye. As follows, briefly :

The language of philosophy professes to be 'clean'. It is also the shortest distance between truth and sign. No metaphoric detours to truth are allowed there. All adventitious material (empirical or exceptional, depending on the kind of philosophy you choose) must be excluded in order to build its route. This cleanliness is not only next to, but on the way to, the godliness of truth, a truth that is vouched for in the name of the god that is its own cleanliness.

It is this obsessive 'cleanliness' or rigour that Derrida questions, and points here and there at how all projects of philosophical cleanliness must conceal their own befoulment, and, more important (though this point is far less often grasped), that cleanliness is constituted by varieties of befoulment which, being implicit in all originary concepts of cleanliness, are methodologically irreducible.

The analogy between Marx and Derrida is located in a set of arguments that can be placed within this particular line of questioning. Derrida applauds J. L. Austin's inquiry into the peculiar 'cleanliness' of the language of traditional philosophy. Yet he also discloses the establishment of certain 'clean' contours within Austinian Speech Act theory. The formulaic cleanliness of Austin's theory is in the service of a certain ambition to discover godliness in speech – a special speech act where Word and Deed are one, where by saying we do – the category of the Performative.[24]

Derrida's response to Speech Act theory is in two parts. The first part, 'Signature Event Context', is a reading of J. L. Austin's *How To Do Things With Words.* The second, *Limited Inc abc*, is a reply to John R. Searle's critique of the first essay. In *Limited Inc*, as Derrida deals with the exclusivism of the Performative, his language often becomes overtly political. For example, he calls 'the system of (il- or per-locutionary) intentions and the systems of ("vertical") rules or of ("horizontal") conventions' 'the language-police' or 'the internal regulation through which the capitalist system seeks to limit concentration and decision-making power in order to protect itself against its own "crisis" '.[25]

Derrida is constructing a loose analogy to the crisis of capital (overproduction, underconsumption, tendency of the rate of profit to fall – can these be pulled into the frame of reference of Derrida's analogy? I do not think so) being partially controlled by mergers and 'equalisation' of profits among competing individual capitals. 'Equalisation' or *Gleichsetzung* carries particular persuasive weight here (see page 35). The control is operated in the linguistic theatre by the assumption that homogeneous intentions are neatly housed and expressed in acts of speech, and in producing an exhaustive taxonomy on the basis of that assumption.

Psychoanalysis has suggested that we might not be fully at home to ourselves, that the presupposition of an intending subject might be constituted by the presupposition of a radically irreducible other, that the sense of a unified self might be made up of temporally (in terms of 'psychic time') unreliable (from the point of view of our picture of self, intention, and experience) animations and connections produced by the work of a psychic machine that has, in its different parts, different 'objectives' that themselves change discontinuously. It is therefore necessary, beyond the outlines of psychoanalysis as a discipline, to entertain the structural possibility that intention is irreducibly heterogeneous. It will not do to say 'Why not get down to discussing the thing bang off in terms of linguistics and psychology in a straightforward fashion? . . . *after*, not before, seeing what we can screw out of ordinary language even if in what comes out there is a strong element of the undeniable' (Austin); for such a postponement leads finally to a position such as the following : 'to know what an intention is, or what any other intentional state with a direction of fit is, we do not need to know the material or psychological properties of its realisation' (Searle).[26]

Against this works a language-police of exclusivist consensus or convention, based upon the convenient assumption that a homogeneous intention is neatly housed in acts of speech. Although Derrida's choice of metaphor is probably incidental, it can certainly be argued that the other term of this analogy may be found in a passage like the following from *Capital I:*

> Commodities cannot go to market and exchange themselves. We must, therefore, have recourse to their guardians, the commodity-owners. . . . In order to relate these things as commodities, their guardians must relate to one another as persons whose will is housed in these things. . . . They must therefore recognise each other as owners of private property. This relationship of right, whose form is the contract, . . . is a relationship of wills which mirrors the economic relation. . . . Here persons exist for one another only as representatives and hence owners of commodities.
>
> (*C.* 178–9)

So that the so-called exchange (inter-communication, or, simply, communication) of intentions (the property – in more senses than one – of the subject as voice-consciousness) can seem to take place successfully, certain conventions must be agreed upon among the custodians of language. All incursions of heterogeneity must be indefinitely postponed ('*after*, not before') or rejected out of hand ('we do not need to know'). 'Persons [must] exist for one another only as representatives and hence owners of [intentions].'

It is interesting to note that Derrida is traditional in his method of constructing the analogy between crisis-management and speech act theory, as clarified by Marx's metaphor of mirroring. By contrast, Marx recommends *decipherment* in the famous passage on the fetishisation of the commodity, where the latter is seen as a text or a transcript that is not merely to be de-*coded* in terms of a reflection theory of intention : 'It does not therefore stand written on the forehead of value, what it is [*Es steht daher dem Werte nicht auf der Stirn geschrieben, was er ist*]; it rather transforms every product of labour into a social hieroglyphic. Later on, human beings [*Menschen*] try to decipher the hieroglyphic, to get behind the secret of their own social product' (*C.* 167).

This does not take away from the fact that Derrida's critique of communication as exchange of intentions can be extended to such diverse areas as bourgeois theories of consumer behaviour, media sociology and its relationship to post-industrial capitalist culture, 'universalist' ethical theories and their foreclosure of the heritage of imperialism and neo-colonialism.[27]

At first glance, the Marxian passage about the 'relationship of wills' (page 48) seems to keep the predication of property grounded in an essentialist way. Is that not the point of Derrida's footnote in 'White Mythology'? That Marx criticises *bad* property, the result of political economy, and contrasts it to the 'intrinsic' senses of the proper?

In a certain sense this cannot be denied. I must therefore force the question a little more. In spite of the burden of evidence to the contrary, is it possible to locate an itinerary of the improper in Marx?

IV

The question of the subject was and remained a problem for Marx. Not only from the point of view of man's self, but equally from the point of view of that process without a subject of which Althusser writes, the process of the self-determination of the Idea most elaborately articulated in Hegel's *Science of Logic*, the book that Marx 'by mere accident' happened 'to leaf through' as he was putting together the *Grundrisse*, 'the seven notebooks rough-drafted . . . chiefly for purposes of self-clarification.'[28] It seems hardly necessary to say that the 'subject' of this process in Hegel is indeed the Idea. As Marx's notebooks make abundantly clear, that which takes the place of the Idea (in the process) for Marx is capital. This is where the genius of Ricardo had failed; he had no clue to the morphology of a concept's self-determination.

To study the development of capital as the Idea develops – this is both Marx's solution and problem. The most obvious problem is that of necessity, so obvious indeed that the charge is brought even on the most ignorant and reactionary plane against all varieties of Marxism. The Idea necessarily determines itself according to the Science of Logic. So does the idea of capital, as indeed the idea of anything. But the subject of the Hegelian science is not the idea of the Idea, or one idea among many. It is *the* idea, the Idea. Thus, although it is commonly explained that capital in Marx, in spite of being studied by means of Hegel's logic, does not carry the aura of necessity that Hegel's object of study – the Idea – does, it is also possible to say that, since capital in Marx is *in the place of the Idea*, it is necessarily contaminated by the burden of necessity.

At least two problems arise here. First, that capital should be dragged into the circuit of irreducible necessity. To say that in order to know it one must know it in its irreducible necessity, although to act with respect to it (to do toward it rather than to know it) one must contradict that knowledge, solves the theory–practice problem in too simple a way. It is rather that Marx questions philosophical 'justice' and 'elegance' (and necessity) even as he uses them to establish his analysis. Otherwise Marx could not write of the extraction of surplus-value, the condition of possibility of capitalist exploitation: 'This circumstance is a piece of good luck for the buyer [of labour-power : the capitalist], but by no means an injustice towards the seller [of labour-power : the worker]' (*C.* 301). A purely *philosophical* justification for revolutionary practice cannot be found.

It is because this heterogeneous concatenation of 'knowing' and 'doing', this possibility of a radical critique of philosophical justice, is most often recuperated within a reading *in terms of* philosophical justice and consistency, that the deconstructive moment in Marx is seen as a blind condemnation of what, according to Marx's own system, is philosophically just. To quote what I think is a representative example: '[In Marx] it is Science and Technology that fulfil the essence of Nature by indefinitely reproducing it as separated.

However, they do this in the name of a finality supposed to be Nature itself.'[29]

The second problematic implication of the filling of the empty place of plenitude in Logic by capital gives rise to the following question : what if the system of the logic only functioned correctly in terms of an irreducibly necessary Subject? Can one sustain the conclusion about capital as 'correct' in that case?

These perplexities are at once caused by, and generate, what I call the mark of the improper. The methodology is doubted by the text, yet the grounds of a practice based on the methodology are endorsed. It is written into the practice of the theory that the example cannot be proper or adequate to the discourse.

A version of this radical impropriety is the theme of Derrida's work. Derrida suggests further that this impropriety represents itself as (a desire for) the proper. The argument that all methodologies are radically improper, has provoked the strongest criticism: irrationalism, nihilism, negative theology, radical scepticism, paralysis. To protect oneself against these presumed dangers, one chooses to understand as nothing but common sense, mere rhetorical gestures, or yet as marginal comments, Marx's own undeveloped admissions: that his analysis must use the same method that makes the object of his analysis an evil : abstracting out individual heterogeneity into a quantitative measure of homogeneous labour so that calculation may be possible: 'In every value-formation-process the higher labour must be reduced to average social labour. . . . One thus saves a superfluous operation and simplifies the analysis by the assumption that the worker employed by capital performs simple average social labour' (*C.* 306).

There is something in common between the method of analysis (reduction) and the property of capital – where the method seeks its own convenience by abbreviation (simplify the analysis). This can pose an unresolvable problem for a philosophy of action. Although he criticises the political economists for their uncritical attitude toward the capitalist mode of production, Marx is obliged to present his own participation in capital's method as no more than a necessary methodological hazard. Derrida emphasises that such a simplification and such an alliance *constitute* the method of all theory, always giving the pre-critical myth of truth the lie. I have tried to suggest that it is in Marx's basic critique of the suppression of heterogeneity that the Derridean analogy is to be found. Derrida's analogy (and indeed all his work, most especially 'White Mythology' and *Limited*

Inc) discloses that the method of all logic – Hegel's science of logic or the logic of the speech act – is allied to capitalism : exclusivism, a common code represented as universal, suppression of heterogeneity. It is not enough to say, as Marx or Althusser does, that freed of its idealistic burden, the method of logic can yield proper science. Putting capital in the place of the Idea, Marx's materialism is more radical than Marx's text allows.

It would of course be absurd to take a diagnostic attitude toward Marx's text in this regard. I should rather attempt to force a reading in terms of what has enabled one to make the diagnosis in the first place; to show the power of Marx's text in terms of the supplement it asks for. I have noticed how Marx's text is improper to itself, needs more than 'itself' in order to be read, gives a reading here that more than matches a reading that is refused there, and uses a method that is originarily contaminated.

The itinerary of the improper in Marx does not stop here. The problem is not simply that capital, the agent of Marx's logic, is contingent and evil. It is also that it is radically im-proper. In the place of self-proximity and self-possession, it must provide itself with the mind of one class of human beings and the body of another. As Marx writes, quoting *Faust*, it is 'an animated monster which begins to work "*as if* it had love in its body" ' (*C.* 302).

The class of human beings whose mind capital must *appropriate* (*an-eignen* – make its own) in order to create its monstrous self is the capitalist class. 'As the conscious bearer of this movement [the movement of capital], the possessor of money becomes a capitalist . . . The *objective* content of the valorization of value becomes his *subjective* purpose . . . and it is only insofar as this is his sole driving force that he functions as . . . capital personified and endowed with consciousness and a will' (*C.* 254).

The class of human beings whose *body* capital must appropriate is the working class. (Here a slight but important difference must be noted. As a 'materialist' in the most colloquial sense, Marx will privilege the body over the mind. Labour itself cannot be usurped, especially not by the transformed power of money, which derives its efficacy by the idealisation of a material gesture. It is the potential of the worker's body actualised in time ['living labour'] that capital usurps.) Time remains constitutive of value. Capital is a determination of value. Its body is made up of the workers' bodies in time. 'Capital is dead labour which, vampire-like, lives only by sucking living labour, and lives the more, the more labour it sucks' (*C.* 342).

But, paradoxically enough, it is not only capital, that monster and vampire, that has no proper being. In this scheme, free human labour can be appropriated by capital because it too can be im-proper to itself. As I have remarked earlier, the distinguishing *property* of labour-power is to be improper, in excess of self-adequation. (This fact does not come about with capitalism; capitalism rationalises it for the purposes of the self-determination of capital.) *Even* if the body is made the privileged pole of the body–mind opposition (and this is by no means always true in Marx), labour-power cannot be adequate to itself. It is in its *nature* to perform *more* than the body's adequation or reproduction. There is room for capital's appropriation within its nature (just as, it can be argued, there is room for appropriation by labour in Nature). To make labour-power adequate to the body so as to release its potential for excess would be the *artificial* obligation of the class struggle, and of social or revolutionary justice.

Although this is clearly Marx's argument, his conclusions are not clearly drawn. We remain caught within the opposition *Fremdarbeit* (alienated labour) and *Eigenarbeit* (proper labour) – work for the capitalist and for oneself. Here Derrida allows us to see that the condition of possibility of this opposition is *Eigenarbeit*'s own 'impropriety' or inadequation to itself. (Perhaps I should repeat that Derrida's critique is of the concept of truth as the concept's adequation to reality and therefore to itself; Derrida shows that the condition of the possibility of the opposition between truth and metaphor is the concept's 'im-propriety' or inadequation to itself.) Marx's well-known conclusions, even when the in- or super-adequation of labour-power to the body is most clearly articulated, is one of opposition, not complicity: 'Suddenly there arises the voice of the worker . . .: "The commodity I have sold you [my labour-power] differs from the rest of the crowd of commodities in that its use makes value, a greater value than it itself costs" ' (*C.* 342). The necessary labour that is adequate to the body's continuation can always be exceeded by the body's potential, which by virtue of time's constitutive agency is *susceptible* to idealisation, that is, transformation into value, the species term of capital. It is by *an-eigen*-ing (appropriating) that *Eigenschaft* (property) of labour-power that capital generates *Eigentum* (property). ('Appropriation through and mediated by divestiture and alienation [*Ent- und VeräuBerung*] is the fundamental presupposition' (*Gr.* 196).) This can be one version of the itinerary of the improper in Marx. I have not gone too far from Derrida's footnote.

The itinerary of the im-proper in Marx runs also through that end-and-origin term, use-value, against which is posed the contingent circuit of exchange value. 'The usefulness of a thing makes it a use-value . . . The very body of the commodity is therefore a use-value. Thus its characteristic does not depend upon whether the appropriation of its useful properties [*Gebrauchseigenschaften*] cost men little or much time. . . . Use-value realises [*verwirklicht*] itself only in use or consumption' (*C.* 126). But this body of the commodity – 'iron, corn, a diamond' – signifies an exchange-situation between man and nature. It is a 'good' exchange, perpetrated by the concrete individual, before the 'bad' exchange organised by abstraction has set in. The presence of a version of exchange ('relationship') in descriptions of the origin of society in an identity of man and nature is to be seen even in the early writings. 'The identity of nature and man appears in such a way that the restricted relation to one another determines men's restricted relation to nature, just because nature is as yet hardly modified historically, and, on the other hand, man's consciousness of the necessity of associating with the individuals around him is the beginning of the consciousness that he is living in society at all.'[30] Here again Derrida's argument from supplementarity helps us. If a hierarchical opposition is set up between two concepts (identity/relationship, use-value/exchange-value), the less favoured or logically posterior concept can be shown to be implicit in the other, supply a lack in the other that was always already there. Although Baudrillard sees this merely as Marx's ideological problem, whereas he can himself speak for 'primitive societies', his remarks are useful here :

> The system of political economy does not produce only the individual as labour power that is sold and exchanged: it produces the very conception of labour power as the fundamental human potential. . . . The system is rooted in the identification of the individual with his labour power and with his act of "transforming nature according to human ends." In a word, man is not only quantitatively exploited as a productive force by the *system* of capitalist economy, but is also overdetermined as a producer by the *code* of political economy.[31]

The opposition between use-value and exchange-value can be deconstructed, and *both* can be shown to share the mark of impropriety. The category of use-value is emptied of its archeoteleological pathos when it is used to describe the relationship between capital and labour-power. The capitalisation of living labour is the realisation of the use-value of labour *seen as a commodity by capital.* Here Marx's complaint may be simply that the monster bred of idealisation should thus be capable of consuming and realising the potential of the human body as a commodity. It may be the anguish of a materialist philosopher, in however restricted a sense, rather than the unexamined idealism of a self-deceived materialist.[32]

Very generally speaking, the objective of *Capital I* seems always to have been to make the philosophical ground accessible to 'the worker' as the considered target for future action. In the *Grundrisse* on the other hand Marx is writing 'for himself' and the 'future action' is the writing of a book. Whereas in the *Capital* the tone is that of an outraged olympian, in the *Grundrisse* the bafflement shows, is worked at, and sometimes controlled by a gesture of postponement.

In the *Capital* Marx can cover in mockery the problem that value (→money→capital) is the agency equivalent to the Idea in Hegel's logic. In the *Grundrisse* the problem remains in the background, a methodological necessity whose implications are hinted at only in rare passages. Here is the mockery in *Capital I*:

> Value differentiates itself as original value from itself as surplus-value, just as God the father differentiates himself from himself as God the Son, although both are of the same age and form, in fact, one single person; for only by the surplus-value of £10 does the £100 originally advanced become capital, and as soon as this has happened, as soon as the son has been created, and, through the son, the father, their difference vanishes again, and both become one, £110. (*C.* 256)

By contrast, when Marx hints at the relationship between capital and the matrix of the self-determining concept in the *Grundrisse*, his tone is remarkably sober. Marx is speaking of capital's effort to reduce circulation time to an impossible zero, because the circulation of *commodities* is a barrier to, as well as a condition of its development, for realisation, and therefore capital-accumulation, depends upon the velocity of the circulation of *money*:

> The continuity of production presupposes that circulation time has been sublated [*aufgehoben*]. The nature of capital presupposes that it travels through the different phases of circulation not as it does in the idea-representation [*Vorstellung*], where one concept turns into the other at the speed of thought [*mit Gedankenschnelle*], in no time, but rather as situations which are separated in terms of time. (*Gr.* 548)

Here Marx implies not only that capital appropriates the mind and body of capitalist and worker but, on a greater level of abstraction, seeks to appropriate the determination of concepts in the Idea. (In economic terms, the progressive minimisation of circulation time is one of the factors leading to the crisis of capital.) I have been suggesting, of course, that on a comparable level of abstraction as well as in the concretest detail of work and writing as work this usurpation occurs in any construction of theory. The method of *Capital* – the title of a book – is the method of capital – the value form – (as Marx points out) not by special dispensation but because making theory has something in common with capitalisation (as Derrida points out).

This is how I force my reading then; but the result is not altogether a consistency. For at the limit Marx will not grant that the definition of mind itself can be brought into the circuit of self-impropriety and monstrosity. The groundstone of idealism with, as it were, a small 'i', is still intact. Circulation being a physical process, dependent upon material exigencies, must take time. Constitutive temporality in Marx is free to side with good or evil. As I have already pointed out, it is time or rather measurement by time that mediates the susceptibility of labour-power to capitalisation or valorisation. In the case of circulation, time, in an older-fashioned way, declares *for* the mind by declaring its kingdom without the reach of capital. The speed of the mind is instantaneous and there capital cannot go. This incipient common-sense (what is 'common sense' if not ideology at its strongest?) faith in mind over matter, this trace of idealism – which must be carefully distinguished from the vulgar rationalism that Marx is usually accused of – that pervades the *Grundrisse* will not let me force a consistent reading.

Why did Marx choose to emphasise *mit Gedankenschnelle* ('at the speed of thought') with words that are in English in the original – 'in no time'? Writing on the idea of the instantaneity of inner discourse in Husserl, Derrida writes of the moment (*Augenblick*, literally 'blink of the eye'):

> The dominance of the now not only is integral to the system of the founding contract established by metaphysics, that between *form* (or *eidos* or idea) and matter as a contrast between act and potency, . . . it also assures the tradition that carries over the Greek metaphysics of presence into the 'modern' metaphysics of presence understood as self-consciousness, the metaphysics of the idea as representation (*Vorstellung*).

Derrida, reading without the ideology of a unified reading, and without the credo that consistency is the mark of excellence, finds in Husserl himself the wherewithal to 'undermine the *im selben Augenblick* argument.' If we allow the pervasive thematics of im-propriety in Marx to operate, we too might find in the Marxian text the wherewithal to undermine its own traces of traditional metaphysics. For capital to occupy (*besetzen*, what in Freud is translated as 'cathect') the place of the Idea, on the one hand, and for use-value to be primordially contaminated by exchange on the other, are transgressions that Marx's text and its ostensible burden cannot come to terms with. And, 'as soon as we admit this continuity between [Idea, Capital, and Labour], . . . nonpresence and nonevidence are admitted into the blink of the *instant*. There is a duration to the blink, and it closes the eye. This alterity is in fact the condition for presence, presentation and thus for *Vorstellung* in general: it precedes all dissociations that could be produced in presence, in *Vorstellung*.'[33]

Can one, only half fancifully, presume that Marx, beset with creditors, knew that the idiomatic expression 'in no time' meant, not in no time, but in the briefest possible time? Should one read the passage within the structure of *Verneinung* (denegation) where a no can mean yes and also, I need to say no so I can say yes, and so on indefinitely? Forced readings open the path of a question rather than close the door with a decidable consistency. This, too, must remain an open question.

It seems appropriate to end these musings in the middle of things, with the opening of a question. There is an informing pathway of the improper in Marx's texts. If one forces a reading of Marx in order to make him consistent with Derrida, the text becomes practicable. It is a peculiar consistency, because it tries to recognise and acknowledge what is not proper to itself. If this seems 'the power of puns', I refer my reader, in search of the place where the pun stops, once again to 'White Mythology', which argues that at the origin is a version of punning.

To make 'literary' in this sense, then, is to 'make practicable'. Not, that is to say, to expose the irreducible self-constitution of the text as self-deconstruction; but to show that the moment of the deconstruction of 'philosophical' justice is the minute foothold of practice.[34] It is the peculiar case of Marx's text that, no consideration of that moment, merely sketched in this essay by way of philosophy and literature, can be broached without recounting the justice–practice heterogeneity in other fields, ideology, history, political economy. And perhaps, with greater difficulty and effort, the field of sexual difference.

The question no longer seems so open. The project of the 'othering of the proper' – *die Welt zu ver-ändern* (eleventh thesis on Feuerbach) – can produce a critique of classical Marxism as well as of deconstruction. Here a deconstitution of the production of the colonial subject seems necessary.

Derrida suspected these limits, indeed signalled them, when in *Of Grammatology* he declared grammatology impossible as positive science, though it must constantly offer the possibility of one. Marking the place of that (im)possibility was an account of the occidentalist project of appropriating the languages of China and Egypt for the purpose of the philosophical and theological vindication of Europe's preferred autobiography as history.

As the proper name 'grammatology' has given way to 'deconstruction', this caution of (im)possibility has been forgotten. The pro-deconstructive Left and certain sections of the sympathetic mainstream in Britain and the US now accept deconstruction as *realia* and ask, respectively: can deconstruction be Marxist, can we live deconstructively? That phenomenon one must think through under the rubric of 'the desire for deconstruction'.[35]

NOTES

1 A shorter version of this essay has appeared in William E. Cain, ed., *Philosophical Approaches to Literature: New Essays on Nineteenth- and Twentieth-Century Texts* (Lewisburg: Bucknell University Press, 1983).

2 'Living On: *Border Lines*', in Harold Bloom *et al.*, *Deconstruction and Criticism* (New York: Seabury Press, 1979), p. 84.

This is a pervasive programme in Derrida. One might look specifically at 'The Exorbitant. Question of Method', in *Of Grammatology*, tr. Spivak (Baltimore: Johns Hopkins University Press, 1976). This, it seems to me, is one reason why Derrida is dissatisfied with the inflation of the model of language to accommodate all structural descriptions. This, in fact, is also why he substitutes 'writing' for 'language'. As he suggests in that book, the study of the heterogeneous writing structure cannot become a positive science because it resists reduction to verbal or linguistic textuality. I read as a related argument Derrida's warning that 'what weighs upon them [two supposedly opposed philosophical traditions] both, transcending this curious chiasmus, are forces of a non-philosophical nature', some of which get spelled out as 'a terrain whose neutrality is far from certain', and 'the political significance of the university' ('Limited Inc.', *Glyph* 2, 1977). I have elaborated this reading in

'Revolutions That As Yet Have No Model: Derrida's "Limited Inc." ', *Diacritics*, 10 iv (Winter 1980), 29–49.

3 *Spurs: Nietzsche's Styles*, tr. Barbara Harlow (Chicago: University of Chicago Press, 1981), p. 113.

4 *Margins of Philosophy*, tr. Alan Bass (Chicago: University of Chicago Press, 1982), pp. 216–17.

5 Karl Marx, *Grundrisse: Foundations of the Critique of Political Economy*, tr. Martin Nicolaus (New York: Vintage Books, 1973); hereafter cited as *Gr.*

6 Derrida, 'From Restricted to General Economy', in *Writing and Difference*, tr. Alan Bass (Chicago: University of Chicago Press, 1978; and 'The Supplement of Copula: Philosophy *Before* Linguistics', tr. James Creech and Josué Harari, in *Textual Strategies: Perspectives in Post-Structuralist Criticism*, ed. Josué Harari (Ithaca: Cornell University Press, 1979).

7 Marx, *Capital: A Critique of Political Economy*, tr. Ben Fowkes (New York: Vintage, 1976), vol. 1, p. 214. Hereafter cited as *C.*

8 Spivak, 'Scattered Speculations on the Question of Value', *Diacritics* 15 iv (Winter 1985), 78.

9 G. W. F. Hegel, *The Science of Logic*, tr. A. V. Miller (New York: Humanities Press, 1976), p. 88 Hegel's history is, of course, the history of philosophy.

10 It cannot be overemphasised that exchange-value is *not* a corruption of use-value but rather is the 'second [form of value] . . . ALONGSIDE use-value' (*Gr.* 177).

11 *Dissemination*, tr. Barbara Johnson (Chicago: University of Chicago Press, 1981), pp. 169–70 (translation modified).

12 *The Standard Edition of the Psychological Writings of Sigmund Freud*, tr. James Strachey, *et al.* (London: Hogarth Press, 1961), vol. 7, p. 598.

13 In a more extended discussion I would plot use-value here in terms of what I have elsewhere called 'the double session of differance' ('Varieties of Deconstructive Practice', unpublished lecture, School of Criticism and Theory, Northwestern University, June, 1982) – the first session a necessary pre-supposition of a pre-originary space, the second the necessary effacement of the tracing of that space.

14 *Of Grammatology*, p. 68.

15 Ernesto Laclau, *Politics and Ideology in Marxist Theory: Capitalism–Fascism–Populism* (London: Verso, 1979), p. 114.

16 See 'The Production of "Post-Modernism": Rei Kawakubo's Minimalist Aesthetics', forthcoming in the Proceedings of *Futur* Fall*, University of Sydney (Australia).

17 This point has been subsequently developed in Michael Ryan, *Marxism and Deconstruction: A Critical Articulation* (Baltimore: Johns Hopkins University Press, 1982).

18 Derrida, *Glas* (Paris: Galilée, 1974), p. 56; hereafter cited as *Gl.*

19 I have touched upon this argument in 'The Letter As Cutting Edge', in Shoshana Felman, ed., *Literature and Psychoanalysis: The*

Question of Reading: Otherwise (Baltimore: Johns Hopkins University Press, 1982); and, '*Glas*-Piece: A Compte-Rendu', *Diacritics* 7 iii (Fall, 1977).

20 It is interesting that in footnote 10 to 'White Mythology', Derrida refers us precisely to those passages in Althusser where the latter investigates the metaphoric logic in Marx. In this connection, it might not be inappropriate to mention that, in the celebrated passage where he contrasts science and history, Althusser 'demotes' science itself to a metaphor: 'When I say that Marx organised a theoretical system of scientific concepts in the domain where previously the philosophies of history reigned supreme [*régnaient*], I am extending a metaphor which is no more than a metaphor' (Louis Althusser, *Lenin and Philosophy and Other Essays*, tr. Ben Brewster (New York: Monthly Review Press, 1971), p. 38). It should be obvious that to learn from Althusser is not necessarily to endorse every specific position he took in the course of a very active career.

21 Louis Althusser, 'Sur le rapport de Marx à Hegel', in *Hegel et la pensée moderne*, ed. Jacques d'Hendt (Paris: Presses universitaires de France, 1970), p. 109. Two years before *Glas*, Derrida commented briefly on Marx's project to turn the Hegelian dialectic upside down ('Outwork', *Dissemination*, p. 31–3). It is well-known that, in the passage where he outlined that project, Marx declared that he 'avowed myself the pupil of that mighty thinker' [Hegel] because 'arrogant and mediocre epigones' had begun to treat him 'as a "dead dog"' and that 'thirty years ago I criticised the mystificatory side of the Hegelian dialectic when it was still the fashion' (*C.* 102–3). This may be compared to Derrida's more circumspect words: 'Though I am not and have never been an orthodox marxist, I am very disturbed by the antimarxism dominant now in France so that, as a reaction, through political reflection and personal preference, I am inclined to consider myself more marxist than I would have done at a time when Marxism was a sort of fortress' (James Kearns and Ken Newton, 'An Interview with Jacques Derrida', *The Literary Review* 14 (18 April–1 May, 1980), p. 22).

22 *Grammatology*, p. 26.

23 *Signéponge/Signsponge*, tr. Richard Rand (New York: Columbia University Press, 1984).

24 Austin, *How To Do Things With Words* (Cambridge, Mass.: Harvard University Press, 1962).

25 *Glyph* 2, pp. 243, 226.

26 *How To Do Things*, p. 123; Searle, 'What is an Intentional State?', *Mind* 88 (January, 1979), p. 82.

27 As general references, see Paul Samuelson, *Foundations of Economic Analysis* (Enlarged Edition, Cambridge, Mass.: Harvard University Press, 1983); David and Diane Cooke, *A Cultural History of Television* (forthcoming from University of California Press); and Spivak, 'Politics of "Feminist Culture"'.

28 Nicolaus, 'Foreword' (*Gr.* 7, 26).

29 Jean Baudrillard, *The Mirror of Production*, tr. Mark Poster (St

Louis: Telos Press, 1975), p. 55. In 1973, commenting on the disappointment attendant upon May 1968 and the academic backlash to the possibility of a Left Coalition government in France, Jacques Rancière wrote bitterly about the change in the intellectual climate: 'If Marx hasn't worked, try Nietzsche' (*La Leçon d'Althusser* (Paris: Gallimard, 1974), p. 14). That change can be described practically by way of the doing/knowing dyad. The asymmetry between doing and knowing in Marx, I am suggesting, is where the opening of practice can be inserted. 'After Nietzsche', on the other hand, '(and, indeed, after any "text"), we can no longer hope ever "to know" in peace. Neither can we expect "to do" anything, least of all to expurge "to know" and "to do", as well as their latent opposition from our vocabulary' (Paul de Man, *Allegories of Reading: Figural Language in Rousseau, Nietzsche, Rilke, and Proust* (New Haven: Yale University Press, 1979), p. 126). Even if doing is conceived of as irreducibly verbal – as, according to de Man, in Nietzsche; or if what is opposed to knowing is structured like a writing, as in Shelley's notion of the imagination, a more plausible, though still idealist, model of deferred practice can be found. Writing specifically of the production of relative surplus-value and division of labour by means of technology – 'a cultivation of the mechanical arts in a degree disproportioned to the presence of the creative faculty' leading to 'the abuse of all invention for *abridging and combining labour,* to the exasperation of inequality' rather than 'lighten[ing] . . . the curse imposed on Adam' – Shelley suggests that 'we want the creative faculty to *imagine* that which we know; we want the generous impulse to *act* that which we *imagine*'. Although the 'we' here is clearly elite, the Imagination is nonetheless that principle of irreducible alterity housed in the Self which is directly opposed to 'the principle of Self, of which money is the *visible* incarnation' (Percy Bysshe Shelley, 'A Defence of Poetry', in *Shelley's Poetry and Prose,* eds. Donald H. Reiman and Sharon B. Powers (New York: Norton, 1977), pp. 502–3; italics mine).

30 Marx, *The German Ideology* (New York: International Publishers, 1970), p. 51.

31 Baudrillard, *Mirror,* p. 31.

32 For an excellent scholarly gloss on this possibility, see A. Allmeeruddy and R. Tortajada, 'Reading Marx on Value: A Note on the Basic Texts', in Diane Elson, ed. *Value: The Representation of Labour in Capitalism* (Atlantic Highlands, NJ: Humanities Press, 1979), p. 11.

33 Derrida, *Speech and Phenomena: And Other Essays on Husserl's Theory of Signs,* tr. David B. Allison (Evanston: Northwestern University Press, 1973), pp. 63, 65.

34 Although obviously determined by European politics in the narrow sense, Derrida's remarks about an 'open Marxism' can relate to what I say about the deconstructive moment in these texts of Marx: 'So an open marxism is one which, without giving way, obviously, to empiricism, pragmatism, relativism, nevertheless does not allow

theoretical restrictions to be imposed upon it by a particular political situation, by a particular political power, as has sometimes been the case in the Soviet Union, and in France too. It is one which does not refuse a priori developments of problematics which it does not believe to have itself engendered, which appear to have come from outside' (Kearns and Newton, 'Interview with Derrida', *Literary Review*, p. 22). It is interesting to compare this with the current position of Svetozar Stojanovic, 'Marx and the Bolshevization of Marxism', part of a forthcoming book.

35 Some good work has emerged in response to this desire. Ryan, *Marxism and Deconstruction*; Christopher Norris, *Deconstruction; Theory and Practice* (London: Methuen, 1982); Gregory L. Ulmer, *Applied Grammatology: Post (e)-Pedagogy from Jacques Derrida to Joseph Beuys* (Baltimore: Johns Hopkins University Press, 1985). As a general comment on such responses, see Stephen Melville's excellent review of some of these books in *sub-stance* 43 (1984).

Texts in history: the determinations of readings and their texts

TONY BENNETT

In recent discussion, 'post-structuralism' has, for the greater part, been equated with the work of Derrida or, more generally, with the ever mobile and flexible strategy of deconstruction. Whilst not entirely shifting this centre of gravity, my concerns tend rather in the direction of a post-structuralist Marxism. I mean, by this, a Marxism which comes after structuralism, which is responsive to its criticisms – and, indeed, to those of other post-structuralisms – and which seeks to take account of them in reformulating its theoretical objectives and the means by which it should both represent and pursue them. I also want to tilt the balance of the discussion slightly in another respect. So far, post-structuralism has been posed largely as a set of tendencies inimical to Marxism and problematic for it in the sense of calling into question a good many of its founding premises and theoretical procedures. That's obviously right so far as the major currents of interaction between the two traditions are concerned. Still, it seems to me to be misleading in at least two respects. First, it tends to neglect the degree to which the anti-metaphysical and de-essentialising orientation of post-structuralist deconstruction has been paralleled by – in turn fuelling and being fuelled by – related tendencies within Marxism. Admittedly, this has often resulted in forms of Marxism which have been so thoroughgoingly revised theoretically that they bear scarcely any recognisable relationship to their classical antecedents. This need not in itself, however, occasion any embarrassment. It is only by being ongoingly revised that a body of theory retains any validity or purchase as a historical force. To construe the relations between the formulations of classical Marxism and those which have been developed in the wake of structuralism as if the latter could be assessed in terms of the degree of their fidelity to or compatibility with the former would be unduly restricting. That way, a body of theory could never be allowed to develop other than via the germination of the seeds of development sown during the crystallising phase of its inception – a profoundly unhistorical conception of the ways in which theoretical ideologies are adapted to changing theoretical and political circumstances. Rather than testing the value of theoretical innovations via such backward-looking glances, the acid test should always be : What do they enable one to do? What possibilities do they open up that were not there beforehand? What new fields and types of action do they generate?

It is in view of considerations of this kind that the construction of relations of *necessary opposition* between post-structuralism and Marxism is not only misleading but counter-productive. This is not to suggest that Marxism could or should even want to ingest deconstruction wholesale. But it is to suggest that post-structuralism confronts Marxism not just with a series of negative problems (although it does that), but with a field of positive possibilities also. I want, therefore, to suggest that, through a critical sifting of the diverse elements of post-structuralism, Marxism may be able to reformulate its problems and objectives – not because it has to in order, so to speak, to keep its theoretical credentials in good condition but because, by doing so, it may open itself into a differently constituted field of political possibilities. Such 'revisionism', that is to say, may contribute to the urgent task of re-thinking Marxism's conception of its relationship to the spheres of political action it constitutes for itself and of the strategies by which it seeks to intervene within them.

I want, then, to consider the relations between post-structuralism, as a general tendency, and post-structuralist Marxism, largely in their potentially positive aspects. First, however, some brief comments on those aspects of post-structuralism which have widely been regarded as posing a series of negative problems for Marxism. What are these problems? 'The work of Derrida and others', Terry Eagleton argues, has '. . . cast grave doubt upon the classical notions of truth, reality, meaning and knowledge, all of which could be exposed as resting on a naively representational theory of language'.[1] Why is this a problem? (The question is rarely put, but it's well worth asking.) The reason it has been *felt* to be a problem – indeed, has sometimes been conceived, and very often perceived as an explicit challenge to Marxism – is that it calls into doubt all those mechanisms (theories of knowledge; metaphysical conceptions of meaning; eschatological or historicist versions of History) which purport to provide a warrant, a certainty of rightness (epistemological, ethical or historical), in the light of which our orientation to and practice within the present might be validated, secured in and by means of some set of criteria that transcends our local, limited and irremediably muddied calculations.

Obviously, acceptance of such criticisms entails that Marxists should critically review all those economistic, scientistic and historicist conceptions by means of which Marxism has traditionally sought to supply itself with such warrants. But need this be a problem? Again, the question is worth asking if only because the major theoretical developments within Marxism over the past two decades have been pushing in precisely this direction. It's singularly odd to expect that Marxists should feel placed on the defensive by the 'discovery' that there neither are nor can be any transcendental guarantees, any absolute certainties or any essential truths since, in recent years, they have devoted some considerable effort to expunging from Marxist thought precisely such residues of nineteenth-century theologies, philosophies of history or ideologies of science. Nor has this been a process of theoretical self-criticism undertaken purely for its own sake. Such essentialising tendencies have been opposed, above all, because of their political effects – the quietism produced by the scientism of the Second International, for example, or the class essentialism which informed the political strategies of the Third International.

To the degree that such tendencies within Marxism have proved politically unhelpful, the only fitting Marxist response to the discovery that there can be no transcendental guarantees is: who needs them, anyway? If it is further argued that Marxism cannot secure its own relation to reality as a knowledge relation, if it must accept its own discursivity and acknowledge that it is submitted to the effects of language and writing: so be it! How could it be otherwise? Still, such acceptance should be accompanied by a demand: that deconstruction prove its worth by showing that it can do more than stand on the side-lines and undermine the terms in which every and any body of theory constructs itself. To argue that Marxism 'is shot through with metaphors disguised as concepts' or that it is dependent on a whole battery of rhetorical and figurative devices is all very well but, in itself, hardly matters a jot.[2] What would matter, what would count as helpful, would be to show that the existing stock of metaphorical, rhetorical and figurative devices used in Marxism had disabling theoretical and political consequences which could be remedied by the use of another set of similar devices. If this is not the point at issue, then deconstruction seems likely to do no more than to lock itself into a historical cul-de-sac in which it keeps alive the demand for transcendence simply by never-endingly denying its possibility – a criticism of essentialism which can rapidly become a lament for its loss, a consolation for the limitations of the human condition which is simultaneously a recipe for political quietism.

To put this another way, it has been argued that one of the major critical effects of deconstruction consists in the claim: 'There is no metalanguage'.[3] That's not true of course. If by 'metalanguage' is meant a language which constitutes other languages or discourses as objects of analysis within itself, then the world is full of them. What, then, does this claim amount to? Simply that there is no meta-metalanguage, no language which can claim an absolute or transcendental validity for its ways of 'fixing' other languages, discourses or texts as objects within itself or which can efface the traces of writing or language within itself. Fine. God is dead and there's no such thing as an Absolute Science which escapes the constraints of its own discursivity. Meanwhile, the struggle between meta-languages – the struggle as to which discursive framing of other discourses is to predominate – continues. What matters for Marxism, as a party to such struggles, is not that it should be able to secure its discursive construction of the 'real' and its framing of other texts and discourses within that 'real' *absolutely*; rather, it is a matter of securing such constructions and framings *politically* in the sense of making them count above contending ones in terms of their ability to organise the consciousness and practice of historical agents.

If it is objected – 'But what can the justification for such a practice be?' – the answer must be 'None' if it's a case of looking for absolute justifications, be they epistemological, ethical or historical. In *Language, Semantics and Ideology*, Michel Pêcheux tells the story of Baron von Munchausen who rode into a bog only to extricate himself from this predicament by dragging himself – and his horse – out 'by pulling with all the strength of one arm on a lock of my own hair'.[4] Pêcheux likens this to the way in which an individual, in being hitched into a subject position within ideology, is also subjected to a 'phantasy effect' whereby, once in place, such a subject represents himself to himself as 'cause of himself'.[5] Whilst I intend the argument only analogically, it seems to me that socialism can extricate itself from the mire of an epistemological and ethical relativism only by means of a political desire which functions as cause and justification of itself (although it is, of course, produced by and within the complex play of social forces and relationships) and which supplies the criteria – always contested – for the determination of the ends to which political and theoretical practice are directed. If that's not felt to be enough, I would ask : what other foundation could there be which is not a demand for transcendence and which – in order to preserve things as they are – simultaneously denies the possibility that such a demand might ever be realised?

MARXISM, DISCOURSE THEORY AND TEXTUAL ANALYSIS

The issues I want now to consider, in the context of these more general problems, concern the ways in which, if at all, texts either can or should be constituted as objects of analysis within a Marxist framework. I shall do so by considering the work of Ernesto Laclau who, perhaps more probingly than anyone else, has sought to reformulate the concerns of Marxism in requiring it to acknowledge and accept the consequences of its own discursivity. The spirit in which he has done so, however, has been consistently positive and political. Whereas Christopher Norris, for example, sees in deconstruction merely a negative challenge to Marxism – particularly to the attempt to constitute the literary text as the object of its scientific knowledge – Laclau translates this challenge into a positive means of expanding Marxism's field of political possibilities.

I should say straightaway, in case the 'if at all' above seems gratuitously polemical, that it's clear that Marxism is and cannot but be concerned with the analysis of textual phenomena. The issues I want to explore concern the means by which Marxism should represent to itself its relationship to the texts with which it engages and the political issues which hinge on such considerations. Laclau expands enormously the significance of these problems in arguing, in effect, that Marxism is concerned with little else other than textual phenomena in the sense that even its primary object – the prevailing system of economic and social relationships – is, Laclau argues, constituted entirely within discourses whose conditions of existence are largely textual.[6]

At the same time, however, Laclau disputes the more usual way in which Marxism has represented its relationship to the textual phenomena it analyses. In its more scientistic formulations, Marxism has typically represented its own relation to reality as one of pure transparency, thereby denying its own discursivity and textuality. Furthermore, in doing so, it has represented its relationship to the texts it has analysed as a knowledge relation. In construing them as forms of the appearance of the real which it knows, (the economy, society, history) Marxism has represented itself as having produced a valid knowledge – or, more accurately, a knowledge that is *tendentially* valid – of such texts 'in themselves'. In opposition to this view, Laclau argues that Marxism, rather than seeking to efface its own discursivity, should conceive of itself as a set of discursive interventions – interventions which must prove their validity through their effects rather than by claiming any kind of prior ontological privilege. Such interventions, he argues, must seek to interrupt, uncouple and disrupt the prevailing array of discourses through which subject identities are formed – and, thereby, forms of political alliance and cleavage constructed – so as to produce new discursive articulations which will produce new subjects, new forms of political alliance and, above all, discursively construct relations of contradiction through which moments of possible historical rupture might be constituted.[7] Since the conditions of existence of discursive practices are, in good part, textual, this is tantamount to saying that Marxism should regard itself as, again in good part, if not entirely, a set of textual practices which seeks to re-articulate the relations between other textual practices so as to produce those systems of ideological interpellation and patterns of political alliance that are calculated, in a particular conjuncture, to be the best bet for socialism.

Whilst I'm not sure I should like to go as far as Laclau in, in effect, collapsing the social into the discursive, I go along with his view sufficiently to think that the way Marxism represents its relationship to the textual phenomena it engages with is not merely a recondite theoretical question but one with far-reaching political implications. I want, therefore, to dispute the view that Marxism should represent texts as possible objects of knowledge (rather than to defend such a view against the criticisms of deconstruction), to review a range of the devices by which it has sought to do so and comment on their, in my view, largely negative consequences.

Texts, so regarded, cannot figure within Marxism, I shall argue, in the sense that there is no space other than a transcendent, ahistorical one within which they can be constituted as possible objects of knowledge. They should not so figure in the sense that such a representation of textual phenomena and of Marxism's relationship to them is both theoretically and politically disabling. It is the former in the respect that it inhibits the adequate formulation and development of what I regard as the proper concerns of Marxist literary theory: namely, the development of a historical and materialist theory of the interactions between texts classified as literary, other ideological phenomena and broader social and political processes and relationships, recognising that the systems of classification within which the 'literary' is produced are always culturally specific and that, therefore, their functioning and effects are a part of what needs to be studied. Whilst that is, perhaps, a fairly uncontentious view, I want to add a rider which calls into question an essentialising orientation which lies behind much of the work that has been developed within the Marxist tradition: that is, that such a theory cannot be adequately developed if predicated on the assumption – an assumption which has usually obtained implicitly – that the relations between literary texts, other ideological phenomena and broader social and political processes can be determined, specified for all time, by referring such texts to the conditions of production obtaining at the moment of their origin. To the contrary, the actual and variable functioning of texts in history can only be understood if account is taken of the ways in which such originary relations may be modified through the operation of subsequent determinations – institutional and discursive – which may retrospectively cancel out, modify or overdetermine those which marked the originating conditions of a text's production.

This is to take issue with the 'metaphysic of origin' which characterises scientistic representations of the relationship between Marxism and the literary texts with which it engages according to which such texts are construed as forms of the appearance of the real which Marxism 'knows'. The characteristic discursive move of such approaches has consisted in the claim that Marxism – through 'the appliance of science' – rescues literary texts from the history of their misunderstanding in revealing, for the first time and via the application of the principles of historical materialism, their objective historical meaning. Such claims are not to be taken at their face-value. Their primary effect has been to disguise the active and interventionist nature of Marxist criticism, to shield from itself and from others a recognition of its own inescapably ideological nature. The stress placed, within Marxism, on returning the text to the originating conditions of its production, whilst *represented* as a scientific move producing a knowledge of the text, has *in fact* functioned as the distinguishing hermeneutic device whereby Marxist criticism, in re-writing the relations of a text to past history, has sought to re-organise its significance and functioning, its meaning in and for the present. In this, Marxist criticism has always functioned in the way Laclau suggests it should: as a discourse of intervention. Interrupting and contesting the ideological production of literary texts effected by bourgeois criticism, it has consistently sought to reorganise the systems of inter-textual, ideological and cultural reference through which reading practices are organised and animated. It has, *in practice*, functioned as a bid to re-order the discursive determinations of reading, an attempt to produce readings and, thereby, to produce the appropriate texts for such readings whilst, *theoretically*, representing itself as producing a valid knowledge of texts 'in themselves'.

This theoretical misrepresentation of the nature of its own activity to itself has had two consequences. First, at the theoretical level, it has entailed that analysis of the functioning of texts within history has been conceived as a once and once only affair. For once a text is coupled to the conditions of its origin by means of 'the appliance of science', the analysis of its subsequent functioning in history prior to the point at which Marxism thus reveals its objective historical meaning is thereby rendered unimportant or is representable only as a history of errors. There are, accordingly, scarcely any – if any – such analyses within the Marxist tradition. Yet it is clear that the determinations and accretions which bear in upon, re-mould and re-configure texts may have a more consequential bearing on the nature of their functioning within the present – and, thereby, on the ways in which this may need to be modified – than do those specified by their relations to the originating conditions of their production. Perhaps more damagingly, and as the second consequence of scientistic representations of the relationship between Marxism and the texts with which it engages, the scope for the political manoeuvrability of texts is thereby severely limited. In effect, one move and one move only is possible: that ordained by the knowledge of the text produced by referring it to the originating conditions of its production.

In view of these considerations, then, I want to suggest that the proper object for Marxist literary theory consists not in the study of texts but in the study of reading formations. By a reading formation, I mean a set of discursive and inter-textual determinations which organise and animate the practice of reading, connecting texts and readers in specific relations to one another in constituting readers as reading subjects of particular types and texts as objects-to-be-read in particular ways. This entails arguing that texts have and can have no existence independently of such reading formations, that there is no place independent of, anterior to or above the varying reading formations through which their historical life is variantly modulated, within which texts can be constituted as objects of knowledge. Texts exist only as always–already organised or activated to be read in certain ways just as readers exist as always–already activated to read in certain ways: neither can be granted a virtual identity that is separable from the determinate ways in which they are gridded onto one another within different reading formations. The consequences of this so far as Marxist criticism is concerned – and the distinction between theory and criticism I have in mind here is that, whereas theory's concern is to analyse the determinations which are operative in the processes whereby meanings are produced in relation to textual phenomena, criticism's concern is to intervene within such processes, to make texts mean differently by modifying the determinations which bear in upon them – is that it should seek to detach texts from socially dominant reading formations and to install them in new ones. The accent here should be placed on the use of the plural mood. Its business is not to subject textual phenomena to a singular move via a scientistically represented revaluation of their objective historical meaning, but to move them about in different ways – to locate them within different reading formations, producing them as different texts for different readers – in accordance with shifting and variable calculations of political objectives rather than with the fixed calculation of such objectives which scientistic formulations produce.

TEXTS, READERS, CONTEXTS

I can think of two major forms of objection that might be advanced in relation to this line of reasoning. The first is that it is merely another version of neo-Kantianism according to which the text is conceived as an unknowable *ding an sich.* I don't think this is the case. If it were, I would certainly be unhappy with it as that is not the sort of company I should like to keep. As I shall try to show, the approach I am advocating is one which aims to suspend the neo-Kantian problematic, to displace its essentialism by means of, following Laclau, an absolute historicalisation of textual phenomena which is, at the same time, uncompromisingly materialist and which thereby affords no space in which 'the text itself' might be constituted as an object, knowable or otherwise. I'll come back to this later. The second line of objection would be that I am merely reducing texts to contexts and I must admit that there is much truth in this. However, I am also proposing a way of re-thinking context such that, ultimately, neither text nor context are conceivable as entities separable from one another. According to most formulations, context is conceived as social; that is, as a set of extra-discursive and extra-textual determinations to which the text is related as an external backdrop or set of reading conditions. The concept of reading formation, by contrast, is an attempt to think context as a set of discursive and inter-textual determinations, operating on material and institutional supports, which bear in upon a text not just externally, from the outside in, but internally, shaping it – in the historically concrete forms in which it is available as a text-to-be-read – from the inside out.

I can perhaps best expand on this concept and its implications by contrasting these with the ways in which the relations between texts and readers are construed in other approaches to the question of reading. Such approaches fall within two broad categories. First, there are those approaches concerned to analyse the formal mechanisms by which a text produces a position or positions for reading, organising its own consumption in the implied, model or preferred reader – the terms vary, but the approach is essentially the same – which it constructs as a condition of its own intelligibility. Clearly, work of this type is of considerable importance and I do not mean to belittle the significance of the considerations with which it is concerned. Nonetheless, the supposition on which it is predicated – namely, that the intra-textual processes through which reading is organised can be specified independently of the extra-textual determinations which mould and configure the reading practices of empirically diverse groups of readers – is problematic. 'No text', Umberto Eco has argued, 'is read independently of the reader's experience of other texts'.[8] If that is so, its implication – although Eco does not draw it – is that reading cannot be accounted for by, first, analysing the fixed properties of the text and only then considering the inter-textual determinations which may explain how those fixed properties come to be differently received and interpreted. Rather, analysis should deal with the ways in which such inter-textual determinations organise the text internally through the specific constitution of the text as a text-to-be-read which they effect. It is clear, for example, that reading practices are, in part, organised by the systems of genre expectations brought to bear on specific texts. It is equally clear that such expectations are largely culturally determined and hence variable. Given that such genre expectations may predispose the reader to relate him or herself to a text in a specific way, it is not clear how or where intra-textual mechanisms of reader positioning might be constituted independently of a set of assumptions concerning the operation of a particular genre, and therefore culturally engendered reader predispositions. Or, to take another example, John Frow has argued that the literary space is marked off by the operation of a 'frame' which establishes 'the particular historical distribution of the "real" and the "symbolic" within which the text operates'.[9] Such frames, he argues, organise the 'inside' and the 'outside' of a text and the relations between them. In the case of texts operating within the constructed space of 'the literary', they produce such texts 'both as an enclosure of the internal fictional space and as an exclusion of the space of reality against which the work is set'.[10] Since the functioning of such frames is culturally dependent, Frow argues, 'changes in the context of reception of a work alter the kinds of expectation governed by the frame and are thus translated into structural changes in the work'.[11] In short, there is no fixed boundary between the extra-textual and the intra-textual which prevents the former from pressing in upon the latter and re-organising it. The intra-textual, in effect, is always the product of a definite set of inter-textual relations.

The second approach to reading has concentrated largely on considerations of social positionality; that is, on the role of class and gender relations, for example, in organising reading practices. The chief difficulty with this approach consists in the tendency to theorise such relations as comprising an extra-textual context of reception since, in this case, no mechanisms are provided for such as could connect such extra-textual determinations to the process of reading. Recent approaches have tried to overcome this difficulty in suggesting that considerations of social positionality bear upon reading only mediately and indirectly as a consequence of the structure of access they produce in relation to the discourses which comprise the ideological level of a social formation. If social position determines the ways in which individuals are exposed to and inserted within ideological discourses, it is the properties of those discourses which actually mould and organise the activities of those individuals as reading subjects. Except for some suggestive comments by Stephen Heath, however, such discursive determinations have been conceived as operating only at a level of highly abstract generality.[12] The concept of reading formation is not meant to displace these considerations but to refine them in requiring that the effectivity of such general discursive determinations be regarded as being conditioned by the way they are processed by the operation of those inter-discursive and inter-textual relations which bear most specifically and most closely on the process of reading.

The concept of reading formation, then, is an attempt to weave a way between these two approaches to the study of reading by conceiving the intra-textual determinations of reading as being over-determined by the operation of determinations which, whilst they cannot be derived from the text concerned, are not reducible to an extra-textual social context either. It is an attempt to identify the determinations which, in operating on both texts and readers, mediate the relations between text and context, connecting the two and providing the mechanisms through which they productively interact in representing context not as a set of extra-discursive relations but as a set of inter-textual and discursive relations which produce readers for texts and texts for readers. This is to question conventional conceptions of texts, readers and contexts as separable elements, fixed in their relations to one another, in suggesting that they are variable functions within a discursively ordered set of relations. Different reading formations, that is to say, produce their own texts, their own readers and their own contexts.

In an interview, Pierre Macherey asked what the study of literature would look like once the supposition that it consisted of fixed works – of texts, given and completed – was abandoned.[13] Well, I think it would look very different. The implication of the perspectives I have been developing is that it would consist not in the study of texts as self-contained givens but in the study of texts as constituted as objects-to-be-read within the different reading formations which have modulated their existence as historically active, culturally received texts. This, it is important to add, would mean not studying texts first and then their readings as if the history of the diverse patterns of readings that have been produced within different reading formations and the different social and ideological relations of reading of which they form a part need not be allowed to complicate or muddy the analytical exchange between analyst and text. To the contrary, it would be a question of studying texts in the light of their readings, readings in the light of their texts. The relations between textual phenomena and social and political processes can be adequately theorised only by placing in suspension the text as it appears to be given to us in our own reading formation so as to analyse the differential constitution and functioning of that apparently same but different text within different reading formations. The aim of such an analysis would not be to reveal the meaning or effects of textual phenomena but rather to make them hum and reverberate to (ideally) the full range of meanings and effects which they have furnished a site for.

None of this in any way queries the objective, material existence of textual phenomena. To the contrary, it stresses it. It is precisely because texts are material phenomena that their social and ideological articulations may be discursively re-ordered, and by social and material means since, of course, discursive processes are social and material processes produced within specifiable institutional conditions. By reverse, the only way of fixing a text as the source of a specifiable range of meanings or effects is by means of idealist constructions according to which there is conjured up the notion that there is somehow and somewhere, at the back of the materiality of textual phenomena, an ideal text – the 'text itself' – which it is the purpose of analysis to reach and reveal, always (if the rhetoric is to be believed) for the first time, or, in an eschatology of meaning, to anticipate. It is for this reason that I do not think my arguments lead in the direction of neo-Kantianism according to which the text is posited as an unknowable *ding an sich*. My argument is not that the text is somewhere 'there' (wherever that might be) but unknowable, but that there is no 'there' in which its existence might be posited other than the varying reading formations through which the actual history of its functioning is modulated and, therefore, that to seek to produce a knowledge of it is to engage in a Sisyphean labour.

FIXING TEXTS IN THE PRESENT BY MEANS OF THE FUTURE DETERMINATION OF THEIR PASTS

In short, and contrary to appearances, it is the concept of the 'text itself', rather than criticisms of it, which rests on idealist principles and procedures. It is a construction and, furthermore, a variable construction since the means by which such a concept of the text is produced vary from one school of criticism to another. In effect, what is constructed as the 'text itself' is the product of a particular bid for the terms of inter-textual, ideological and cultural reference which are to prevail in organising reading practices, and therefore cannot supply the means of arbitrating between readings. It follows that to seek to determine the limits of what can and cannot be said on the basis of the 'text itself' is to engage in a pursuit that is necessarily metaphysical since it rests on the supposition that the discursive wrappings that have been placed around a text within different reading formations can somehow be peeled away to yield an unfettered access to its irreducible kernel, thereby establishing analysis in a relationship of pure and unmediated transparency to its object. Either that, or it is merely myopic, overlooking the history which, in determining the forms in which a text is currently available as an object-to-be-read – the whole ensemble of material, social and ideological relations which condition the apparent givenness of 'the text on one's desk' – simultaneously occludes itself.

However, this is not to suggest that all the readings that either have been or might be produced in relation to textual phenomena should be regarded as of equal value. It is merely to argue that the differences between them cannot be resolved epistemologically by claiming for a particular reading the warrant of a relationship to the 'text itself' such that all other readings are thereby automatically disqualified in its favour. Rather, readings can only be assessed politically in terms of a calculation of their consequences in and for the present. Texts, according to such a view, cannot be conceived as extra-discursive points of reference which may be appealed to as a means of adjudicating between readings. Rather, they exist only as variable pieces of play within the processes through which the struggle for their meaning is socially enacted : kept alive within the series of bids and counter-bids which different critical tendencies advance in their attempts to organise reading practices – to make texts mean differently by re-writing their relations to history – texts are thus kept alive only at the price of being always other than 'just themselves'.

Paradoxically, it is precisely at this level – the level of the social struggle for the meaning of textual phenomena – that the concept of the 'text itself' is produced and has effects as an essentially rhetorical device used to enhance the claims of a particular ideology of reading. It provides the means by which a new reading seeks to clear a space for itself and to displace the cultural power of prevailing readings in producing, in its construction of the 'text itself', the criteria of validity in relation to which other readings can be found wanting. It is for this reason that the functioning of the concept of the 'text itself' is always paradoxical. Whilst forming a part of activist and interventionist critical projects which implicitly recognise the 'moveability' of texts in the very form of their attempts to shift them, to make them mean differently, that movement is always represented as a final movement, as, at last, pinning texts down so that their intrinsic nature can be recognised. There are, of course, a variety of means by which such a concept of the 'text itself' may be discursively produced. Barthes argues that the category of the author typically functions in this way. 'To give a text an Author', he writes, 'is to impose a limit on that text, to furnish it with a final signified, to close the writing'.[14] Whatever the details of the devices used, however, a necessary condition for and complement to the discursive production of the 'text itself' consists in the discursive production of a unified subject by whom that text can, even if only tendentially, be recognised.[15]

This is as true of Marxist criticism as of any other. I argued earlier that the distinguishing hermeneutic gambit of Marxist criticism has consisted in the contention that the objective historical meaning of a text can only be understood by placing it in the context of the originating conditions of its production. The precise way in which this move operates, and its consequences, are, however, considerably more complicated than this bald description suggests. In fact, detailed analyses of texts in the light of the originating conditions of their production are somewhat rare in the Marxist tradition, and they rarely stop at that. Indeed, there is a sense in which such considerations are the last things to be taken into account. To take Lukács – and I would argue that, on these matters, Lukács is the paradigm case – the way he construes the relations between a text and the social and ideological conditions of its period is always informed by a prior conception of that text's relations to earlier and subsequent texts, and of the social and ideological conditions of their respective periods, as specified by the degree to which it does or does not continue the realist tendencies of earlier texts or anticipate and pave the way for those of subsequent texts. In short, the objective historical meaning of texts is determined not so much by relating texts to the conditions of their production as by locating them within the meta-text of a History which Marxism claims to know but yet whose final judgements – which can only be delivered once the process of History has been completed – it can only anticipate. Hence Lukács's constant insistence that the meaning of a period and its texts will become clearer to us the more distant we are from it – not just because, with time, perspectives settle, but because, with the unfolding of each stage of historical development, we move a little closer to the post-historical unified subject, Man, to whom the meaning of the text of History and, therefore, of each text within it will finally be rendered luminously transparent. In Lukács's work, the means by which the text itself is fixed and its objective historical meaning deciphered is thus via the determination which the future is allowed to exert on that text and its history.

The idealism of such an approach is apparent. The 'text itself' which such a criticism posits turns out to be that text which achieves a full and adequate relationship to itself only when the text of History has been completed. It is an ideal text which assumes a social and material form which is fully adequate to itself only at the end of History and which, pending this consummation, exists only as a shadowy presence, an ideal form lodged behind the diverse social, material and ideological relations which regulate the real history of its reading, until it is given in such a form that its 'in-itselfness', in being completed, is made transparent. Not only idealist but ideological : the critical project that is produced and supported by such a view ends up constituting literary texts as a privileged region for the reproduction of an ideological view of history. Althusser has argued that an ideological conception of history 'far from functioning as a (provisional) truth for the production of new knowledges' presents itself 'as the *truth of* History, as exhaustive, definitive and absolute knowledge of it, in short as a system closed in on itself, without any development because without any object in the scientific sense of the term, and only ever finding in the real its own mirror reflection'.[16] This perfectly describes Lukács's criticism and, indeed, the entire tradition of Marxist criticism which constitutes texts as the pre-texts for the elaboration of a historicised humanist aesthetics. For such an aesthetic can only ever find in the real historical lives of texts the mirror reflection of its conditioning premise : namely, that texts are a reflection of the historical process through which Man makes himself, as will eventually be made clear once they slot into the foreordained hermeneutic sprocket-holes which await them at the end of that process.

It's not the fact that there can be no surprises within such an approach that I object to, nor even its manifestly ideological nature since it seems to me that any critical practice which hopes to be a historical force must be deeply ideological in the sense that its concern will be to engage in the struggle for the terms in which individuals are to be produced and mobilised as subjects in history. Rather, it is the form of this ideology and, therefore, the subject it produces that must be taken issue with. I argued earlier, following Laclau, that Marxism should be conceived as a set of discursive interventions which seeks to interrupt, uncouple and disrupt the subject identities and forms of political alliance constructed by dominant ideological discourses so as to forge new ones. The implications of this for Marxist criticism are that it should contribute to such struggles by seeking to disarticulate texts classified as literary from the system of ideological connections in which they are inscribed via the functioning of bourgeois reading formations and to order their ideological articulations differently – to make them mean differently – by re-organising the systems of inter-textual, ideological and cultural reference, the reading formations, within which they are constituted as objects-to-be-read. I also argued that, in practice, this is how Marxist criticism has mostly functioned, albeit that it has misrepresented the nature of its activity to itself through the application of scientistic formulations with the result that it has permitted itself one move and one move only in relation to literary texts – that of bringing them into line with the knowledge of their objective historical meaning produced by Marxism.

I'll take the case of Lukács again since it's clear, first, that his criticism was motivated by a definite political project – the attempt to produce an alliance between the progressive wings of the bourgeoisie and the proletariat – and, second, that this project depended on the idealist principles I've just outlined whereby Lukács sought to fix texts into history. The system of articulations Lukács sought to weave via his studies of literary texts can be roughly summarised as follows: literary texts are reflections of the process, yet to be completed, of Man's historical self-creation; the texts which most adequately reflect this process are those which embody the maximum form of Man's historical self-consciousness available in a particular epoch; the supports for such forms of historical self-consciousness are provided by the world-views of progressive social classes – the bourgeoisie yesterday, the proletariat today; therefore, the progressive sections of the bourgeoisie should support the working class in order to support those humanist values they had once championed. In this way, Lukács's criticism formed an attempt to construct a system of political alliances – particularly in the context of the struggle against fascism – that would operate not along class but along cultural lines. It sought to reformulate an essentialist conception of class struggle as being articulated around a single contradiction – the proletariat versus the bourgeoisie – as a cultural struggle conceived in equally essentialist terms. The struggle between the proletariat and the bourgeoisie was thus conceived as merely a contingent stand-in for the struggle between a system of opposing cultural values: reason versus unreason; socialism versus barbarism;

Man versus the inhuman. In short, the way in which Lukács related texts to history, fixing them within it by referring them forward to the imminent *telos* of their soon-to-be revealed objective historical meaning, served as a means of articulating bourgeois humanist values to those of socialism, but only at the price of re-presenting the struggle between the proletariat and the bourgeoisie as merely the given, contingent form of the more essential struggle between the humanising and dehumanising forces in history. Clearly, once texts have been shifted by being moved into such an interpretative system, there is no other way they can be moved which is not, at the same time, a breach with that system and the fixing of texts it proposes. All criticism can do, so long as it remains within the confines of such a system, is to perfect its anticipations of the judgements of the post-historical unified subject it posits as a condition of its own practice.

What can be done with such a criticism today? Not very much, it seems to me. Apart from the fact that the way of fixing texts in history it proposes rests on a secularised eschatology of meaning, the political calculations of which it formed a part have been surely called into question. It is clearly not the case that all of the struggles which need to be coordinated in the struggle for socialism can be grouped around an essential contradiction expressed in terms of the proletariat versus the bourgeoisie. To the contrary, the successful articulation of such struggles into a provisional unity depends on a recognition of their relative autonomy, of the separate interests of women and blacks, for example, which cannot be subordinated to an essential class contradiction. This being so, the political value of producing for literary texts an objective meaning within history is called into question. If such texts are to be regarded as strategic sites for the contestation of dominant ideological subject identities – and I think they should – it needs to be recognised that, as such, they are implicated in different struggles, and not just one, and that, therefore, they may need to be moved around differently – and then only provisionally – within different social and ideological relations of reading, rather than being moved just once by an attempted scientistic fixing of their meaning. As to whether the 'text itself' might encounter, at the end of history, the unified subject of judgement which can sustain and recognise it, that, it seems to me, together with a good many other issues of the same nature, is an issue we can safely leave to the future since there are more pressing problems to be dealt with.

NOTES

1 Terry Eagleton, *Literary Theory: An Introduction* (Oxford: Basil Blackwell, 1983), p. 143.
2 See Christopher Norris, *Deconstruction: Theory and Practice* (London: Methuen, 1982), pp. 74–5.
3 Ibid., p. 84.
4 Michel Pêcheux, *Language, Semantics and Ideology* (London: Macmillan, 1982), p. 17.
5 Ibid., pp. 108–9.
6 See Ernesto Laclau, 'Politics as the construction of the unthinkable' (unpublished paper).
7 Laclau deals with the problem of the discursive construction of relations of contradiction in 'Populist Rupture and Discourse', *Screen Education* no. 34 (Spring 1980).
8 Umberto Eco, *The Role of the Reader: Explorations in the Semiotics of Texts* (London: Hutchinson, 1981), p. 21.
9 John Frow, 'The Literary Frame', *Journal of Aesthetic Education* 16 ii (1982), p. 25.
10 Ibid., p. 27.
11 Ibid., p. 28.
12 See Stephen Heath, 'Difference', *Screen* 19 iii (Autumn 1978).
13 See the interview with Pierre Macherey in *Red Letters* no. 5 (Summer 1977).
14 Roland Barthes, 'The Death of the Author' in *Image–Music–Text*, ed. Stephen Heath (London: Fontana, 1977), p. 147.
15 In this respect I believe that the discursive conditions for the production of the 'text itself' are similar to those required by theories of value. I have discussed the latter in 'Marxism and Popular Fiction', *Literature and History* 7 ii (Autumn 1981).
16 Louis Althusser, 'The Conditions of Marx's Scientific Discovery', *Theoretical Practice* nos. 7–8 (1973), p. 7.

Criticism and institutions: the American university

JONATHAN CULLER

One of the most common themes these days in the realm of critical theory is the call for criticism and for literary theory to take up a relationship to history, by confronting the question of their insertion in social and political history and by taking account of their own history. Most often, this call to history comes from those who proceed not to show how this might be done but rather to write books arguing that others are failing to attend to history. One recent version of this enterprise, for example, notable mainly for its shrillness, convicts Paul de Man and post-structuralism of fatalism and avoidance of history but then proceeds not to show how criticism might promote social change or become properly historical but to celebrate Kenneth Burke for conceiving of criticism as a political activity.[1]

A more serious recent attempt to set criticism in relation to history is Terry Eagleton's lively account of the fortunes of criticism since what he calls 'the rise of English' : *Literary Theory: An Introduction.* The call to history here comes, first, as a demand that criticism and theory take some responsibility for the historical plight of their societies and work for change, but also as a demand that criticism take account of its own historical character, as a product of the society to whose culture it contributes. The first emerges as a concluding complaint about each mode of literary theory : whatever its virtues, it proves unhistorical, neglecting concrete social and political issues. This reproach not only provides a way of bringing together otherwise disparate theoretical orientations – as different styles of evasion – but also permits the easy, engaging tone of the exposition. Eagleton can dip into New Criticism, or phenomenology, or reader-response criticism for a reasonably sympathetic account and then disengage swiftly and easily with the observation that this is all very well, but 'will reading Mallarmé bring down the bourgeois state?' or how will 'responding to Marvell around the seminar table transform the mechanised labour of factory workers' ?[2]

The procedure is somewhat flip, but the question he raises is serious and difficult: how can one determine whether, as he suggests, 'the great majority of the literary theories outlined in this book have strengthened rather than challenged the assumptions of the power system' (p. 195)? It is hard to show whether even Eagleton's own criticism has weakened the power structure, given the argument that the university and its pluralist ideology are strengthened to the degree that Marxist discourse becomes an internal variant rather than external opposition. But Eagleton is right to carry on without waiting for a convincing resolution of this intractable historical issue.

In fact, the question of whether literary theory or criticism can have strong social and political effects is somewhat murky in Eagleton. Swift to dismiss such claims by twentieth-century critics, he is strangely eager to grant claims put forward in the nineteenth century that literary study would prevent social revolution by providing a pacifying substitute for religion, giving the children of the working classes the sense of a stake in the culture, and offering instruction in timeless truths that would distract them from their immediate circumstances. As Eagleton puts it, 'if the masses are not thrown a few novels, they may react by throwing up a few barricades' (p. 25). But can one not just as well retort that you won't keep the working classes from throwing up barricades by throwing them a few novels?

The other call to history comes in Eagleton's argument that critical theory derives from historical circumstance. A convincing case is made for the rise of literary study, but in later chapters the connections become less specific and convincing: theoretical approaches are presented as responses to the 'nightmare of modern history' or as imaginary solutions to real historical dilemmas: 'Phenomenology sought to solve the nightmare of modern history by withdrawing into a speculative sphere where eternal certainty lay in wait; as such it became a symptom, in its solitary, alienated brooding, of the very crisis it offered to overcome' (p. 61), or Heidegger's philosophy 'provided one imaginary solution to the crisis of modern history as fascism provided another' (p. 66).

If the historical analysis of the first chapter is more convincing than these later historical explanations, which make critical theory a series of deluded responses to so-called 'historic collapse', it is because of Eagleton's concern there with the institutions of literary study. The problem in later chapters, it seems, is the lack of a well-thought-out model of critical history which would focus on institutions of criticism.

This is a general problem for those who would do history. In *The Republic of Letters*, an ambitious attempt at a history of recent American criticism, Grant Webster seeks to supply the lacking 'model of critical history which will account for the rise, flourishing, and fall of various schools of criticism' by adapting Thomas Kuhn's model of scientific paradigms.[3] A powerful and original critic creates a new paradigm : 'an extra critical standard of value or ideology is transformed into a new critical charter' (p. 8), which becomes the source of authority for a practice of 'normal criticism'. *The Republic of Letters* describes the charters established by T. S. Eliot (for the New Criticism) and Lionel Trilling (for the New York Intellectuals). A second volume will explore the paradigms of myth criticism, structuralism, deconstruction, and what he reportedly calls the 'Erotic Revolution', which includes pornography, gay liberation, and feminist criticism.

Webster's model allows for the representation of change in critical approaches but, like Kuhn's model itself, it does little to account for the phenomenon of change which inspired it. A new charter is created when a powerful, original critic draws up an authoritative programme or vision, imposes an ideology. One reason Webster's method fails to explain what produces change is the role it grants institutions. They are seen as the avenues to fame and fortune, the means of institutionalising a practice and thus spreading influence, rather than a context that generates criticism and critical innovation. Since criticism has become a university activity, part of the functioning of universities, one must ask what sort of pressures institutions exert on criticism and what role they play in producing critical change.

Once we begin thinking about institutions, however, we may find ourselves questioning the Webster/Kuhn model of the paradigm. Webster defends his claim that criticism is organised as a series of contrasting paradigms by arguing that critical approaches are mutually exclusive and no real debate between them occurs (p. ix). However, we have become more accustomed of late to complaints of a different sort: that deconstruction is really just a pretentious variant of New Criticism, or that the radical force of some theoretical and political project has been watered down into American close reading. Defenders of critical innovations frequently wish that there *were* mutually exclusive critical paradigms, so that they could be sure of doing something new and different, so that the new things they were doing weren't always getting mixed with other things, or assimilated. But since the producers and consumers of criticism are members of a profession organised into competing departments, with a reward structure based on the publication of new critical contributions, there is, on the one hand, pressure for critical innovation (which can be hailed as changing the way we think about a work or a problem) and, on the other hand, an inclination to look to criticism for new insights about literary works or new questions to ask, which can be incorporated in the discourse of one's teaching or critical writing. Though innovation may take the form of new programmes for criticism (claims about the nature of literature or interpretation that look like new paradigms), there is pressure to assimilate innovations to an ongoing critical practice, to put them to use.

In a critique of Kuhn's model, Stephen Toulmin argues that the switch from Newtonian to Einsteinian physics – the scientific revolution on which Kuhn places greatest weight – does not in fact illustrate his notion of incommensurable paradigms with a breakdown of communications between them. On the contrary, scientists accustomed to the old views were able to consider the new proposals and, in numerous cases, adopt them, offering scientific arguments for the change in theoretical standpoint.[4] Toulmin goes on to argue that investigation of the rationality of a discipline should be concerned not with particular systems – Newtonian physics, etc. – but rather with the conditions under which, and the manner in which, changes occur. 'The rationality of a science', he writes, 'is embodied not in the theoretical systems current in it at particular times, but in its procedures for discovery and conceptual change through time' (p. 84). Critical theory encourages us to think of criticism as warring schools or, in more recent parlance, interpretive communities, each with its own axioms of criticism. If we think about critical change, however, we need to focus not on the doctrines of individual schools but on institutions and their role in the generation of new ideas and their reception. Normal criticism, in Webster's model, follows the principles of a particular charter: New Criticism, myth criticism, deconstruction, and so on. I submit, on the contrary, that normal criticism in our day is not a practice enclosed within a well-defined paradigm but a shifty or sloppy eclecticism that is always engaged in change. It changes not by dramatic shifts of paradigm but by assimilation of novelty, reducing forceful claims of a theoretical perspective to usable insights, escaping contradiction by taking the view that different approaches or emphases suit different works: feminist criticism helps with some works, deconstruction with others. (It is precisely because normal criticism takes this form that we must constantly argue against eclecticism.)

We speak, for example, of the hegemony of the New Criticism in the forties and fifties, but in fact most of the criticism from this period does not remain within the paradigm of explication that resolutely ignores authors, readers, and history. Normal criticism here is interpretation that joins such techniques of close reading as attention to imagery with an interest in authors and in literary history. The study of literature remained organised, for the most part, by historical periods; critics were expected to be experts in a period, as were graduate students, since jobs were defined in this way. Normal criticism was not by any means an orthodox New Criticism. I want to argue that institutional practices of teaching and writing about literature create a shifting, eclectic 'normal criticism' that at once fosters innovation and recuperates it.

One way to think about the role of institutions would be to consider several of the salient differences between British and American institutionalisations of literary study. For example, in Britain, university teachers were, until recently, granted tenure after a brief probationary period. Critical writing has little to do with tenure and thus is not made to seem the decisive activity of teachers of literature. In America, the central role of criticism in decisions we take seriously, such as tenure reviews, produces the assumption that critical publications should be serious scholarly or critical contributions, not works of popularisation or journalism, for example. In general, the British academic system is not based, as the American is, on continuous evaluation (promotions, hiring at all levels, external reviews, fellowship panels, etc.). American teachers of literature spend a vast amount of time evaluating – not literature, but one another – so that critical writing and proposals for critical writing become crucial to academic careers. The need to innovate or 'advance knowledge', as we still say, is built into the system, in ways it is not in Britain.

Second, the different status and structure of graduate education in Britain, where it is a relatively recent activity, less central to the definition of the university, and where it involves primarily supervision of research projects rather than systematic training in classes and seminars, has made methodological issues and theoretical debate less central to the institution than they are in America.

Third, since English undergraduates generally study a single subject, critics teach literature not, as in America, to heterogeneous groups of students often more committed to other disciplines, but to those already specialising in a national literature – a difference whose effects one ought to explore.

Fourth, in Britain a national salary scale prevents departments from competing with one another to attract noted critics with higher salaries and lower teaching loads, as happens in America's capitalist university system. There is thus less possibility for critical writing to function as a way of attracting offers and as a medium for departmental competition.

Finally, professionalisation is considerably less advanced in Britain. Organisations of university teachers, which negotiate salaries and conditions of employment, are more important than professional organisations concerned with literary studies. Teachers of literature are likely to think of themselves either as intellectuals or as university teachers, while in America the professor of English is perhaps above all a member of the profession of teachers of literature, of the literary critical guild. This is an important issue on which much could be said; but with these sketchy indications of institutional differences, let me return to the matter of recent American criticism.

The major critical development of the past 20 years in America has been the impact of various theoretical perspectives and discourses: linguistics, psychoanalysis, feminism, structuralism, deconstruction. A corollary of this has been the expansion of the domain of literary studies to include many concerns previously remote from it. In most American universities today a course on Freud is more likely to be offered in the English or French Department than in the Psychology Department; Nietzsche, Sartre, Gadamer, Heidegger, and Derrida are more often discussed by teachers of literature than teachers of philosophy; Saussure is neglected by linguists and appreciated by students and teachers of literature. The writings of authors such as these fall into a miscellaneous genre whose most convenient designation is simply 'theory', which today has come to refer to works that succeed in challenging and reorienting thinking in fields other than those to which they ostensibly belong, because their analyses of language, or mind, or history, or culture offer novel and persuasive accounts of signification. Of course, there had been earlier borrowings from other disciplines in American criticism – in the Marxist criticism of the thirties and in psychoanalytic criticism focused on authors, characters or readers – but these attempts had often seemed reductionist, ignoring complexities of literary language and making the text, in effect, a symptom, whose true meaning lay elsewhere: in the authorial neurosis or social contradiction or philosophical truth it reflected. The versions of European philosophical and psychoanalytical thought that became influential in the 1960s and 1970s, however, had themselves included extended reflection on language and meaning and were attractive precisely because they offered richer conceptual frameworks than did the New Criticism for expounding the complexity of literary signification. Instead of reducing literature to something non-literary, of which it would be a manifestation, these various theoretical enterprises – in fields as diverse as anthropology, psychoanalysis, historiography – discovered an essential 'literariness' in non-literary phenomena.

These discourses roughly assembled under the nickname 'theory' identify the literary not as a marginal phenomenon but as a logic of signification that generates human meanings of many sorts. Their engagement with irreducible complexities of language provides a link with the New Criticism that has facilitated the American reception of these interdisciplinary theoretical discourses, even though they challenge the specificity of the aesthetic and eschew the New Critical project of demonstrating the organic unity of individual works.

The question is, how did institutions make this possible and influence the directions it took? First, university expansion in the 1960s favoured critical innovation and the proliferation of critical possibilities by permitting universities to add new courses and programmes, without having to choose between one and another way of teaching and studying literature. College catalogues show that most institutions have added new courses without eliminating the old.[5]

Second, the expansion of universities and demand for more teachers of literature brought changes in their conditions of employment, with subsequent effects on criticism. In 1968 Michael Shugrue wrote in *English in a Decade of Change*:

> A growing college population, the shortage of qualified college teachers of English, and federal funds for curriculum research and teacher education have enabled the college English teacher to broaden the range of his activities significantly. With higher salaries, research grants from foundations and the government, and freedom from the need to moonlight, he can undertake research in libraries around the world . . . Salaries at the upper end of the schedule have risen even more than beginning salaries . . . Some colleges still maintain an aura of genteel poverty for faculty, but the limited supply of college English

teachers . . . is gradually forcing them, too, to acknowledge a changing academic world . . . Hundreds of excellent college departments spread across the country, however, find it increasingly difficult to attract faculty members from the small pool of approximately 500 new Ph.D.'s in English produced in 120 institutions in America each year . . . The need to recruit and keep qualified teachers of English leads, inevitably, to higher salaries, better working conditions, and a richer professional life for the college teacher of English, with or without the Ph.D.[6]

The reduction of the teaching load at research universities and elite colleges (from six or eight courses per year to four, in general) has encouraged the notion that the primary task of professional professorial critics is research and publication. We speak of teaching and administrative tasks preventing us from 'getting on with our work'. The later job crisis further reinforced the importance of criticism since, as current wisdom has it, you need more publications now to get a job interview than you needed ten years ago for tenure. One can argue that the system of publication exists not just to accredit professionals (a system of degrees would do that) but to distinguish those accredited from providers of services (such as nurses and school teachers), to accredit them as participants in an autonomous enterprise, where in principle projects are not imposed by outside forces but flow from the critic's own curiosity or from the so-called 'needs' of the field itself. Professionalism, as Jencks and Riesman note, is 'colleague-oriented rather than client-oriented'.[7] In the academy, professionalism ties one's identity to an expertise and hence to a field in which one might be judged expert by one's peers. This induces a proliferation of subfields as the job market becomes tighter: as writers of letters of recommendation we find that we have a stake in defining some area – say, psychoanalytic interpretations of Shakespeare – such that our candidate may be deemed one of its most accomplished experts. The connection between criticism and the continuing professional evaluation on which appointments, promotions, grants, and prestige depend may thus generate a more specialised and innovative criticism than might other arrangements, such as the British system I mentioned earlier.

Third, criticism has been affected by the primacy of departments – that distinctively American contribution to the system of higher education. The structure which makes the university a consortium of departments competing for students and money may encourage visible, innovative enterprises. As resources for expansion have disappeared, competition for money and positions often takes the form of competition for students and thus encourages ventures into new areas – film studies, women's studies, psychoanalysis, intellectual history, neglected philosophical writings – which are not claimed by other departments and offer possibilities of stimulating courses and research. The combination of the professionalisation of faculty (which makes one's peers the principal audience for one's work) and the organisation of the university into competing departments creates a situation in which departments are expected to vie with departments at other universities for eminence, both by attempting to hire their most distinguished critics and by encouraging their members to seek greater professional standing. Parsons and Platt note in *The American University* that institutions have not been content to excel in some fields while letting other departments remain less eminent.[8] Provosts and deans apply pressure that makes even conservative chairmen willing to encourage publication that will attract attention. For deans in our system, 'visibility', as we call it, may have become more important than what is called 'soundness'.

Criticism has also been affected by changes in the membership of university faculties. Commentators suggest that before the Second World War, literary scholarship in America was a marginally acceptable genteel vocation for white Anglo-Saxon protestant males of a certain social standing and economic status. The New Critics who challenged the Old Scholars were of the same sex and class, but they were followed, Leslie Fiedler writes, by a second generation of modernist critics :

> not renegade WASP bearers of infectious aesthetic doctrines, but many of us the offspring of non-English-speaking stock, with a veneer of Anglo-Saxon polite culture no more than a generation thick. . . . By the last years of the fifties, we former outsiders had established ourselves as insiders. The end of World War II had seen the influx into colleges and universities of vast hordes of government subsidized students, ex-G.I.s, many the first of their families ever to have been exposed to higher education. To teach the succeeding waves of the continuing invasion, new faculty had to be recruited out of the first waves: sons and daughters of working class or even petty-bourgeois parents, not even predominantly North European, much less *echt* Anglo-Saxon, after a while overwhelmingly East European Jewish (and to make matters worse, graduates of land-grant universities or city colleges) . . .[9]

This is something of an overstatement, since as late as 1969 only 7% of English department faculty were Jewish (13% in what one survey identifies as the 'better' universities); the humanities seem to have been the last disciplines to accept Jews,[10] but change has come, though it is hard to trace its direct effects on criticism, except in the case of the slowly increasing number of women faculty members. Energised by feminist thinking, they have produced changes in the literary canon (each new edition of the *Norton Anthology of English Literature* contains more women authors than its predecessor), an increasing number of popular and successful courses on women's writing, and a lively, polemical feminist criticism which treats traditional male authors and general issues relating to gender and sex, as well as women's writing. A new area of critical debate has emerged; and while these developments in criticism are in part a consequence of wider social movements, criticism has also been an instrument of social change. Pioneering works of feminism, such as Simone de Beauvoir's *The Second Sex* and Kate Millett's *Sexual Politics*, which played an important role in the growth of feminist movements, are in large part readings of literary works.

One cannot, though, discuss these issues fruitfully without considering the models by which universities operate and how they may affect critical writing. One can distinguish two general models at work in this period. The first makes the university the transmitter of a cultural heritage, gives it the ideological function of reproducing culture and the social order. The second model makes the university a site for the production of knowledge.[11]

The first model is linked with the experiments in general education that were so prominent in the years between the wars. By this model the university should be integrated : agreed upon and focused on the heritage it is seeking to transmit. The New Criticism succeeded as well as it did, one could argue, because it could function as a way of making the literary heritage accessible to a growing and more diversified student body entering universities. This model would lead one to expect literature departments to devote considerable energy to controlling the content of offerings and debating what ought to be required of an undergraduate major or a graduate student. It gives criticism the role of interpreting the canon, elucidating that 'core' of knowledge to be transmitted.

The other model casts the university as producer of knowledge. Its success is related to the growth of the sciences and of funded scientific research. A university is not an integrated unit commanded by a concept of education so much as an administrative apparatus for managing a series of loosely-integrated activities, each of which follows a particular logic, determined by developments in the discipline, priorities set by funding agencies, or pressing social issues. Aside from elementary courses, what gets taught and what research is conducted will depend more on professors' sense of the important problems in their specialities, or the availability of grants and their success in obtaining them, than on departmental decisions about what should be transmitted to the young. This structure can be conducive to the production of knowledge, because it encourages individual faculty members to pursue, in their teaching and writing, whatever sort of enterprise seems most likely to bring them recognition.

The increasing availability of research grants, a major feature of this model of the university, is a decisive change for literary studies in the post-war period. There is a dramatic increase in the number of Guggenheim Fellowships awarded for literary study – from 16 in 1937–40 to 176 in 1961–4 and 149 in 1977–80.[12] While Guggenheim panels have been conservative, fellowships awarded by the National Endowment for the Humanities and the American Council of Learned Societies have supported work on theory. Most useful, perhaps have been Mellon Fellowships, which let universities take in for a year or two young theorists they might be loath to hire permanently. The availability of grants affects criticism by producing a new goal : to devise research projects that will obtain awards, and thus to imagine what will impress granting bodies, which encourage one to cast one's project in terms that suggest novelty and breadth of perspective. In addition to encouraging the *appearance* of innovation (which sometimes does generate innovation) the grant system reduces the power of departments and universities over their members, making critics think of a professional peer group as their most important audience. And since this group judges writing, critical writing becomes the chief activity by which one's standing is determined. The increasing availability of grants encourages critics to reflect on their critical activity : in seeking to justify what they propose to do to an audience they take to be representative of the profession, critics help enunciate the rationality of a discipline, generating a *lingua franca* in which new approaches or projects are justified in familiar terms and traditional research is given some new, attractive twist.

The model of the university as producer of knowledge seems designed for the sciences and is frequently resisted by teachers of literature, but it has benefits for the humanities. The emphasis in the first model on shared values and the integration of the university can manifest itself as intolerance of dissidence and difference. Analysts have had difficulty in explaining why the percentage of women faculty members *declined* between the 1920s and the Second World War, but this model of the university as reproducer of culture may well bear some responsibility. The university as loosely-knit producer of knowledge can be more tolerant, allowing people to go their own way as long as they attract students, or research money, or the esteem of their professional peers.

The first model gives criticism the function of elucidating the masterpieces of the cultural heritage that is taught. The second model gives criticism no specific educational function but makes critical progress or innovation the goal of teachers of literature. Critical investigation, in this second model, is simply what professors do: to write criticism is to generate knowledge, and though a canonical body of texts may serve as a starting point, the only prescribed goal is to advance one's understanding of cultural phenomena. This, incidentally, is one reason why the situation of criticism seems confusing today. The model of the university as a site for the production of knowledge has altered the function of criticism and the role of critical invention.

American universities are structured by the conflict between the model of the production of knowledge and the model of the reproduction of culture. There is tension between them, with local variations that may be quite difficult to interpret. Though the vast expansion of funded scientific research led the second model to become dominant after the War, the play of the two models continues, especially in educational rhetoric. The resistance to literary theory and speculative criticism often takes the form of appeals to the importance of reproducing or transmitting the cultural heritage. Harvard, which has been one of the world's most successful entrepreneurial universities or research consortia, has devoted considerable energy to proclaiming the other model of the university: in the Redbook, *General Education in a Free Society* (1945), and then in its recent Core Curriculum. The relation between these much touted projects and the fortunes of literary criticism at Harvard might repay investigation. One can say in general, though, that despite the importance for recent developments in criticism of the pluralism and interdisciplinarity fostered by the model of the university as producer of knowledge, American criticism is distinguished by the links, produced by universities, between criticism and pedagogy: specifically, between criticism and a pedagogy attempting to cope with America's unparalleled experiment in mass higher education.

For instance, European criticism has frequently encouraged

consideration of readers and reading, but in America reader-oriented criticism has received a pedagogical and democratic inflection. Stanley Fish was only the first to equate the meaning of a literary work with the reader's experience, including hesitations, erroneous conjectures, moments of puzzlement, and so on. The recent fortunes of reader-oriented criticism here seem linked to relevance to the common American pedagogical situation in which a teacher confronts a class of inexperienced, puzzled, somewhat recalcitrant readers. Teachers find it productive to maintain that a student's puzzlement is not grounds for silence but part of the meaning of the text and thus grounds for discussion.

The pedagogical connection has also helped to advance feminist criticism, since the study of women's literature and women in literature is frequently thematic and can be pursued in elementary courses, whose success has stimulated work in feminist criticism and given teachers leverage with their departments. In our entrepreneurial university, good enrolments may permit a faculty member to pursue projects his or her seniors find dubious.

Third, the pedagogical context in which criticism is produced has encouraged theories and methods that help generate interpretations, for discussion of the meaning of a work is the form that literary instruction most commonly takes. Marxism and structuralism, which are not methods of interpretation but urge analysis of elaborate mediating systems, have been relatively unsuccessful, while the attention to problematical textual details fostered by deconstruction (and its productive framework for thinking about such matters) has been encouraged and assimilated by our interpretative critical practice.

But criticism's link with pedagogy is double-edged. For the most part, appeal to teaching is a conservative, even reactionary gesture: the suggestion that thinking and writing about literature ought to be controlled by the possibilities of classroom presentation is usually an attempt to dismiss new lines of investigation or abstruse critical writings without confronting them directly. The traditional link between literary studies and the reproduction of culture gives such appeals a plausibility that they would not have in other fields. Few would seriously suggest that physicists or historians should restrict their work to what can be communicated to 19-year-olds. A further complication for literary criticism is that critics teach in departments that devote considerable time to the teaching of foreign languages or of English composition. These tasks fall most heavily on the young and badly paid; and in this situation someone is always prepared to argue that instead of writing another book or teaching a graduate seminar, critics should devote more of their energy to basic education. Those whose critical orientation is out of favour may be especially vociferous in calling their colleagues to abandon difficult speculative or interpretative projects for freshman composition.[13] The American pedagogic context may have a fundamentally conservative impact, ensuring that theoretical reflection cannot go very far by forcing it to justify itself – as it is not forced to do in France or Germany, for example. Moreover, the teaching of composition can encourage a functional attitude to language, as critics find themselves adopting an ideology of lucidity; and despair at the awkwardness of student prose can encourage a sentimental reverence for anything well-written. The activities of departments where criticism is produced give it a situation unlike that of any other form of writing and research. The professional pressure to publish is always countered by forces working against advanced or innovative critical speculation.

Whatever one thinks about these factors, a crucial condition of recent critical change seems to have been the availability of money in the late 1960s and early 1970s, which helped make accessible European influences and American work stimulated by them. Conferences, visiting professorships, and especially new journals permitted the exploration of these new critical possibilities. *New Literary History* (1969), founded when the centenary of the University of Virginia made available money to give the university and its strong English department greater visibility, quickly became a major forum for translation of foreign theoretical work. *Diacritics* (1970), founded in the interests of the 'visibility' of a Romance Studies department, discovered that its most successful issues were those explicitly concerned with recent French theory. These two journals provided not only examples of new work but above all a sense that something significant was happening in criticism. In retrospect, it seems as though the student protest movements which energised and disrupted universities in the 1960s had the effect of permitting a questioning of orthodoxies of all sorts, so that when new methodological and critical possibilities emerged, as they very shortly did, they could be explored and exploited, even though they bore little direct relation to the concerns and goals of student movements of the sixties.

In America, unlike Britain, the assimilation of foreign theoretical work has been almost entirely a university activity. In the 1960s *Partisan Review* showed an active interest, publishing articles by de Man and Hartman, several translations of Barthes and Lévi-Strauss, and some discussions of structuralism, but eventually joined the opposition to structuralist and post-structuralist thinking. *The New York Review of Books*, which a 1972 survey by Hover and Kadushin claimed was far and away the leading intellectual forum,[14] was first cool and then hostile, eliminating critics who became involved from its list of contributors, rejecting sympathetic reviews of theoretical criticism, avoiding participation even in feminist theory and criticism; but surprisingly, its attacks seem to have had little effect. When the *New York Review* joined *Time* and *Newsweek* in middle-brow opposition it succeeded only in depriving itself of influence in the domain of contemporary criticism, and revealing to what extent criticism was a university enterprise, part of the functioning of what had arguably become the most important American institution.

This relation to the academy gives contemporary theoretical criticism a problematical character. Interdisciplinarity, in the academic world, involves competition for funds, positions, and students, but above all, arguments about disciplines that would not necessarily occur in the sphere of public criticism. When a professor of French or English teaches or writes about Freud or Heidegger, this is anomalous in the university world, which is organised into departments that supposedly represent distinct intellectual fields. 'Theory', as we call it, thus occupies a strange position : studied and practised within universities, disseminated by the academic media, 'theory' is an academic activity, yet within the university it is anti-disciplinary, challenging not only the boundaries of disciplines, on whose legitimacy the university structure seems to depend, but also these disciplines' claims to judge writing that touches their concerns. In practice, 'theory' contests the right of psychology departments to control Freud's texts, of philosophy departments to control Kant, Hegel, and Heidegger. Yet since this subversion of the university's articulation of knowledge takes place within the university structure, there is considerable scope for disagreement about what is happening – radical claims and charges of inescapable conservatism.

If, as Gramsci says, intellectuals in the capitalist state function as 'experts in legitimation', then theoretical criticism might be deemed the place where critiques of legitimacy are continually being carried out – in a quarter where they may seem to pose the least direct threat to social and political institutions. Whatever the political potential of these critiques, which is by no means clear, this possibility appears to have arisen through a transposition of a certain power of literature. The power of defamiliarisation, previously associated with the literary avant-garde, behind which academic criticism lagged, has now passed to criticism. The quality of the 'modern', the sense of crisis that literature provokes, now inheres in the critical process of exposing and questioning the assumptions on which prior critical, literary, cultural activities depend. Criticism has built into critical reflection the defamiliarising analysis of the conditions of possibility of discourse; so that criticism becomes, among other things, the practice of generating questions about discursive knowledge, of reflecting on interpretation itself and pursuing the contestatory movement that used to be associated with avant-garde literature.

I am suggesting that institutional pressures and the interested activities of departments and individuals within professional and disciplinary systems have contributed to criticism's taking on the disruptive, defamiliarising power of literature. This is an ironic result, of course, responsible for much of the confusion about the politics of criticism that surrounds us, for these institutional influences cannot but vitiate the innovating, critical effects which they have helped to promote.

A different way to conclude would be to say that formerly the history of criticism was part of the history of literature (the story of changing conceptions of literature advanced by great writers), but that now the history of literature is part of the history of criticism, dependent upon what is canonised, what is explicated, what is articulated as a major problem for literature in the critical communities in universities. Even if one resists that reversal of the traditional relation between criticism and literature, one must recognise that criticism today, because of its reorganisation around an interdisciplinary critique of signifying processes and its entanglement with the entrepreneurial structure of universities and the processes of professional advancement, is in a new relation to literature. Any attempt to move beyond criticism as it is presently constituted will itself be part of the system of questioning that criticism and its institutions have developed.

NOTES

1 Frank Lentricchia, *Criticism and Social Change* (Chicago: University of Chicago Press, 1984).

2 Terry Eagleton, *Literary Theory: An Introduction* (Oxford: Blackwell, 1983), pp. 190 and 43. Further page references are included within the text.

3 Grant Webster, *The Republic of Letters* (Baltimore: Johns Hopkins University Press, 1979), p. 4.
4 Stephen Toulmin, *Human Understanding* (Princeton: Princeton University Press, 1972), p. 104.
5 For discussion of curricula, see Elizabeth Cowan, ed., *Options for the Teaching of English: The Undergraduate Curriculum* (New York: MLA, 1975) and Thomas W. Wilcox, *The Anatomy of College English* (San Francisco: Jossey-Barr, 1973).
6 Michael Shugrue, *English in a Decade of Change* (New York: Pegasus, 1968), pp. 86–7.
7 Christopher Jencks and David Riesman, *The Academic Revolution* (New York: Doubleday, 1968), p. 201. See also Richard Ohmann, *English in America* (New York: Oxford University Press, 1976), pp. 234–51.
8 Talcott Parsons and Gerald Platt, *The American University* (Cambridge, Mass.: Harvard University Press, 1973), p. 146.
9 Leslie Fiedler, *What Was Literature?* (New York: Simon and Schuster, 1982), p. 60.
10 Stephen Steinberg, *The Academic Melting Pot: Catholics and Jews in American Higher Education* (New Brunswick, N.J.: Transaction Books, 1977), pp. 119–22. These figures agree with those of Seymour Lipset and Everett Ludd, 'Jewish Academics in the United States', *American Jewish Yearbook* (1971).
11 See Alain Touraine, *The Academic System in American Society* (New York: McGraw Hill, 1974).
12 John Simon Guggenheim Memorial Foundation, *Reports of the President and Treasurer* (New York, 1979), p. xxxii.
13 For example, E. D. Hirsch, who urged critics to discover authors' intentions (*Validity in Interpretation*, 1967), and Frederick Crews, champion of the psychoanalysis of characters in fiction (*The Sins of the Fathers*, 1966), have turned to Freshman Composition and exhorted others to follow them.
14 Julie Hover and Charles Kadushin, 'The Influential Intellectual Journals', *Change Magazine* 4:2 (March 1972), 38–47.

Difference and history

History traces

MARIAN HOBSON

'Certainly any reading method like Derrida's – whose main ambition is both to reveal undecidable elements in a text in lieu of some simple reductive message the text is supposed to contain and to shy away from making each reading of a text part of some cumulatively built explicit thesis about the historical persistence of and the agencies for Western metaphysical thought – certainly any method like that will finally be unable to get hold of the local material density and power of ideas as historical actuality.'[1] Edward Said's is not the first, though it is probably the most cogently argued attack on Derrida for lack of historical purchase on ideas. But it is based on a quite stunning lack of understanding of the status of Derrida's work, and in particular of the status of Derridean terms like 'différance' and 'trace'. What is being criticised, beyond a different intellectual orientation, is in fact, in coded form, lack of explicit political position. Now Derrida, as Said and others acknowledge, has shown no merely passing interest in the politics of philosophy; in the institutionalisation of thought; in the socio-political anchorage of a text. Moreover, he has devoted time and energy to practical work and discussion in these fields.[2] The practical doesn't then provide ground for attack. What is not liked is that Derrida does not ground his work in an already-provided analysis of western society, nor on the whole does he marshal those highly abstract concepts which, because they claim to refer to the real, are somehow thought of as more material. Said claims that Derrida reduces 'everything we think as having some extratextual leverage in the text to a textual function' (p. 692). This claim renders undifferentiated what are complex striations in Derrida's work. Not merely does Derrida point out the local anchorage of the texts he is operating on (Heidegger, for instance, in 'Restitutions', or Kant, in 'D'un ton apocalyptique adopté naguère en philosophie'), his work tends to show a way of thinking the historical structure of thought in general. Moreover, it could and should be argued that his work is in turn both anchored locally, and part of wider more inclusive historical structures – and that Derrida also takes account of this or at least indicates this, hence the 'booting' effect of his writing, its looping between levels. Here, however, I shall develop only part of this argument, first by redifferentiating, and then by tying together into a pathway some Derridean concepts. (In a sense, however inadequately, this is applying concepts of 'différance' and 'trace' to themselves.) It should then be apparent that, far from collapsing what Said deems to be outside the text back on and into it, these concepts are exploring what could be called the historical nature of thought without using any kind of position of even momentary transcendence, any kind of cosmic exile, to borrow Putnam's phrase.

Books about Derrida or deconstruction have often shown a *homing* instinct : they fix on one term, like *différance*, from Derrida's writings and terminate it – they treat it as if it were both determinable and privileged. They assume it to be *indifferent* that the term is part of a collection : powered by a kind of critical homesickness, they homologise or bring together in indifference what are in fact sets or pluralities of terms. The most obvious collection is that associated with *différance* (with an 'a'). It has been given preference – but actually *espacement* and *trace* occur sometimes side by side, in harness so to speak, and sometimes one after the other, but in close connection (e.g. *Positions*, p. 44).

This set of words : *trace*, *différance*, *espacement*, is marked by a structural delaying. To defer is to cause to differ – etymologically they have the same root, and the spelling of *différance* with an 'a' is a reminder of this, as it is of their divergence. The structural delay isn't preceded by unity : differentiation, lapse of times makes identity impossible. *Espacement* seems to mark that delay which is also a movement away from. *Différance* and *espacement* show that no moment of experience can present itself except as *re*ference again to what it is not, what differs from it : and this differential network is called 'trace, gramme, espacement' (*Positions*, p. 44) – as in the 'observation' of elementary particles, one is left with a track (etymologically related to trace) that is a movement in space–time, and with certain effects the particles are supposed to have left behind. *Différance*, *espacement*, *trace*, refer then, though in different ways, to trajectory – in non-coincident fashion. I want to follow this trajectory, but first to put a marker forward. It is trace, track, which makes identity impossible. But this impossibility is itself plural, not simple. It is not a straight negative – not simple, identical, non-identity. Trace, lack of self-coincidence, is on the contrary a plurality of impossibilities, a disjunction of negatives.

So: the members of the incomplete set *différance*, *espacement*, *trace*, (one could add *frayage*) are not homologous: it is precipitate to home in on one and assimilate the others. It's not in fact clear whether they are the same or whether they are different. (Neither should they be called a series – that's misleading because in a mathematical series, even an infinite one, any member can be placed, sited, localised and bounded). But these concepts have itchy feet. They are on the move, they're not really guessable in advance. They are unstable in the literal sense of not being stabilisable. They can't be made to stand still. (This is one of the reasons – only one – why it is unwise to speak of theory and practice in relation to Derrida or deconstruction. It is not clear whether such instability can be marshalled into a theory as such, especially if theory is placed in a binary opposition with practice. A theory is 'of' something, it requires a genitive, a beat which it can police or process. Its beat, its area of application is *opposite*, *over against*, in some sense, for there is a visual model at work (*theorein* meant to watch a competition), but Derrida's work has not usually been over against another work: on the contrary, there is a host text off which it has lived, or at least has referred to in a glancing way. Sometimes, and at some points – as in *Glas* – his text and the host texts (Hegel, Genet) are hard to prise apart. This makes the notion of theory even more doubtful.)

A different tactic has often been tried. A good many writings on Derrida have taken this instability in tow, so to speak, and treated it as an effect of deconstruction. They talk of the 'free play of the signifier', or of sense.[3] There is a lot wrong with this: first and foremost '*free* play' doesn't seem to occur in Derrida at all. No wonder. The phrase, which refers to Kant's *freies Spiel*,[4] the free play of the power of judgement, brings with it notions of spontaneity and freedom which are inappropriate, to put it mildly. 'Free' is in fact an addition by the first translator of the paper read by Derrida in the US in 1966, 'La structure, le signe et le jeu.'[5] 'Jeu' *tout court* is not much used after *Grammatology* in 1967, though it appears in *Eperons*. Even if *jeu* is understood as 'play' or 'game' and not as 'play' in a machine, that is the necessary wobble in a tautly set-up structure, it seems wrong to privilege it instead of relating it to, for instance, Eugen Fink (*Le Jeu comme symbole du monde*) and the circle round *Kantstudien*. And it is because 'free play' has been privileged that there has been a neglect of some of the most important – politically important – elements of deconstruction : the concern with hierarchies of forces, with the changes that can be wrought in an intellectual set-up by such practices as 'reinscription'. It is to render undifferentiated and thus probably ineffective the unstabling effect of deconstruction.

To talk of the 'free play of the signifier' is to play around. Concepts like *différance*, *trace*, *espacement* don't go round in a ring. Their relation to each other is problematic : they supplement each other, but not quite, not completely nor without remainder. Neither the same nor different, they appear to be delayed versions of each other ('delay' is probably derived from the frequentative of 'defer'). (And here their lack of self-identity becomes paradoxical : is 'différant' différant? If it is, then it is identical with itself and so not différant and v.v. The resemblance to Grelling's paradox, built round the terms autological and heterological, is not fortuitous. Self-reference, with *différance*, *trace*, *frayage*, doesn't have a clarifying but a perturbing effect.) *Trace, espacement, différance*, relay each other. They form tracks which are probably not arrangeable chronologically nor vectorisable in time. But they are all concerned with trajectory and they seem to be going somewhere, as a somewhat straggly group (and can be compared to Deleuze and Guattari's 'rhizomes' and 'nomades'). That there is this movement is unsurprising when one thinks of Derrida's attentiveness to where texts are going, especially the places they are going which are not openly acknowledged. One can think too, of his recent account of his own work given in English, where he says : 'If I saw clearly ahead of time where I was going I really don't believe that I should take another step to get there' but he adds that this 'did not mean . . . I never know where I'm going'.[6] It looks as if the shifting movement between *différance*, *trace* and *espacement* is powered by the slight tensions created by their lack of sameness – the 'pas sans pas' the 'step without a negative' of the writings on Blanchot : like the mathematical paradoxes of the beginning of the century, perhaps they're shifting the ground under our feet, forcing a change of gait, the limp necessary to walking somewhere.

These have been so far liminary remarks, but they are liminary marks which aren't going to stay at the edge. One of the most important recent works by Derrida, 'Spéculer – sur "Freud" ', is concerned with the course of Freud's argument in *Beyond the Pleasure Principle*. Freud frequently applies the term 'speculation' to this work and in particular to his investigation of the question: can all elements of psychic life be subsumed under the pleasure principle? Derrida develops 'spéculer' to refer not merely to themes in Freud's text, to the impulse to repetition, to the problem of the self and its relation to death, but to Freud's whole mode of posing a problem in order to solve it. 'Spéculer' is in fact trajectory through a discourse. Freud states that neurotic behaviour like repetition of the circumstances of traumatic injury seems on the surface difficult to bring under the pleasure principle. In the face of such evidence Freud moves out from the pleasure principle as the fundamental explanation of psychic events; he speculates, as he says, tries out other explanations, but until the last chapters returns to it as the key to psychic life. 'Spéculer' describes then Freud's havering, haltering gait in the argument, his movement out from and return to the pleasure principle. But this movement is epitomised by – 'etched into' is the literal meaning of the Greek – the account Freud gives of his grandchild Ernst's game with a cotton reel threaded on a piece of string. The child threw it away from himself, making a sound diagnosed by his mother and by Freud as 'fort' and pulled it back uttering 'da'. Freud proposes several explanations of this game: as a revenge impulse for his momentary abandonment, or as self-conquest, in that displeasure at his mother's disappearance is turned gradually into a pleasurable game. But no proposal satisfies Freud: he starts out again, as if there were an irreducible remainder in each piece of evidence, not resolvable into the pleasure principle. Grandchild's game and grandfather's speculation are both trajectories; both have the same rhythm: *fort/da*, out and back.

Derrida goes beyond this. The child's game is speculation, in that something is ventured, sent out, for profit. The sending/retrieving of the reel constitutes the self, not as a present kernel, but as a relay: the self is kept going through the repetition of the game, and mastery is obtained through the game of repetition. Likewise the grandfather plays a game with his writing, he speculates, keeps starting it up, strings it out (Derrida puns on fils/fil, son/string); he tries *out* his ideas; *Jenseits des Lustprinzips* becomes a meta-psychological text, part of the constitution of the analytic movement.

For this constitution to take place, both of the child and of Freudianism, both as intellectual doctrine and powerful social force, there has to be more than repetition. The movement, in the play of the child, in the discursive argument of the grandfather, doesn't merely ply between bounds, between *fort/da*, like a shuttle. The repetition involves a change of level, the first bounds, *fort/da* become a part of what must be repeated. 'It's a question of the repetition of the couple disappearance/reappearance not only of reappearance as a pole in the pair, but of the reappearance of the pair which must come back' (*La Carte postale*, p. 339). The child's repetition of his game is an *auto-affection*, an operation on the self : passive genitive – the disappearance of the mother and of self, becomes active genitive – the making disappear of the mother. The self is maintained as a trace, as the thread, as a relay, through his own disappearance and reappearance. 'He gets himself to disappear (he masters himself symbolically), he plays with the dead boy as he would with himself, and he gets himself to reappear from that moment on without using a mirror, in this very disappearance, keeping himself like his mother at the end of the line [*fil* : thread but also telephone cable]' (*CP* 340). This movement forward, applied to either grandchild or grandfather, takes the same path : that of speculation, that of uncertain and incremental return to a starting point, where it is the movement back which presupposes the movement out. 'This . . . speculates starting with the return, from the beginning of what owes it to its self to return' (*CP* 335). Derrida is playing on at least three senses of speculation : speculation with ideas; speculation as the creation of money and thus power through circulation; and then speculation from speculum, mirror, where an image of what is reflected in the mirror is relayed back, and reappropriated. (There is a deformation of Lacan here.) Derrida plies between speculative possibility, speculation as economic and social power; speculation as mirror reflection, the relation of self to self where there is no proper self but only a relayed series of reappropriations :

I consider the whole game's over after these first pages, in other words, he will only repeat his halt, his not moving or his walking step [*pas de marche*] but it's precisely a question of repetition here. The speculative possibility of the entirely other (than the pleasure principle) is written in it in advance, in the letter giving him the job, which he thinks he's sending himself circularly, specularly, it's written there like something that can't be written into him, opening him up to being written on by the other at the same level as the principle. This very surface of the 'same level' doesn't belong to itself any more, it's no longer what it is in the way it is. The writing affects the very surface of what holds it up. And this not belonging to itself unleashes speculation.

Already you must think that I'm myself twisting the 'properly freudian' use of speculation, of the notion of concept and of the word. Where Freud seems to make it into a mode of research, a theoretical attitude, I'm considering it as the object of his discourse as well. I act as if Freud wasn't only getting ready to speak speculatively of this or that (for example of a beyond for the pleasure principle) but as if he were already speaking about speculation. As if he weren't content to move around in it, but wanted to treat of it as well, in sideways fashion. And it's the sideways of this procedure that interests me. I act as if what he appears to analyse, for example the relation between the two principles, were already an element in speculative structure in general, at the same time in the sense of specular reflexion (the pleasure principle can recognise itself or not, or no longer recognise itself at all in the reality principle) in the sense of production of surplus value, calculation and betting on the stock market, or even the issuing of holdings more or less fictitious, in the sense, at last, of what goes beyond the edges of the given presence of the present, the given of the gift. (*CP* 303–4)

Derrida speaks of the 'singular path of speculation' (*CP* 287). Speculation havers – its possibility is that of a disjunction of negatives; it is explicitly distinguished from Hegelian speculation, which constitutes itself through absorbing its dialectical negative; speculation's meandering path is neither the dialectic nor the hermeneutic circle; speculation constructs and deconstructs itself in an interminable detour. For in 'speculation' what is written about doesn't precede the writing; the child's game isn't prior to Freud's account of it, on the contrary it describes its own description. Freud's text like the child's persona is constituted by a process of overwriting which is both prior as well as posterior to any apparent 'event'. For the persona, 'autos', as for text, we have a set of differential pathways rather than localisable elements, we have networks, traces, which are tracks going backwards (da) as well as forwards in time (fort). The coherence of a text or of self is not one of identity or self-identity, but one of self-replication and self-repetition through reappropriation. Another term, 'télé', is applied to the child's or Freud's playing/writing: but it raises difficult questions of Derrida's rewriting of meaning and of intention that I can't go into here. One can just say that it presents itself at least at first glance as a differentiated version of *spéculer*.

There is another group of concepts that imply movement to and fro under *tension*. The plying between the directions of the path is a tension between deferred versions of the game – death of life and life of death, or lifedeath as Derrida calls it. Out of this tension comes the set and the self: (Etymologically the German *spannen*, to put under tension, and *sponte*, 'spontaneously', are related).

Set: if this word must refer to a unity, which is rigorously neither that of the subject nor of the conscious, the unconscious, the person, of the soul and or the body, of the *socius* or of the 'system' in general [a disjunction of negatives again] then the set as a set must liaise with itself to constitute itself as such. All being-together, even if its modality is limited to none of those we have just put in a series, begins with a liaising with itself, with a *binding* of the self in a differantial relation to itself. (*CP* 429)

Lier then represents this differential substitute for unity. It is the translation of the Freudian *binden, Bindung* : cathexis : the fixing of certain drives and then their resolution in behaviour through secondary processes. In that sense *lier* represents psychic energy under tension; the replacement of a primary process by a supplement, by a secondary process: the drive to satisfaction is mediated by a complex set of partial processes which delay, string out the pleasure. But as part of the group *lier*, *lyse*, *analysis*, it once again, like 'spéculation', refers both to the trajectory of the psyche and to the institution of psychoanalysis. Derrida goes further : *lier*, *binden* is related by him to a concept, *stricture*, used in *Glas* and in *La Vérité en peinture.* Once again, as at the beginning of this paper with *différance et al.*, we have a set of concepts *lier, stricture, bande/bander* (the sexual pun is intended) which seem to be delayed versions of each other. *Stricture* is a trajectory under tension between life/death, between the death from no pleasure and death from too much. *Spéculation* of the grandfather or of the child's game leads to mastery, to a self created not as identity but as network of criss-cross references. *Stricture* seems to be the tension of opposites which instead of being opposed, are looped under high tension into a pathway. 'Stricture produces pleasure by binding it. It plays between two infinities, betting and speculating on the surplus value this restriction will get it' (*CP* 427). As such, it is not dialectic, it merely creates dialectic effects : its negative is not lack of opposition, but *pas sans pas.* The mastery it makes possible in Freud's theory is not created by power of one principle, that of reality, over another. On the contrary it is tautological, it is caused by deferring, by a trajectory which, looping back to near its point of departure creates tension and difference with an 'e'. It is a transcendental tautology (*CP* 430). In traditional philosophy the transcendental principles are what form the grounds of possibility of experience, what logically precede it and make it possible. But *stricture* in *Glas represents* a deconstructive force : pulling together what traditional philosophy would like to separate (form/content, sensible/intelligible, etc.), it forces what is set up as transcendental to collapse on to what it is opposed to : it sets up a pathway between what is postulated as separate (*Glas* 242, 250, 271).

Stricture, *lier*, *bander* are then another set of Derridean concepts whose relation is problematic. They represent the impossibility of conceptual opposition (in *Glas* the opposition between Holy Spirit and Virgin Mother produces Christ). They are then the trajectory under tension between impossible opposites to which Derrida gives the acronym IC, Jesus Christ. This tension creates for Hegel, says *Glas*, an effect of transcendence, of mastery, of standing outside the network. Now such an effect underpins much writing of history or about history. In practice, such writing will not explicate fully its own position in regard to the past (it also cannot, by a necessary impossibility which is not recognised, by a kind of wilfulness); in its theory, it invokes the name of History to make it act as backstop, as that which judges and limits other codes, other writing.[7] But such a stance is an 'effect', a 'leurre', a trap, and will collapse back into the network which it seemed momentarily to transcend :

> This is why this history of the postal services . . . can't be a history of the postal services : first because it is concerned with the very possibility of history, of all those concepts then, of history, of tradition, of transmission or interruptions, reroutings. Then because such a 'history' of the postal services would only be a minute parcel in the network that it would be claiming to analyse (no metapost), only a card lost in a sack, one which a strike or a sorting error can always make indefinitely late, lose without recall (*CP* 74). [This is of course a contradiction of Lacan's famous statement that a letter always arrives at its destination.]

But it might seem, against Derrida, that to write history, some kind of transcendence is necessary, even if a momentary one : you have in some way to stand sideways to the process. This transcendence can be provided by an origin, placed outside and supporting the historian's web, or else provided by telos, by an end towards which the whole historical process can be seen as moving. But the effect of *différance* is to make that transcendence impossible. What Derrida provides is a way of thinking radical contingency : there is no origin, nor proper direction of meaning (*sens propre*) from which history can be measured. But this doesn't mean that a trajectory is impossible. There is no tidy seriality, but a complex pattern of forward and recursive loops : contingency like Freud's *spéculation* isn't part of a logic of opposition : the trajectory is pathed out not in any comforting dialectic of good/bad, true/false, confirm/accuse but in an uncomfortable *athesis* as Derrida calls it. There is a 'necessary heterogeneity, an interminable network, branching out in listening posts to somewhere else [*en allo*] (*Glas* 136).

I want to relay this account of the history of the postal service, and at a second level, the problematic relation between the sets of Derridean concepts, to one of the first published texts by Derrida, an introduction to Husserl's *Origin of Geometry*. The problem history posed for Husserl was considerable. The aim of his whole philosophy is to get beyond mere facts of experience and of wordly presence to what he calls 'eidetic structures', that is, forms of experience which are prior to facticity. From his first writings, from the *Logical Investigations* (1900), Husserl opposed both empiricism and historicism: phenomenology was 'to have as its exclusive concern experiences seizable and analysable in the pure generality of their essence, not experiences empirically perceived and treated as real facts'.[8] With Husserl as with Descartes, maths seems the purest example of such essences: geometry or maths in general seem to make possible ideal repeatability of thought without interference of language except as pure meaning. Why then does maths have a history? What is the relation between mathematical thought and the objects of mathematical thought? What is the relation, to use Husserlian terms, between the constituting act and the constituted sense? Husserl, in the text translated by Derrida, argues that history is incomprehensible unless it explores the 'powerful structural a priori which is proper to it'. Geometry is not a chain of successive facts; on the contrary, to understand geometry is to bring together genealogy and epistemology. Geometry is a tradition, an activity of transmission. The present whole of culture, says Husserl, implies a continuity of parts which entail each other, each constituting a present for us of *past* culture; a present which is a sediment of originary sense, but which the act of understanding reactivates and makes living. Yet the events of geometry's history were once projects, that is, acts creating sense. This sense turns into sedimented geometric objects (mathematical objects); but these are in turn justified by the present's power not to treat them as dead but to give them meaning, to bring them alive in understanding. This process is called by Husserl *Rückfrage* and to it Derrida applies in his introduction what he himself terms a postal analogy:

Like its German synonym, return inquiry (*question en retour*) is marked by the postal and epistolary reference or resonance of a communication from a distance. Like the *Rückfrage*, return inquiry is made from a position where something has first been sent. From a received and already readable *document,* the possibility is offered me of asking again and *in return* about the originary and final intentions of what has been handed to me by tradition. The latter, which is only mediacy itself, and openness to telecommunication in general, is then, as Husserl says, '*open to continued inquiry*'.[9]

Husserl develops then a view of history which could be called a network of return calls: movement back to reactivate discoveries which in their time had been a movement forward, a project for sense. This movement forwards, this anticipation then takes the form according to Derrida of a Kantian Idea. The Kantian Idea is brought in by Husserl in the discussion of unity of intuition in *Ideas* (1913).[10] The Kantian Idea tenses in both meanings – it makes temporal and it injects sense. It is a task and it founds ideation – it founds that orginary process of consciousness which is temporalisation, woven out of protentions and retentions, in that it retains what was once protention and project. The Absolute of Living Presence then, says Derrida apropos Husserl, is in fact a consciousness of indefinite announcement of the future in the present, or of the past which is in the present. Time is not phenomenologically successive: it is unified by this net of protentions and retentions, of castings back and projectings forward and the unity of this movement appears to consciousness as indefinite.

Derrida's account of the construction of a tradition, a pathway out of tension between protentions and retentions, projections forward, and retainings of the past is clearly a version of his account of the child Ernst's constitution of self through the fort–da trajectory of the reel; or a version of Freud's speculation, his constitution of his psychoanalytic theory and his psychoanalytic movement. But like Derrida's *stricture* or *lier*, Husserl's Kantian Idea is a tension, it is never thematised by Husserl. For as a task for consciousness, it isn't extra-historical, but exists throughout history, *as* history. With a disjunction of negatives and a pattern of argument which should now be familiar, Derrida says that the Absolute of the Idea as telos, aim, of infinite determinability (though practical interminability) is the Absolute of intentional historicity:

> The 'of' points neither to a simple objective genitive nor to a simply subjective one; it is neither a question of an objective Absolute independently revealing itself to an intention relative to it, which is waiting and conforming itself to it; nor is it a question of a subjective Absolute, creating meaning and absorbing meaning into its interiority. (*OG* 157)

It is the Absolute of genitivity itself, pure possibility of a genetic relation. It is an activity of consciousness arising out of a dialectic created by temporalisation – the play between protentions and retentions, and a non-dialectic, the absolute identity of the Living Present, the universal form of consciousness.

There is then nothing outside this openness which is tradition: no Platonic Ideas, no telos, no mathematical objects separate from history. The origin of history and the telos of history only exist in relation to each other. The Absolute is only passage towards. It is traditionality which circulates from one to the other, illuminating one by the other in a movement where consciousness invents its own path by an indefinite reduction which is always already begun, where every event is a turning, and where every turning back to origin is a venture towards a future horizon.

Derrida's accounts of the *Rückfrage*, of temporalisation as a tension between protentions and retentions, of the constitution of a historical tradition are then versions of the account given in 'Spéculer' of the child Ernst's constitution of self; or of Freud's speculation. They seem relayed versions of each other, repetitions after lapse of time without identity, *différant*. But something more can be said. Derrida at the end of his introduction to the *Origine de la géométrie* articulates Husserl with Heidegger, and implicitly himself with both. Husserl's phenomenological treatment of the origins of geometry has uncovered for our geometrical knowledge eidetic structures which are not an axiomatic, not given once and for all, but which show in general how it is possible to have a tradition of truth at all (with all that that implies of non-fixity). Husserl seems to have shown that a historicity can be thought which is neither purely empirical history nor merely an historical rationalism. In doing so, says Derrida, he has led us to the ontological question: why is there history, why is there facticity at all? But then there can only be, it seems, retreat: only phenomenology can deal with this, though it cannot answer. For Being is that which appears and disappears, and Discourse is always already late. So, says Derrida, the phenomenological approach which seemed to be a propaedeutic, a preliminary set of methods, can only be continued. It is interminable. The phenomenological reduction, the attempt to get beyond psychological and historical experience to the structures of those acts which constitute our knowledge, is doomed, structurally doomed, to be constantly iterative. Being has always already left us with a remainder. So that Husserl is after Heidegger. The phenomenological reduction is an awareness of Discourse's absolute lateness. This awareness appears in the criss-cross, the net of protentions and retentions which is the Living Present:

> The impossibility of resting in a simple maintaining of Living Present, an origin . . . always other in its self-identity, the incapacity to close oneself in the innocent indivision of the originary Absolute, because it is only present in ceaselessly deferring itself, this impossibility and incapacity give themselves as a pure and originary consciousness of Difference. (*OG* 171)

'Transcendentale serait la Différence' – Derrida uses the conditional and a capital. The conditional is the tense for reporting speech, or for reporting the implications of Husserl's work. Typically then, what could be taken, in reference to later work of Derrida, as a setting up of *différence*, as a transcendental, is also a drawing back of the position into a philosophical tradition. The transcendental contingent, *différence*, is thus made *différant*, contingent. There is no archaeology of a past present, only a projection forward and a pointing back.

The telephone or postal analogy used by Derrida in the *Origin of Geometry* calls forward to the 'télé', and to the 'coup de fil' of 'Spéculer – sur "Freud" ', and to the post cards of *La Carte postale*; projecting back from 'Spéculer – sur "Freud" ', *différance*, *spéculation*, is not a new name for empiricism, nor navigation according to circumstance; looking forward from the *Origine de la géométrie*, the criss-cross of the *Rückfrage* points to the indecisive gait which is yet going somewhere, the looped deviancies of the networks of 'Spéculer'. Derrida's *trace* is itself a trajectory.[11] The back and forth makes a set of plies – strands in a yarn or rope, which provide the strength through tension. We are left not with a scatter of points but with a trajectory.[12]

NOTES

1 Edward W. Said, 'The Problem of Textuality: two exemplary positions', *Critical Inquiry*, 4 (1978). 673–714. The quotation is from p. 701.

2 For instance, in the group *Greph*, and in the *Collège de philosophie*. The concern to reappropriate Derrida's work for 'history' has been discussed by Geoff Bennington, 'Outside Story', a Review Article of *Marxism and Deconstruction* by Michael Ryan in *LTP: Journal of Literature Teaching Politics*, 3 (1984). Ryan's book is a subtle and sustained equivalence or comparison – it is both – between deconstruction and Marxism. For instance: 'Although the terms are not

identical, the critical, anti-ideological charge carried by the words "history" and "relation" in Marx is matched by that implicit in the words "trace" and "difference" in Derrida. If "history" is Marx's word for the breaking up of nature and for the onset of institutions and production, it bears a relation to Derrida's term, the "becoming-unmotivated" of the trace, the breaking of signification with the "natural attachment within reality". There is no nature of language or of thought which is not already institutionalized or becoming-unmotivated. Assuming that motivation names the natural attachment in general, we might weave Marx and Derrida together in a slightly illegitimate way by substituting the word "history" for the word "unmotivated" in the following passage from Derrida' (p. 57). And he proceeds to quote a passage from *Grammatology* effecting the substitution. But Ryan does not recognise that in this part of the text, history is being contrasted with nature in a very different sense, and one that is made entirely clear: 'Tout cela renvoie, par-delà l'opposition nature/culture. à une opposition survenue entre *physis* et *nomos*, *physis* et *techné* dont l'ultime fonction est peut-être de *dériver* l'historicité', *De la Grammatologie* (Paris: Minuit, 1967), p. 50. All references to Derrida's work will be given in the text, and all translations will be mine unless otherwise stated: Edmond Husserl, *L'Origine de la géometrie*, tr. et intro. de Jacques Derrida Paris: PUF, 1962) (referred to in the text as *OG*); *L'Ecriture et la différence* (Paris: Seuil. 1967); *La Dissémination* (Paris: Seuil, 1972); *Glas* (Paris: Galilée, 1974); *Epérons* (Venice: Corbo e Fiori, 1976); 'Restitutions', in *La Vérité en peinture* (Paris: Flammarion, 1980), 291–436; *La Carte postale de Freud à Socrate et au delà* (Paris: Flammarion, 1980) (referred to in the text as *CP*); 'D'un ton apocalyptique adopté naguère en philosophie', in *Les Fins de l'homme, à partir du travail de J. Derrida* (Paris: Galilée, 1981), 445–79.

3 Cf. Christopher Norris, *Deconstruction: Theory and Practice* (London and New York: Methuen, 1982), p. 67; Frank Lentricchia, *After the New Criticism* (London: Athlone, 1980), p. 168.

4 Kant speaks in the *Kritik de Urteilskraft*, section 9, of the 'freies Spiel der Erkenntnisvermögen'.

5 *The Structuralist Controversy: the Languages of Criticism and the Sciences of Man*, eds. Richard Macksey and Eugenio Donato (Baltimore: Johns Hopkins University Press, 1972), originally published as *The Languages of Criticism and the Sciences of Man* in 1970, contains a translation of Derrida's text which uses 'free play', and it is this translation which was associated with the original conference of 1966, and with Derrida's first celebrity in the U.S. Alan Bass's translation of the article in his translation of *Writing and Difference* (Chicago: Chicago University Press, 1978), uses 'play'. It looks rather as if the excessive weight put on ideas of play in deconstruction in the U.S. derives from the first translation, which has to be regarded as a mistranslation; 'jeu' in Derrida's work should be related to ideas of 'alea', which is very far from a concept of 'freedom' of play or of anything else.

6 Jacques Derrida, 'The time of a thesis: punctuations', in *Philosophy in France today*, ed. Alan Montefiore (Cambridge: Cambridge University Press, 1983), pp. 36–7.

7 See Geoff Bennington, 'Not Yet', a review of Fredric Jameson, *The Political Unconscious: Narrative as a Socially Symbolic Act* (London: Methuen, 1981), in *Diacritics*, 12 (1982), 23–32, for an analysis of the use of 'History' as an absolute tendency in argument.

8 Edmund Husserl, *Logical Investigations* (1900–1), tr. J. N. Findlay, 2 vols. (London: Routledge and Kegan Paul, 1970), Vol. 1, p. 249.

9 My adaptation of John P. Leavey's translation, quoted by Gregory L. Ulmer: 'The Post-Age', a review of Derrida's *La Carte postale*, *Diacritics* 11. iii (Fall, 1981), 39–50. Ulmer's consideration of this passage reveals the problems in understanding Derrida, and in particular, his use of the negative. Ulmer says baldly that 'according to the postal principle, tradition and translation consist of an idealized communication' (p. 48). He states that Derrida privileges Joycean equivocity of language, which makes translation impossible and tradition of meaning perilous, privileges it against Husserlian univocity. But Derrida does not say this. It is true that he balances Joyce against Husserl: but it is to point out that Husserl's project of univocity is the transcendental parallel of the Joycean project; they are each dependent on each other. Some limiting value of univocity is necessary for Joyce, or his text would be unintelligible, for it presupposes that the repetition of univocity in Husserl's purified mathematical language is possible. Derrida here is producing that ni, . . . ni, that disjunction of negatives which places them not under dialectical tension, as perfectly balanced opposites, but brings them together as *stricture*. See Marian Hobson, 'Derrida's Negatives', in *Cross-references: Modern French Theory and the Practice of Criticism*, ed. David Kelley and Isabelle Llasera (London: Society for French Studies, 1986).

10 Edmund Husserl, *Ideas* (1913), tr. W. R. Boyce Gibson (London: Allen and Unwin, 1931), section 83.

11 There is an interesting parallel (which I shall explore elsewhere) between Derrida and Dummett here. Dummett gives a sketched version of the anti-realist's view of time: 'For the anti-realist, the past exists only in the traces it has left upon the present', 'The Reality of the Past', in *Truth and Other Enigmas* (London: Duckworth, 1978), p. 370. The anti-realist is, of course, he for whom to grasp the meaning of a statement is to recognise of a situation whether it justifies that statement.

12 This account of Derrida's work and its relation to the *Origine de la géométrie* will be developed in other texts.

Derrida and Foucault: writing the history of historicity

ANN WORDSWORTH

In the conclusion to *Pre-Capitalist Modes of Production* Hindess and Hirst observe that 'by definition, all that is past does not exist. To be accurate the object of history is whatever is *represented* as having hitherto existed'.[1] A Marxist analysis registers these representations as the effect of social and political ideologies. Idealist and positivist historians claim that the real is reached *through* these representations, either because history is a rational order and its movements express an essence accessible to knowledge, or because knowledge of history can be got through given facts. By posing the historian's conception of history as the unity of the hitherto existent, Hindess and Hirst make it clear that there is no real object 'history', only a philosophy of history; the historian's work reduces to its ideological positions.

The mechanisms of ideology are used to account for the construction of literary texts as well as of historical ones; yet when Derrida says that 'literary criticism has already been determined, knowingly or not, voluntarily or not, as the philosophy of literature',[2] he does not use the theory of ideology to identify idealist or positivist readings. For this reason, among others, the political effectivity of Derrida's work comes under suspicion: he is readily accused of turning everything into a scene of writing, a play of undecidables as elegant as it is reactionary. As the confrontation between Derrida and Foucault concentrates both the radical claims of Derrida's work and the fiercest attack on it, we might take the moves opened by Derrida in his questioning of Foucault's strategy in the pages which make a kind of prologue to the second chapter of *Madness and Civilization*, that is, Foucault's reading of Descartes and the Cartesian Cogito.[3]

In *Madness and Civilization* (1961) Foucault argues that an epistemological break occurred between the medieval and classical periods: while in the medieval era reason and madness enjoyed a 'free exchange', the inauguration of the Age of Reason was predicated upon the silencing and banishment of madness. According to Foucault two exemplary and complementary instances of this historical shift can be found in the thesis of the Cartesian Cogito and the redeployment of the empty lazar-houses for the incarceration of the insane. Foucault's project in his book is to write a history of madness by constructing an archaeology of its silence since the medieval period.

In his 1963 review 'Cogito and the History of Madness', Derrida poses two major questions: if history is a rational concept, how is it possible to write a history of madness? And second, if Foucault claims to speak for a madness that by definition must remain silent does he not risk reappropriation by the very mode of exclusion that he claims to avoid? His attempt to use a language that refuses the support of reason is not without problems: 'we have the right to ask what, in the last resort, supports this language without recourse or support . . . ? Who wrote and who is to understand, in what language and from what historical situation of logos . . . this history of madness?' (*WD* 38). Derrida then examines Foucault's reading of the text from Descartes's *Meditations* and denies the claim that Descartes excludes madness from the identification of doubt.

Foucault's reply, 'My Body, This Paper, This Fire', makes in turn a bitter and powerful accusation against Derrida's work which has been returned to frequently by many of Derrida's critics: 'in his reading Derrida is doing no more than revive an old old tradition . . . the reduction of discursive practices to textual traces; the elision of the events produced therein and the retention only of marks for a reading . . . what can be seen here so visibly is a historically well-determined little pedagogy. A pedagogy which teaches the pupil that there is nothing outside the text.'[4]

The reading that Foucault denounces as a fetishising of the text is provoked by the work of translation that Derrida continuously performs as the process of deconstruction. Psychoanalysis provides an example: 'every language has its own dream language. The latent content of a dream . . . communicates with the manifest content only through the unity of a language – a language that the analyst must thus speak as well as possible.' Derrida emphasises this obligation in order to elaborate the processes of resistance to any reading – clinical, everyday, philosophical, critical, etc. – that language maintains. He goes on:

As well as possible: progress in the knowledge and practice of language being by nature infinitely open . . . are not the insecurities and insufficiences of analysis axiomatic and irreducible? And does not the historian of philosophy, whatever his method or project, abandon himself to the same dangers? Especially if one takes into account a certain embedding of philosophical language in non-philosophical language. (*WD* 308)

The gain of Derrida's initial work in his first series of questions is the opening of a certain space that Foucault's description cannot use and is prevented from using by the very articulation of the project – to write 'a history of madness itself before being captured by knowledge, an archaeology of silence'. In Derrida's eyes the effect of an archaeology is simply to reproduce the conditions that already accuse and objectify madness, the very process that Foucault sets out to displace. Hence his question, 'Is not an archaeology, even of silence, a logic, that is, an organized language, a project, an order, a sentence, a syntax, a work?' (*WD* 35). It is only by ignoring the force of this questioning that Foucault can then reduce deconstruction to textual tracing; and by similarly ignoring these questions, the demand to archaeologise, historicise, contextualise, continues to remain dangerously naive.

The problems seem to centre most clearly around the assumptions of 'a history'. Thus:

A history, that is, an archaeology against reason doubtless cannot be written, for, despite all appearances to the contrary, the concept of history has always been a rational one. It is the meaning of 'history' or *archia* that should have been questioned first, perhaps. A writing that exceeds, by questioning them, the values 'origin', 'reason', and 'history' could not be contained within the metaphysical closure of an archaeology. (*WD* 36)

From here the underlying requirements of each project can more easily be gauged. For Foucault to write the history of madness will mean the execution of a structural study of an historical ensemble. For Derrida such a writing must first submit to a translation of the terms that establish its terrain, that these may then be spoken '*as well as possible*'. In this speaking, the terrain will change insofar as the language of classical oppositions – reason, unreason – will lose its defining order and different articulations will take place. Taken from its archaeology, silence, for instance, will have different effects: 'within the dimension of historicity in general, which is to be confused neither with some ahistorical eternity, nor with an empirically determined moment of the history of facts, silence plays the irreducible role of that which bears and haunts language, outside and *against* which alone language can emerge' (*WD* 54).

Reading Foucault, in his turn, against that 'most powerful, extended, durable, and systematic formation of our "culture" ',[5] Derrida finds the most productive moments emerging first from Foucault's need to speak madness in 'a language without support', one refusing 'in principle, if not in fact, to articulate itself along the lines of a syntax of reason' (*WD* 37); and second, from Foucault's sense of the profound link between the articulation of madness as historically constituted and the 'possibility of history' (*WD* 42). Both these moments, however, are obscured and hampered by the premises of archaeology: by the homogenising of madness as 'madness itself' with a specific 'history'; by the need to 'speak it'; and by an objectification of the link madness/history at a certain moment and in a certain text, viz. the creation of the houses of internment for the mad and the Cogito. Derrida works both these moments out of the archaeology and reinscribes them as effects in what he calls 'a cleavage . . . interior to meaning *in general*' (*WD* 38), a first dissension of logos, more ancient by far than the emergence of classical reason in the enlightenment, and constitutive of the logical–philosophical inheritance which marks the project of archaeology. It is necessary to unsettle the symmetrical relation of madness and reason and to trace the exclusion of madness to a crisis of the logos; without this re-staging, Foucault's project and language are bound within the tradition they work to dissolve.

In taking the opposition of determined reason and determined madness back to the interiority of the logos, to language, Derrida uses Foucault's definition of madness: 'madness is the absence of work'. He proceeds via the Cogito whose 'mad audacity' would consist in a return to an original point 'which no longer belongs to either a *determined* reason or a *determined* unreason, no longer belongs to them as opposition or alternative . . . It is therefore a question of drawing back towards a point at which all determined contradictions, in the form of given, factual historical structures, can appear, and appear as relative to this zero point at which determined meaning and nonmeaning come together in their common origin' (*WD* 56). The economy of this point which Descartes enacts and represses as the Cogito exceeds every finite and determined totality and institutes meaning and nonmeaning, the order of reason and silence. In seeing the Cogito as re-enactment of this 'hyperbolic extremity', Derrida reinscribes the rhythms of history in a deconstructed version of Foucault's linking of madness and history:

Descartes knew that, without God, finite thought never had the *right* to exclude madness etc. Which amounts to saying that madness is never excluded, except *in fact*, violently in history; or rather that this exclusion, this *difference* between the fact and the principle is historicity, the possibility of history itself. Does Foucault say otherwise? '*The necessity* of madness is linked . . . to the *possibility of history*'. (*WD* 310)

Similarly, using the same work of translation on Foucault's text, its conclusions are reinscribed : 'the extremity of hyperbole' found in the Cogito re-enacts the originary economy of language : there are two separate tendencies at work within the Cogito, the function of the first, certainty, being to limit the force of the second, hyperbole, or excess. According to Derrida the very historicity of philosophy can be located in the movement between the two :

The historicity proper to philosophy is located and constituted in the transition, the dialogue between hyperbole and the finite structure, between that which exceeds the totality and the closed totality, in the difference between history and historicity; that is, in the place where, or rather at the moment when, the Cogito and all that it symbolizes here (madness, derangement, hyperboles, etc.) pronounce and reassure themselves then to fall, necessarily forgetting themselves until their reactivation, their reawakening in another statement of the excess which also later will become another decline and another crisis. (*WD* 60)

There is a rhythm, a temporality of crisis and repression, but this is not the timing of a chronology. It is rather 'the movement of temporalization itself' (*WD* 61).

If it is possible to register this description and somehow to make it, not familiar certainly, but to some extent *thinkable*, then Derrida's critique of Foucault's archaeology or history of madness becomes clearer. The Cogito does not as a point in a determined historical structure inaugurate a new era in which madness is excluded; the Cogito is inhabited by the structure of writing : 'The relationship between reason, madness, and death is an economy, a structure of deferral whose irreducible originality must be respected . . . It is more written than said, it is *economized*. The economy of this writing is a regulated relationship between that which exceeds and the exceeded totality : the *différance* of the absolute excess' (*WD* 62).

If this economy, structure of deferral, *différance*, inaugurates historicity in general, well, to put it flatly, the pedagogy of textual traces has come a long way. And it is not surprising that other discourses, critical, political etc. will have their own systems of predicates shaken and put at risk.

This effect is felt (and manfully repressed) throughout Derrida's interview with Houdebine and Scarpetta first published in *Promesse* in 1971. Persistently, Houdebine tries to assure Derrida that:

> dialectical materialist logic, whose general economy is articulated on the basis of the conceptual series 'matter . . . /contradiction/struggle of the contraries, unity–inseparability–convertibility of the contraries in the process of their transformation etc.' . . . is necessarily caught in an economy whose double register appears fundamentally in the *dual unity* . . . historical materialism/dialectical materialism. (*P* 60)

Dialectical materialist logic and deconstruction, in short, have a reciprocating vocabulary and could use, perhaps further, each other's terms with advantage. Houdebine specifies: Derrida's problematic of writing and the materialist text have common grounds; they encounter in the process of the deconstruction of the logocentric discourse insofar as the materialist text 'has long been the historical text repressed–suppressed by logocentric discourse (idealism, metaphysics, religion) taken as the discourse of a ruling ideology in its different historical forms' (*P* 61). Similarly, Houdebine goes on, the Marxist concept of ideology puts in question the self-certainty of consciousness as does *différance*, though it does not use that particular motif; so too does contradiction, despite its metaphysical name, insofar as it acts as a 'radical heterogeneity' (matter/meaning) and in its double moment surpasses the notion 'spacing'.

The eager flurry of Houdebine's claims stems from the wish to assimilate Derrida's thought and to take from it, let's say, the 'rational kernel'. Perhaps the relation to deconstruction should be seen as a sort of extraction process, or a laundering: certainly the movement of Houdebine's assimilation of Derrida's work is suspiciously simple – as indeed has been that of more recent assimilations. However, there is a further more critical movement that Houdebine continues in the correspondence after the interview and which stems from his discreetly unstated suspicion that deconstruction hatches idealism. *If* these idealist tendencies could be corrected, chief among them the reduction to language, there would be gains for both dialectical materialist logic and deconstruction. To effect this, Houdebine proposes isolating spacing/alterity from their relation to *différance* and then, with an ease that surprises Derrida (he asks in his reply, 'is it not rather new to define the system spacing/alterity, on which we agree, as an essential and indispensable mechanism of dialectical materialism?'), reclaims them as heterogeneity, 'the materialist motif par excellence', thereby inscribing the differences that have not 'fallen from the sky' in a 'necessary articulation with the entirety of a differentiated social practice' (*P* 93). The system of differences, read through a logic of contradiction, can then be linked, via Lacan's 'symbolic', to 'social practice in the aspect of its signifying means of production (language)' – thereby saving the whole system of predicates, history, ideology, practice etc. from Derrida's cautionary quotation marks.

Nevertheless, such adaptation of terms is not successful – nor indeed possible; nor are the parallels that Houdebine claims to make. The terms of deconstruction are not detachable. Perhaps Derrida's explanation of the strategic necessity of a kind of paleonomy, the maintenance of an old word in a deconstructed operation, can help to make this clear :

> Taking into account the fact that a name does not name the punctual simplicity of a concept, but rather a system of predicates defining a concept, a conceptual structure *centered* on a given predicate, we proceed: (1) to the extraction of a reduced predicative trait that is held in reserve, limited in a given conceptual structure . . . *named X*; (2) to the delimitation, the grafting and regulated extension of the extracted predicate, the name *X* being maintained as a kind of *lever of intervention* in order to maintain a grasp on the previous organization, which is to be transformed effectively. (*P* 71)

Extraction, graft, extension : this is the process that Derrida calls *writing*. If it now comes back to writing it is not by chance – though all the assumptions that lie behind that cliché are now at risk : we have not reached our destination or any proper conclusion and we have not returned to acknowledge the ancient model of an old, old tradition. We are back to writing.

Terry Eagleton has recently praised the force and centrality of style in Fredric Jameson's work : 'Jameson composes rather than writes his texts, and his prose . . . carries an intense libidinal charge, a burnished elegance and unruffled poise, which allows him to sustain a rhetorical lucidity through the most tortuous, intractable materials.'[6] But Derrida's writing cannot be praised as the release of an effective style. Extraction, graft, and extension decompose rhetorical lucidity : 'one must speak several languages and produce several texts at once'.[7] This is the strategy of *Glas* and of *La Carte postale* and of Derrida's insistence that modern teaching of philosophy must take into account, not thematically but as a form of expropriation, the techno-politics of the media. It is these interventions in academic practice, the effect of structures of expropriation (*différance*, pharmakon, hyperbole, *technē* etc.) working across texts and disciplines, that are forgotten when Derrida is accused of a reactionary pedagogy.

If we now return to Derrida's work on the Cogito it is perhaps to see more clearly the expropriating structure working against the historical and anthropological reading of Descartes and the historical and linguistic assumptions of Foucault's writing. The Cogito enacts both temporal originality (hyperbole, 'the project of exceeding every finite and determined totality' (*WD* 60)) and the movement of temporalisation that presents it as discourse. That this enactment necessarily inaugurates writing and simultaneously recasts it, and that every work bears the mark of this economy, makes for a difficult kind of reading and commentary. Derrida's 'several texts at once', the styles, the expropriating words make up a writing that works this scene. Recognition of it becomes easier when Derrida relates a particular piece of commentary to the (inadvertent) enactment of such a scene: Foucault's reading of Descartes's Cogito makes it possible to open the Cogito by what in both Foucault and Descartes resists such an opening.

The same opening appears through similar strategies in Derrida's essay 'Freud and the Scene of Writing' (*WD* 196–213) and shows how Freud in his struggle to describe the initiation and trajectory of memory finds (and loses) this opening in the change from a traditional use of scriptural metaphor (writing as transcription or translation from thought to expression) to the use of writing and writing machines as the enactment of locations, processes and chronicities. For Freud, the Mystic Pad, with its erasable writing surface, its retention of legible marks on the underlying wax and the periodic nature of the actions needed to lift the top sheet and clear the surface, represents structuring of the psychic apparatus. But the clarification of Freud's neurological and metapsychological thinking does not interest Derrida; *his* interest lies in showing the effects of Freud's metaphor, not as an expository device (whose limits Freud points out), but from the moment when, rejecting the machine because it cannot reproduce from within as the psychic apparatus can, Freud returns to the metaphysical structure of oppositions: passive machine/active psyche, life/death. Its contribution to Freud's theory is finished; not however its effects in the scene of writing. By working Freud's metaphor out of its metaphysical alignments Derrida can then demonstrate what its pathbreaking work had really shown – the enactment of what is called writing inscribing itself always already in what is presumed external to it: matter, consciousness, discursive practice.

That writing is not a mere transmission of content, however eloquently or rigorously performed, is only one of the disruptions that Derrida makes. The space of communication that extends classically from the limited range of voice and gesture to the written, from thought to speech, from sender to receiver is also put at risk, that milieu 'that is fundamentally continuous and equal to itself, within a homogeneous element across which the unity and integrity of meaning is not affected in an essential way' (*MP* 311). To back out of this voluminous element is precisely to move from the isolation of texts in their pre-given orders, the certainties of destination and identity, and to attend to the non-ideal exteriority of writing, the graphics of expropriation, *différance*, the trace, supplementarity etc.

This is the radical demand of Derrida's work and the source of its resistance to both accusations of pedagogy and to forms of academic re-assimilation. As he himself puts it at the moment of his thesis presentation :

> The reproductive force of authority can get along more comfortably with declarations or theses whose content presents itself as revolutionary, provided that they respect the rites of legitimation, the rhetoric and the institutional symbolism which defuses and neutralizes whatever comes from outside the system. What is unacceptable is what, underlying positions or theses, upsets this deeply entrenched contract, the order of these norms, and which does so in the very *form* of works, of teaching or of writing.[8]

NOTES

1 Barry Hindess and Paul Q. Hirst, *Pre-Capitalist Modes of Production* (London: Routledge and Kegan Paul, 1975), p. 309.
2 Jacques Derrida, *Writing and Difference*, tr. Alan Bass (London: Routledge and Kegan Paul, 1978), p. 28. Further references will be cited in the text as *WD*.
3 Michel Foucault, *Madness and Civilization: A History of Insanity in the Age of Reason*, tr. Richard Howard (New York: Vintage/Random House, 1973).
4 Michel Foucault, 'My Body, This Paper, This Fire', tr. Geoff Bennington, *Oxford Literary Review* 4:1 (1979), 26–7.
5 Jacques Derrida, *Positions*, tr. Alan Bass (London: Athlone, 1981), p. 102. Further references will be cited in the text as *P*.
6 Terry Eagleton, 'The Idealism of American Criticism', *New Left Review* 127 (1981), 60.
7 Jacques Derrida, *Margins of Philosophy*, tr. Alan Bass (Chicago: Chicago University Press, 1982), p. 135. Further references will be cited in the text as *MP*.

8 Jacques Derrida, 'The Time of a Thesis: Punctuations', in *Philosophy in France Today* (Cambridge: Cambridge University Press, 1983), p. 44.

The practice of historical investigation

MARK COUSINS

What is the relation of historical investigation to theoretical argument within the human sciences? On the one hand those sciences establish themselves through the production of their own objects, their own problems, and their own procedures. On the other hand historical work continuously shadows those sciences. Monuments, documents, all of what we call remains, whatever has been left over, are collected, collated, published and restored. They are endlessly questioned for the human activity that might be discerned in them, activity which knows no a priori bounds. The past can seem both like a test of the human sciences and also a principle of excess, a realm in which the limits of the present are lifted. For the objects which circulate as the greatest problems in the human sciences are always able to be displaced and redeployed as a *history*, a displacement which is frequently presented as a promise and procedure for the resolution of those problems.

Language and sexuality are presently two such objects within the human sciences. What is language? What is its relation to other signs?[1] What is writing? Or what is the sexuality which is referred to? How far can sexuality differ between one culture and another? Did Freud initiate a Copernican Revolution in the analysis of sexuality or was he just the ethnographer of a Viennese tribe? Indeed it is no accident that the problems of language and sexuality impregnate each other. Contemporary ideas of representation and signification have themselves been caught up by the consideration of what distributes humans into sexed beings. It is in fundamental accord with the movement of the human sciences that problems of representation be taken with problems of sexuality, conditions of a symbolic order. And yet within these theoretical arenas in which problems of language and sexuality are played it can seem extremely unclear how the various disputes about them might be, if not resolved, then at least argued out. For it can seem undecidable as to what shall count as evidence, so radically internalised has the evidence become to the theories which contest each other. Grammar, syntax, semantics are all objects which withdraw into discrete theories to receive their determination; so too does desire, the body and all its bits. This should cause no surprise. At other times other problems can be produced whose categories seem just as incommunicable. Madness, law and culture itself have all often appeared in this way. It is a kind of movement which has frequently appeared in the human sciences, and it brings in its train a scholarly temptation – that the human sciences should turn their backs upon themselves and appeal to another court – that of history.

The grounds of such an appeal usually take two forms. First, they seek to remind us that the emergence of such problems in the human sciences has itself a history, and that one way of addressing a problem is to address the conditions of its 'necessity'. Secondly, grounds are adduced in favour of the claim that historical phenomena exceed the limitations which our conceptual categories impose. A parallel with ethnography is implied. For if attention to anthropological difference can protect us from ethnocentrism then attention to historical difference should protect us from what we might call chronocentrism, what is more usually called anachronism. So for example the histories of sexual or linguistic phenomena are held to reveal a wealth of variation of difference whose excessive character might break our conceptual chains. Has not research on the Homeric odes reformulated anachronistic distinctions between writing and speech? Has not research on the sexual categories of the Greeks thrown doubt upon the status of the lines we draw between different object choices? In all this, historical investigation appears to guarantee the truth of this excess and its product, History, can seem like a new horizon which theoretical work must strive to encompass and by which it will be measured.

The purpose of this paper is to reject this view. It certainly may appear that if we expose the conditions of the emergence of a problem, then the problem itself becomes a different sort of problem. No longer is it a problem by which we are caught, but a problem whose story we may tell. Pathos and distance replace anxiety, mastery follows a theoretical fatigue. After all, this tendency in the human sciences to historicise has a history itself, one which it would be a pleasure to tell. But it is worth forestalling this pleasure and arguing that historical investigation cannot simply be used to bypass the theoretical problems which necessarily define the human sciences. Moreover, historical investigation is itself subject to theoretical problems; it is condemned to jostle uneasily with the human sciences. It cannot establish itself as a distinct and privileged mode of existence which displaces the human sciences.

Before this denial is dismissed as the delusion of an anti-historical passion, I should make it clear what is not argued in the paper. Nothing opposes historical investigation as such; nothing denies its importance; nothing undervalues its humane pleasures. All that is opposed here is the claim that such investigations can *resolve* problems within the human sciences. Such investigation has to hang with other forms of investigation in a tissue of uncertainty. What are opposed here are the attempts or assumptions that a historical ground can be established which provides a certain test of knowledge in the human sciences. For such attempts demand but cannot secure a philosophy of history, which would reign as queen of the human sciences. In particular the problem which this paper addresses is that within many justifications of historical investigation any philosophy of history is manifestly rejected. The disrepute into which speculative schemes of historical forms of being have fallen do not provide a temptation for the claims of historical investigation. But I shall argue that the claim that historical investigation can resolve theoretical problems by themselves is in fact nothing but a special case of a philosophy of history.

Consider the following aspects of any historical investigation and its writing. It must deal with problems of identity and difference. Any analysis has to group objects which are referred to in terms of an identity or difference. Phenomena must fall under the same class as other phenomena, or they must differ from them; or at least some definite ratio must be established. In this sense historical investigation must establish differences. But the differences which it establishes and represents must have a limit. The impossible project of establishing an infinite series of differences would in effect prevent any object from having a history. For something to support a history there must be a space of sufficient identity. Historical writing is then caught up in the play of representing differences through identities which differ from each other. This point is not criticism of historical investigation but it underlines the fact that there is a level of irreducible theoretical decision within historical writing. What sorts of objects can be referred to, what objects have a sufficient difference to be considered different objects, what objects have a sufficient identity to be considered the same objects – all these issues will crucially affect the product of historical investigation but will not themselves be part of that product. I want here to glance at two opposed responses to this problem of theoretical decision of the differences between objects and the type of identity which is necessary to be deployed as the history of an object. Furthermore, I want to suggest that despite their apparent opposition they may share a common ground. The first response, a general doctrine of History, I shall pass over briefly.[2] The second response, a rejection of any philosophy of History in favour of a professional practice of historical investigation, I shall deal with at greater length, for it is this response which has a greater contemporary allure.

The first response privileges the construction of a general doctrine of the past as a distinct form of existence, History in the upper case, a philosophy of History. Historical interpretation in this sense depends upon a theoretical structure through which representations of the past may be sorted, analysed and assigned their significance. In this, History is the product of investigations which are supported by distinct theoretical protocols which in turn purport to provide a particular character both for a particular type of knowledge, historical knowledge, and a particular form of existence, the historical. In short, History is a category which is supported by philosophical categories of epistemology and ontology.

Now whenever the category of History is deployed as a distinct form of being, the question of difference must always be handled in terms of identity, for in the end, or rather from the beginning, all historical differences are subordinate to the identity of History itself. The structure of the category of History, be it an evolution, Hegelian or Marxist form, is a little theatre in which the representations of the past are assigned their part. Differences are employed merely to provide details of a process, the historical process as such. In a rigorous form, such as in Hegel, there must finally be a complete identity of a conceptual scheme of knowledge with the order of the real and its past. Historical differences are sublated into the order of identity, a process in time which is increasingly present to itself.

It hardly needs to be said that such a position is rejected not only by those who are anti-Hegelian. More significantly it is not so much rejected, as found without interest by those who for more than a century have been concerned to establish historical investigation as a non-philosophical practice, as a 'craft' with skills and rules, as a definite technique of discovery. It is this second response that I want to consider. As this professional enterprise, historical scholarship has largely sought to avoid philosophical schemes or at least to draw the sharpest distinction between research and its representation from any subsequent reflection upon it. It is commonplace to read praise for an historian's research coupled with a tut-tutting over the vagaries of the Hegelian or Marxist arguments into which it is inserted. These vagaries are at least held to be eminently distinct from the research, and are thought to be superimposed when, in the profession's odd figure, the research is 'written up'. What seems to be at stake in this judgement is that whatever philosophical or political preferences the individual historian may exercise, they have nothing to do with the practice of historical investigation itself. The core of that practice is held to be one which neither requires nor supports any general conception of History at all. There is, quite simply, the past which may be known through its representations. Historical investigation may be modestly proposed as the discovery of the past through a range of techniques and standards of evidence. Because of this, historians have been able, if and when they wish, to turn away from theoretical debate since there is no requirement for them to determine the status of History as such. Yet in its wake this conviction can also lead to the unjustified assumption that the representation of differences and identities between objects of the past can evade theoretical decision.

This is one reason why, from time to time, historical investigation suggests itself as the way out of certain impasses in the human sciences. For those who wish to make a detour around certain theoretical problems, historical investigation seems to promise a dimension in which even if the problems are not solved, they are at least deployed as an intelligible history. It can also seem to promise a harvest of evidence which contrasts with the endless drought of argument. But this turn, which is itself deeply determined by the structure of the human sciences themselves, is not without its problems. For whatever are the attractions of a practice which attempts to establish its own criteria, which refuses any philosophical majesty, it can at a certain point exhibit a philosophical blindspot. The particular blindspot of historical investigation, I will argue below, is the blindness to the fact that its truth claims are established ultimately only within a definite practice which is not without its own conditions. As a claim to produce and evaluate evidence, in general, the modest craft of historical investigation can come to involve a philosophical claim as powerful as those openly declared by philosophies of history.

It is usually stated that the rise of modern historical scholarship involves a non-theoretical but a decisive technical distinction between primary and secondary sources.[3] This distinction is held to control the central issue of evidence and its evaluation. Classical and Renaissance historians may be praised for their attempts to approximate the ideal of making a case which rests upon secure evidence, but it is only with the professional penetration of archives that the distinction is said to be non-theoretical; it advances no general propositions about what can or cannot exist historically. It is held to be technical in the sense that it is merely a means of discovery, the means of the inquisition of the past. Yet if this is held to be the crucial condition of historical investigation it is worth examining the presuppositions which are involved.

A primary source is preferred over a secondary source because – why? Because it is close to – what? A complex of relations is opened up by this question. A primary source is closer to what it refers to than a secondary source.[4] This word 'closer' has itself two connotations. It is closer to the truth and it is closer to the event. Truth is the adequate representation of the event. The event is the object which may be referred to in truth. A primary source is then the more reliable witness to the event. The event is most reliably represented by a witness, by testimony which can be best trusted. Secondary sources are tainted, less reliable; they cannot be treated as convincing testimony; they lack reliability. Secondary sources function as a kind of hearsay; their evidence is less admissable. They may in fact be true but their truth will be so contingently. They cannot establish truth. The question of truth within historical scholarship then starts from the question of truth as evidence. And the category of evidence is one which profoundly privileges the notion of the *event*, a singular entity in time whose existence and identity it is the task of investigation to establish. Two sorts of question emerge as the locus of historical investigation. Did the event happen or not? If it did, into what class of event did it fall?

It is clear that the professional historian's attempt to avoid the problems of any philosophy of history by privileging the craft of investigation, by opposing investigation to philosophy, in fact leads to another scene altogether. The circuit truth/witness/event has the strongest parallel with another practice, law, whose magisterial categories will certainly be different from theoretical argument in the human sciences but whose practice maintains a jealously guarded order of procedure. The elementary and privileged place accorded to the category of event in law may be thought of as a violation, be it civil or criminal. The object of legal argument is to establish whether or not an event-as-violation occurred. In respect to an alleged crime, legal practice asks the questions as to whether the event in question did or did not occur, whether suspicious reports or allegations that an event has occurred correspond to the best evidence of the existence of such an event. And then, or rather at the same time, it is asked whether the event which has been described falls into this or that legally defined class of events. Is it murder, manslaughter, an accident, or whatever? Who and what are responsible for the crime? What are the lines of causality to be drawn in respect to the event? What degrees of responsibility do or can particular persons here bear? And all this is to be established in due legal process, in hearings, trials, and appeals, each of which is conducted in accordance with definite procedures. There are definite rules of evidence concerning admissability. Hearsay may be discounted; clearly motivated witnesses may be impugned. In the absence of a plea of guilt and a full and uncoerced confession partial forms of evidence must be assembled into an edifice which is to be accepted as a representation of the event which is beyond all reasonable doubt. The truth is the most certain representation of the past. But this 'past' is not the past in general, but only the past as it concerned the event and the questions of responsibility which such events raise. The truth as found by a court is of course subject to appeal but such an appeal will merely extend reasoning about the event and responsibility for the event. The production of new evidence will permit a representation which was not available to the previous court. Arguments concerning failures of reasoning in the previous court will seek to overthrow its representation of the event.

Historical scholarship bears more than a fleeting resemblance to this jurisprudential complex. It is not just that historically the emergence of historical scholarship and techniques of, especially, common law arguments have gone together. Nor is it just that the historian's skills might be described as forensic. It is that there is a parallel between the way in which the question of truth and evidence privilege the category of event. In law, especially in criminal law, the violation as event is central. By definition, however, the category of event is rigorously defined by law. The question is not what happened in general but whether what happened is legally pertinent or conversely whether what is legally significant happened at all. It might appear that the legal process attempts to establish what really happened in the past, but 'really' is used in a specialised sense.

'Really' is what is relevant to the law, what is definable by law, what may be argued in terms of law and evidence, what may be judged and what may be subject to appeal. 'Reality' as far as the law is concerned is a set of representations of the past, ordered in accordance with legal categories and rules of evidence into a decision which claims to rest upon the truth. But this truth of the past, the representations of events, is a strictly legal truth.

This type of representation of events is also produced by historical investigation. It too is dominated by the category of event, in the sense that not everything that may be said of the past is relevant but rather only what may be the product of this form of investigation. The practice of historical investigation is to produce (uncover) events, whose representations are called historical facts. To this end the best evidence and the best witnesses are sought, primary sources. Forms of reasoning are employed to establish the events, to establish the agents of the event and to establish responsibility for the event. The quest for historical facts is indeed central to the historian's practice. It is part of the reasons why, as in law, the category of event is a central if unacknowledged a priori of historical thought.[5]

At this point a confusion may have arisen. It can be reasonably objected that historians deal with far more classes of objects than simply events; they deal with periods, nations, classes, ideas. They cannot be restricted to the usual sense of event. That is true if event is contrasted to something else such as the category of structure or thought. But I use the term 'event' here in an enlarged sense to indicate what historical investigation establishes as a fact through the sifting of evidence. Whatever is an historical fact is an historical event. The point is precisely that historical discourse treats objects as events, whether the event be the murder of the King or the decline of the West. The category of event is the condition which enables historical discourse to establish the truth of alleged facts. This would explain why there is a tendency to treat historical objects as events, as if indeed historical objects were events which were the action of an agent.

Perhaps this is why in historical writing there is so much action. Others have sought to explain this in terms of the structure of historical writing, above all through the requirements of narrative. But it might equally be because the objects of historical reference, being considered as events, require the presence of agents. The question of what happened leads as fluently in historical investigation as in law, to the question of who did it. And in both arenas questions of causation are embedded in questions of responsibility, of what is responsible for the event. Such responsibility is not restricted in any way to human beings as such. Nations, churches, classes, ideologies can all partake in the problem of assigning responsibility for an event. But by handling the issue of causation in this way, as an issue of responsibility, what is entailed in that causality is conceived as the action of agents, as if events are precipitated by agents.

The proximity of the law is again implied. For it is the law which enables us to consider non-humans as agents, a world in which non-human agents act, bear responsibility, have motives, pursue interests, as if indeed they were bearers of human attributes. Within the law non-human agents exist, and are slandered, and can even be guilty of culpable homicide. The law is a world in which not only the event is privileged but in which causation appears as a problem of the assignation of responsibility and its degrees. As a consequence the legal subject is central to legal reasoning but exists not as a distinction between subjects and objects, between persons and things, but is anything designated as a legal subject such that it can be reasoned about as a person. Whether it be a limited company, a branch of the executive or a private citizen it can be a legal subject, can be legally reasoned about, can be said to act and to cause events.

To some extent this is the world which is borrowed for the purposes of historical investigation especially in the matter of the cause of events. In terms of historical investigation as such there is a parallel with legal process in the circuit of evidence, fact and truth. In terms of the world postulated, a world which is the condition of historical argument, there is a parallel with jurisprudence insofar as it is a world of events and a world of agents. It is a world created out of the residue of an action. The poles of events and agents of responsibility create a definite world produced by a definite practice of investigation. To say this is not to criticise historical investigation but to insist that like other forms of investigation it has definite conditions and definite consequences, and it can have no general foundation or privilege beyond itself. But to reject any general foundation to historical truth or any general truth of History does itself not undermine a notion of historical truth as such. There is no need to enter a form of scepticism about statements about the past. It is enough to recognise that the justification for truth claims about the past are part of the particular practice of historical investigation. Historical facts are not illusions; we may well say they are true. But their truth is the finding of a particular mode of instantiation, and one which has particular effects on the type of objects which may enter its canons of verification. Its objects are events and because of this it follows that since historical investigation follows a particular sort of object, facts as events, then historical investigation has no monopoly in dealing with other types of object in which the distinction between the past and the present may not be pertinent. No one expects that the type of truth, the whole truth and nothing but the truth, which the court hopes to elicit from witnesses shall stand as the exhaustion of all that might be said without error. The language of the past, the sexuality of the past, can of course be investigated historically, but historical investigation cannot claim to exhaust that past without also claiming that the past had only one form of existence, that is History in the upper case. That is the unexamined means whereby historical investigation is installed as having a privilege within the human sciences, the philosophical blindspot of the historian's practice.

Routine historical scholarship and the most fantastic philosophies of history can easily slip into a common condition, a privilege accorded to historicity as the one and only proper court for the enactment of a truthful discourse on what has existed. History and truth merge at the point where interrogation and judgement produce a verdict. Against this it can be argued that to be historical is one and only one possible mode of the existence of objects. If that mode is privileged above all others then the most determined event is in play, one which may properly be called *logocentric*. It is the fantasy that the past may not only be represented as history, but also exhaustively and truthfully represented. It is fantasy that cancels all other claims so that the concept and referent of history may be joined according to the due processes of law.

NOTES

1 Michel Foucault, whose work does nothing to resolve problems within linguistics, nonetheless demonstrates with great rigour why it is within the human sciences that the *problem* of language should create such a prevalent anxiety. The emergence of an autonomous linguistics, which he dates from the work of Grimm and Bopp, leaves a vacuum in the human sciences which can be named as the problem of *representations,* those objects which are scattered through culture, whose scattering is at a certain point culture itself but for which there is no general doctrine. What relation do representations have to language? This is a problem that haunts the human sciences from their inception. The emergence of structuralism or a general

semiology, far from being the esoteric fad its detractors held it to be, promised to answer this enduring and fundamental question. Neither a structuralist nor a semiotician, Foucault was nonetheless able to chart the determined character of this moment in the *Order of Things* (London: Tavistock, 1970).

2 I do not intend to be dismissive of the problems that are raised by philosophies of history. They do not constitute, however, the main object of this paper. Many contemporary problems in assessing philosophies of history and their relation to the practice of historical writing are taken up with lucidity in P. Q. Hirst, *Marxism and Historical Writing* (London: Routledge and Kegan Paul, 1985).

3 See R. G. Collingwood, *The Idea of History* (Oxford: Clarendon Press, 1946), Part V.

4 It might of course be objected that this parallel between legal and historical practice breaks down in the face of the objection that while the 'events' with which the law deals are positively defined at law no such delimitation occurs within historical investigation. In a sense this is true; there is no limit to the questions which the past may be put to. But each and every question will contain protocols which determine what will count as a possible answer, what will function as a pertinent event. Moreover, legal practice itself, while subject to legal rules, is nonetheless open to the perceptions, forms of argument and mundane notions of course which enter the courtroom in the persons who will speak. See H. L. A. Hart and A. M. Honoré, *Causation in the Law* (Oxford: Clarendon Press, 1959).

5 But perhaps the most striking demonstration that historical events *are* subject to a definite form of specification is the frequent complaint made by historians against the category of 'event' as it appears in psychoanalysis. The evident irritation expressed with a concept of event which does not measure up to its canons of evidence, the shock expressed at a practice whose interpretations refer to events which 'historically' may not have happened, all too clearly reveal the specific and legislative character of the historical event. Imagine a practice of interpretation which prefers secondary sources, and unreliable witnesses!

Aesthetics and history

Of aesthetic and historical determination

RODOLPHE GASCHÉ

As innocent as the prefix *post-* in front of *structuralism* may sound, it is burdened with the formidable task of blaming and overcoming structuralism's alleged ahistoricity. The mere linguistic event of a formation such as 'post-structuralism' alone suggests that history-in-person has come to belie the theoretical ambitions of the previous ahistorical doctrine. Under the banner of diachrony and the factual, empiricism, now disguised as post-structuralism, pretends to have come to grips with pure synchrony, and through it to have overcome nothing less than the ideology of platonism. Yet, in spite of all these claims, it is, in practice, not very easy to distinguish post-structuralism from what precedes it. Recent collections of essays featuring so-called post-structuralists are a perfect case in point. One of the reasons for this difficulty lies, undoubtedly, in the fact that the question concerning the difference and the relation of structure and genesis, system and history, platonism and empiricism, had itself been opened up by structuralism. Hence, it would be preferable, if one does not consider post-structuralism to be an object of wish-fulfilment rather than anything else, to speak of neo-structuralism. Indeed, the controversy of structure versus history, whether it haunts structuralism already from within, or follows it disguised as post-structuralism, presupposes a minimal consensus, at least, and therefore a hope of mutual reconciliation. This consensus consists of nothing less than the agreement upon the essential complicity between structural and genetic analysis, history and ahistory, synchrony and diachrony, platonism and empiricism.

Yet, in claiming as we do here that the question 'history versus structure' has been opened up in structuralism itself, we do not merely want to say that structuralism's assertion of the priority of structure and system is a function of a conscious theoretical choice by which genesis and history are relegated to the status of border-phenomena. On the contrary, the thesis is that structuralism, with its insistence on structure, is the dream-come-true and goal of historicism. Indeed, we would contend that there is no concept more historical than the concept of structure.

As Derrida has noted in *Writing and Difference*, structural consciousness is 'consciousness in general, as a conceptualization of the past . . . , of facts in general. A reflection of the accomplished, the constituted, the *constructed*. Historical, eschatological, and crepuscular by its very situation.'[1] The seemingly ahistorical doctrine of structuralism is, indeed, tributary to the notion of end-time-oriented history, that is, to history as such, since mere chronological series of facts are not history at all. The structure by which facts become conceptualised, and in which the essential relations are laid out, represents the final outcome, the fulfilled telos of history. As the result of history, it is also that in which history culminates, and comes to an end.

No one was more aware of this complicity between structure and genesis, between platonism and empiricism, than Husserl. As Derrida has demonstrated in *Edmund Husserl's 'Origin of Geometry': An Introduction*, as well as in the essay ' "Genesis and Structure" and Phenomenology', it was precisely this recognition of the complicity in question, and the ensuing interrogation of both the idea of system and history, which led to Husserl's development of phenomenology. From the outset, phenomenology has been interested in overcoming the theoretically unsatisfactory state of a presumed conflictive difference of the genetic and the structural approach, a difference that, because of the polemical rift between the approaches, also implies an essential interdependence. By its transcendental quest, Husserl's phenomenology represents, indeed, an attempt at reconciling the alleged differences between the two approaches. Navigating between the Scylla of logicising structuralism (with its systematic structures that are perfectly closed upon themselves) on the one hand, and the Charybdis of psychologistic and historicist genetism on the other, Husserl, after having exposed the empiricist – that is scepticist – nature of the principles informing both structuralism and genetism, opened, as is well known, a new direction of attention. This new attention, as Derrida has pointed out, is concerned with the original unity, the common root of both structure and genesis. This root is thought by Husserl to be the structurality of an opening of what one used to call structures, or as the structural a priori of historicity, as it is called in his later works.

Although it may well be the case that Husserl reproduces in the field of phenomenology many of the problems he set out to overcome, the new philosophical attention of phenomenology, it seems to us, remains – to the extent that it seeks the best in structuralism, i.e. means to explore iterability, and through it, historicity itself – the sole tradition in which the problem of structure versus genesis can be posed in a philosophically exigent manner. It is, we believe, the only viable tradition of philosophical questioning in the aftermath of dialectic and speculative thought, in which the difference and complicity, the double bind, between structure and history, platonism and empiricism, can be accounted for. From a phenomenological perspective, these differences, instead of appearing as primary differences, are understood as being derivative upon the transcendentality of a structural opening. Whether one conceives that opening in Husserlian terms, as the irregionality of the *noema*, the non-intentionality of the *hyle* of *Ideas I*, in Heideggerian terms as Being as dif-ference, *Ereignis*, *Lichtung*; or in Derridean terms as differance, iterability, supplementarity, etc., this attention to a fundamental passivity of a priori structures of an opening for structures (in the common sense) and temporality not only precludes the one-sided possibilities of closure in the structuralist approach, or of hoping to be able to do without a minimum of fundamental structures in a purely historical approach; it altogether displaces the traditional debate. It is no longer a question of pro and contra. As already for Husserl, the occasional privilege accorded to one approach over the other is a function of the space of description to which they are applied as operative concepts. What changes the parameters of the traditional debate concerning the truth values of structure and genesis is the interest in their underlying unity, whatever the terms in which that unity is thought.

In what follows, we would like to address a debate intimately linked to the one mentioned. It is the debate currently raging in literary criticism, opposing textual (merely aesthetic) criticism, concerned with the structures of the works of art themselves, and (extrinsic) historical criticism. Without truly engaging in a 'transcendental' analysis of the difference in question, that is, without developing in detail the type of unity that these different trends of conceptualisation presuppose, the following remarks will mainly limit themselves to asserting that for mere historical, if not systematical, reasons, it is, indeed, impossible to choose clearly between aesthetics or history.

In order to begin displacing the controversy and the polemics that take place in the name of history against text-oriented criticism and aesthetics and vice versa, we will turn to an analysis of an eighteenth-century text, a text emanating from a century that simultaneously gave birth to the twin disciplines of 'aesthetics' and 'history'. The text we will consider is Alexander Gottlieb Baumgarten's dissertation of 1735 entitled *Meditationes philosophicae de nonnullis ad poema pertinentibus*, hereafter to be referred to as *Reflections on Poetry*.[2] This relatively short text is to be viewed as already containing *in nuce* the major ideas that Baumgarten displayed in his *Aesthetica* between 1750 and 1758.

Baumgarten's contribution to the problems of aesthetics is often seen as limited to his having named the science of aesthetics. In that perspective, his dry and pedantic work, following that of the rationalist philosopher Wolff – himself a disciple of Leibniz – is viewed as bringing a certain type of reflection on the beautiful to an end, rather than giving birth to a new approach. Undoubtedly, Baumgarten's philosophy reflects his age, and his aesthetics, because of its merely formal nature, remains tributary to the rationalist conception of the beautiful. And yet, was it not Baumgarten who, by recognising the dignity of aesthetic experience – an experience judged common by the rationalist philosophers – laid the grounds for the distinct sphere of the science of the beautiful? Was it not Baumgarten who, by introducing a number of decisive categories and concepts into the study of the beautiful, anticipated Kant's *Critique of Judgement*, and through it the speculative systems of the aesthetics of German Idealism as well as those of German Romanticism? Indeed, Baumgarten's science of the beautiful 'survived the complete destruction of its shell, the rationalist metaphysics, through Kant's transcendental philosophy'.[3] It would be naive to believe that contemporary philosophical aesthetics or literary criticism have left that tradition behind. As the continuing debate over the relation between history and aesthetics shows, even some of the more technical aspects of Baumgarten's aesthetics continue to inform the contemporary debates. As we hope to demonstrate in the following by centring on one of Baumgarten's major concepts – a concept concerning the possibility of distinguishing the historical and the aesthetical – a detour through Baumgarten's *Reflections on Poetry* could represent a first, and indispensable, step in coming to grips with the essential complicity and unity of history and aesthetics which underlie the current controversies.

In his essay 'Art History and Pragmatic History', Hans Robert Jauss notes:

The decay of the traditional form of literary history, shaped in the nineteenth century and now drained of all exemplary scholarly character, makes it almost impossible for us to realize the great status that was enjoyed by art history at its birth, with the formation of historical perception in the thought of the Enlightenment, in the philosophy of history of the German idealists, and at the beginning of historicism.[4]

As Jauss remarks, the form of history that claimed philosophical interest by contrast to the traditional 'histories', up to the middle of the eighteenth century, was a history that borrowed its paradigm from art history. This process, we claim, can be seen to begin with Baumgarten's reflections on art in his dissertation. In our analysis of that text, we will be concerned, above all, with the conceptual nexus between the disciplines of aesthetics and history, with what makes it both possible and necessary that art history could enjoy the status of a paradigm with respect to historical knowledge.

Aesthetics as understood by Baumgarten is a science of perception, the science of things perceived, or *aistheta.* It is a science that Baumgarten, aware of the inner limits of conventional logic, had the courage to juxtapose with the oldest and most eminent philosophical doctrine as a second sphere within the totality of reason. This other sphere within reason as a whole is endowed with a specific autonomy with regard to the logical sphere. Although the law that rules it is not the same as that of the logical concept, it is not merely a simulacrum of it. It is, on the contrary, an *analogon rationis.* In the aftermath of Leibniz's doctrine of a succession of distinct steps of cognition – that is thought – Baumgarten recognised that the lower powers of cognition have their own *logos.* Contrary to the superior faculty of logic exclusively concerned with *things known* or *noeta*, the *gnoseologia inferior*, that is aesthetics, amounts to a sort of cognition concerned with things of sense, with things that, contrary to the things removed from sense, are endowed with a certain obscurity. Whereas thought has as its objects things which are *distinct*, sensate representations (*repraesentationes sensitivae*), the objects of perception are *confused.* It is important to note that this notion of confusion is not to be understood in a derogatory sense. The notion of *perceptio confusa* refers to a distinction made by Leibniz in paragraph XXIV of the *Discourse on Metaphysics.* Leibniz writes : 'When I can recognise a thing among others, without being able to say in what its differentiae or properties consist, the knowledge is *confused.*'[5] The confusion in question concerns a lack of distinction with regard to the characteristics of an object, or to the specific differences that distinguish it from other things. Hence, as Ernst Cassirer has remarked, one must understand 'confusion' here in its strict etymological sense. This meaning, to quote Cassirer, is 'that in all aesthetic intuition a confluence (*Zusammenfluss*), a fusing together, of elements takes place, and that we cannot isolate the individual elements from the totality of the intuition. But such a confluence creates no disorder; for this complex presents itself to direct perception as a definite and harmonious whole (*als ein durchgängig-bestimmtes und als ein durchgängig-gegliedertes Ganzes*).'[6] The discriminatory activity characteristic of conceptual (symbolic or intellectual) cognition as demarcated from sensate or intuitive cognition is a function of conceptual knowledge's aspiration to ground the manifold of the properties of a thing in the unity of its essence. The confused perception of sensate cognition lacks this progression or regression toward a ground or essence, and is, thus, necessarily indistinct. Yet this does not mean that confused perception could not be *clear* perception. Indeed, confused representations can be either obscure or clear.

Let us recall here that Baumgarten's aesthetic, as a logic in a broader sense, is supposed to serve as a guide for the lower faculty in the sensate cognition of things. It serves, according to Baumgarten, to 'improve the lower faculties of knowing, and to sharpen them', in other words, to help sensate perception achieve perfection (*RP*, 78). Perfection is meant to achieve unity in variety. Such perfection in sensate cognition depends on the clarity of sensate, or confused, representations. Clear representations in contradistinction to distinct representations (i.e., to concepts), are representations that permit everyday orientation in our sensible environment. In addition, clear representations, contrary to obscure ones, are communicable, because they alone are sufficiently distinguishable from one another, and hence recognisable to sense. Now, what constitutes clarity? And what is it that demarcates it from distinctness? Baumgarten argues that the difference between obscure and clear representations is a function of the number of characteristic traits (*notarum repraesentationes*) they contain, and which serve to distinguish and, thus, to make them recognisable. Clarity in sensate representation stems from the quantity of representative elements that it includes. Obviously enough, concepts are clear too, but their clarity is said to be one of *intensity*. Whereas concepts are *intensively clear or clearer* than others – 'through a discrimination of characteristics (*per notarum distinctionem*)' plumbing 'the depth of cognition' – sensate representations are *extensively clear or clearer* than others. Whereas intensive clarity, the clarity of ideas – 'complete, adequate, profound through every degree' – follows from the reduction in depth of the whole of an intuition to a few fundamental or essential distinctions in which the essence of the thing is beheld, extensive or aesthetic clarity, which does not suffer any such conceptual reduction, is a function of the sole quantity of representation (*RP*, 42). Baumgarten notes: 'In extensively very clear representations more is represented in a sensate way than in those less clear . . .' (*RP*, 43). The more elements a sensate representation contains, the clearer it is, and since perfection is a function of clarity, the clearer it is, the more perfect it is.

Yet what is of special interest to us here is the fact that the clearer a sensate representation becomes, that is, the greater the unity that it achieves in variety, the more *determinate* it is said to be. Indeed, determinateness is grounded in the perfection of clarity of sensate representations, in an increased extensive accumulation of characteristic sensate traits. Now, determinateness, according to Baumgarten, is the criterion *par excellence* of clear representations. Since determinateness is the mark for a type of unity that characterises individuals it is that type of unity that most radically distinguishes clear representations from the generality and universality of concepts, essences or grounds. The difference between confused, but clear sensate representations and distinct representations or concepts, is that the former constitute individuals. 'Individuals are determined in every respect', Baumgarten notes (*RP*, 43). They are, indeed, most determined (*determinatissimus*). Determinateness, because it achieves an individualised unity-in-variety in sensate perception, is the hallmark of what Baumgarten understands under the aesthetic object. As Alfred Baeumler has remarked: '*perfectio cognitionis sensitivae* – that means a *direction*, a *road*. The road of *determination* that leads to the *individual*, the road, thus, toward the aesthetic *object*.'[7] This category of determination, or determinateness, later to be translated by Kant and the German Idealists as *Bestimmung*, and by the Romantics as *Characterisierung*, is a category constitutive of that very specific logical realm that Baumgarten's aesthetics has wrenched from the logic of the Schools. Determination as a connecting of sensate representations into individuals is the *analogon rationis* that constitutes the realm of aesthetics as a realm in its own right. It corresponds to a sensate type of connecting of characteristic elements into the concrete unity of an individual, and is, consequently, similar to – but also very different from – the sort of connecting that distinguishes *ratio*. In short, then, if Baumgarten can be said to have effectively laid the ground for the sphere of aesthetics, a sphere thoroughly distinct from that of rational cognition, it is because of the category of determination that brings about unity as individuality.[8] This hallmark of aesthetics is the true survivor of Baumgarten's science of the beautiful, as all the major aesthetics since the end of the eighteenth century clearly prove.

But determinateness is not only a fundamental category of aesthetics, but, from Baumgarten on, of history as well. As mentioned above, the eighteenth century is the cradle of both philosophical disciplines. Historically speaking, the rise of the historical view of life in the eighteenth century is intimately linked to the appearance of aesthetics. In fact, history from Dubos, Muratori, and Vico to Herder, etc., is a child of the individualising spirit of the eighteenth century. Without hesitation, one can follow Baeumler who claims that 'Aesthetics is the precursor of Historiography.'[9] Historical and aesthetical knowledge, then, are the two new modes of non-rationalist cognition that correspond to individualities constituted in analogy to reason through extensive determinateness into concrete and sensible unities. The eighteenth century juxtaposed these new sciences with the traditional ones.

It now remains to be seen how the concept of determination does indeed characterise both aesthetics and history in Baumgarten's *Reflections*. Let us therefore first recall that Baumgarten, having introduced the idea of aesthetics in paragraph 116 as the science of perception, laid out, within the sphere of aesthetics, a special domain among *things perceived* – the domain of the rules of presentation (*propositio*). That part of aesthetics that treats of presentation, and that 'is more extensive than the corresponding part of logic', (the latter by presenting its thoughts as it thinks them, need observe only a few rules), comprises a *general rhetoric* that deals with unperfected presentation, and a *general poetics*, 'which treats generally of the perfected presentation of sensate representations' (*RP*, 78). General, or philosophical, poetics is the science concerning the body of rules regarding presentation, and to which a poem, if it is to be 'a perfect sensate discourse', must conform (*RP*, 39). What contributes to the perfection of a poem as a discourse of confused, yet clear, representations – that is, to the extensive clarity of these confused, because fused, representations – is called *poetic*. From what we have already seen, the poetics of a perfected sensate discourse must hinge on its determinateness. Baumgarten writes : 'The more determinate things are, the more their representations embrace. In fact, the more that is gathered together in a confused representation, the more clarity the representation has . . . and the more poetic it is . . . Therefore, for things to be determined as far as possible when they are to be represented in a poem is poetic.' Since 'extensively clearer representations are especially poetic', and since 'particular representations are in the highest degree poetic', the criterion of the poetic nature of a poem or perfect sensate discourse is its determinateness (*RP*, 43). The more determined a discourse is, the more poetic it is. Or, in other words, individuals are highly poetic, since they are completely particularised representations (*RP*, 69). That which has been determined to such an extent that it represents a concrete unity, a *repraesentatio singularis*, is poetic. Baeumler writes : 'The activity of the poet consists in determination.' It consists in accumulating determining traits that lead to what Baumgarten called in his *Aesthetica* 'venusta plenitudo', the beautiful plenitude of a sensible totality.[10]

But such an individualising and determining formation of representations characterises history and historiography as well. In both cases concreteness, or individualising determinateness, represents the criterion that distinguishes them from logical, rational cognition. This brings us then, to the question of what in fact distinguishes history and aesthetics, since, obviously, they cannot be identical. Yet since determinateness is *the* informing category of both, the constituting element without which there would be no aesthetics and no history, the distinction cannot be fundamental. Indeed, since, for Baumgarten, history is a perfected sensate discourse of confused and extensively clear, that is, determined and individualised, representations, it is obviously a distinction within aesthetics in general. But history is a mode of *perfect* sensate discourse, and therefore it remains ambiguous whether history is a part of poetics, or whether it is opposed to poetics. The sole distinguishing feature between both may be found in what Baumgarten designates by 'lucid order'.

Although the clarity and perfection of the poetic discourse can only be achieved through determination, determination alone appears insufficient to bring about that goal. What is needed, in addition, is an interconnection of the determinate representations. Baumgarten remarks: 'The interconnection of poetic representations must contribute to sensate cognition' (*RP*, 62). But interconnection is not made possible through a principle different from the one of determination. It is achieved through a second-degree type of determination, through a determination of determination. This second and higher concept of determination by which the interconnectedness of representations becomes secured, and discursive order becomes realised, articulates a second meaning implied in the term 'determination', namely, direction and tendency toward a certain end. Within the context of our analysis of Baumgarten's *Reflections*, we will conceptualise the determination of determination as *thematic determination*.

What is a theme? For Baumgarten, as the following definition reveals, it is another word for what Leibniz called the principle of sufficient reason. 'By theme', Baumgarten writes, 'we mean that whose representation contains the sufficient reason of other representations supplied in the discourse, but which does not have its own sufficient reason in them' (*RP*, 62). In the scholia to paragraph 71 of his *Reflections*, Baumgarten makes it quite clear how he wants us to understand the status of the theme. By analogically comparing the order of perfected sensate discourse to 'the rule of order by which things in the world follow one another for disclosing the glory of the Creator, the ultimate and highest theme of some immense poem, if one may so speak', the theme is elevated to the status of a transcendental and self-sufficient cause or principle that serves as the sufficient reason for all other subservient themes or representations. Because of its self-sufficiency, the theme is unique and one, and subordinates all other representations to itself, which, in this manner, also become 'connected among themselves' (*RP*, 63).[11] The theme thus functions as that which determines the already determined representations in such a manner as to integrate them into an individualised whole. The *determination of determination*, or the individualising of the manifold individualities – that, precisely, is the task of the theme. Paragraph 68 insists that representations that are not determined by the theme are not connected with it, and thus fall outside poetic order. The scholia to that same paragraph reads as follows: 'Now we are in a position to see that representations may be altogether good independently of each other, but that in the co-ordination of them every sense idea, every fiction, every fantasy must be excluded' (*RP*, 62). Only where such subjection of determined representations to a determining theme occurs does one find the highly poetic order of a unified totality or individuality.

But such determination of individualised representations by a theme through which these representations become interconnected in one global unity does not happen all at once; it follows a certain order. The lucid method (*methodus lucidus*) referred to above, concerns, precisely, the manner in which representations are to succeed one another in every poetic discourse. Lucid method is the order by which a sensate discourse must exhibit its determinateness by a theme. To cite again: 'The general rule of the lucid method is this: poetic representations are to follow each other in such a way that the theme is progressively represented in an extensively clearer way' (*RP*, 63). The lucid method of poetic organisation, consequently, corresponds to a progressive manifestation of the (transcendental) principle of determination of the manifold determined individualities, contributing in return to the progressive determination or individualisation of the primary theme. The lucid method is the method of thoroughly totalising and specular determination, of the exhibition of the one principle of determination as the totality of all interconnected individual representations. Extensively clear, the poetic order achieves this clarity by fusing all individualities into one, and by exhibiting to one pure glance the principle of this totalisation in its ordering function as a thoroughly articulated whole. In short, poetic discourse in general requires, as such, not only singularising determination, but a step-by-step linkage of all its representations to one unifying teleological principle or theme that confers an individualising unity to the whole of these representations.

To achieve this *analogon rationis*, the lucid method can take three different forms, all of which concur within the poetic discourse in general as a perfected sensate discourse: 'Since . . . certain of the co-ordinate ideas can cohere as premises with conclusions, certain as like with like and related with related, certain through the law of sensation and imagination, therefore there is available for lucid presentations the method of reason, the method of wit (*ingenii*), and the method of the historians, respectively.' The latter is also called the method of memory (*methodi memoriae*). The poet, in order to create a perfect sensate discourse, a discourse thoroughly interconnected, must make use of all three methods. It is, indeed, poetic 'to go over from one method to another,' Baumgarten claims (*RP*, 64). This becomes evident, especially, in the poetic representation of 'philosophical or universal themes' where the historical method, for instance, must be supplemented by the other methods – by the method of wit, in particular. Indeed, says Baumgarten, if 'the historical part is not rich enough, heterocosmic fictions [i.e., fictions that are not impossible in all possible worlds] are likely to be necessary' (*RP*, 58). The historical method is in need of determination: 'determinations have to be added to the poem about those things concerning which history is silent' (*RP*, 59). But, more importantly, history as a historical method geared toward exhibiting the universal and primary theme, has to supplement its already considerable determinateness by having recourse to prophetic fictions, to prophecies, says Baumgarten, that 'become the poet beautifully'. Indeed, since 'future events are going to exist', it is from them that things past receive their ultimate thematic determination (*RP*, 60 and 61). Probable heterocosmic fictions as to the future thus contribute to render the historical method perfect. But what follows from this is also the implication that a perfected historical method is, because of its lucidity, intrinsically poetic.

At this point we can circle back to our question concerning the difference between poetic and historical discourse. Poetic discourse and history are clearly aesthetic discourses. Considered in itself, history is characterised by the method of memory, that is, a method that makes presentations cohere through the law of sensation and imagination. Imagination here means not only the reproductive faculty, but, according to Wolff's psychology, the faculty of non-rational unification of sense impressions through images as well.[12] But as a method that achieves thematic determination of already highly determined representations through totalising images, history is one form of *perfected* sensate, or aesthetic, discourse. It is one form of lucid exposition contributing to the perfection and clarity of confused representations. Yet, in that quality, history is poetic. It thus seems that history, rather than being a discourse different in nature from poetic discourse, is after all only one of the latter's possible articulations. As the need for the supplementation of the historical method demonstrates, history fulfils its goal of thematising determination only by giving way to other methods. Poetic discourse is the larger concept by which historical discourse is determined. Of the method of history one can say what Baumgarten stated with respect to individual representations, namely, that though they may be altogether good independently, their truth is in the interconnection with other representations. It is only through the interconnection with the two other methods that history can fully achieve what it sets out to do – to co-ordinate representations in such a manner as to progressively reveal the primary determining cause.

As seen, the very task of determination characteristic of the historical discourse leads to history's progressive poeticisation. It is the need inherent in aesthetic discourse to achieve greater and greater clarity of its confused representations that causes history to turn into poetics. The logic of increased individualisation or concreteness brings about the transformation of history into poetic discourse as that discourse in which the telos of determination is achieved through the progressive manifestation of that telos itself. To speak of history, then, as in conflict with aesthetic discourse is doubly wrong. First, because historical discourse is one form of perfected aesthetical discourse, and, secondly, because, as such a perfected discourse, its truth lies in poetry as the totally transparent and concrete sensate discourse. Poetry, as that discourse that achieves full determination of its object through individualising determination and teleological thematic determination, is the encompassing type of discourse of which history is one form. The deep reason for both the intimacy between poetics and history, and the subordination of the latter to the former, thus clearly lies with the category of determination – the operator of the *analogon rationis.*

At this point of our development, one can easily imagine the objection that the complicity outlined between history and aesthetics would hinge entirely upon the mere contingent linguistic fact, on the good fortune, that the word 'determination' has a clear double meaning in both Latin and German. Thus, nothing universally valid could be deduced from that wordplay. Moreover, outdated speculations of this kind would have no bearing whatsoever on the present discussion on what is historical or aesthetical.

Since these objections touch at the very heart of the problem of the relation of the generality of philosophy to the natural languages, this, for obvious reasons, cannot be the place to answer this complex question. Let us, therefore, confine ourselves to a few remarks only. Anyone who consults an English-language philosophical dictionary on 'determination' will certainly be confirmed in his assumption that that term is philosophically insignificant: at best, he will find a reference to the logical meaning of that word.[13] He will miss all reference to either the meaning of boundary, limit, fixation, characteristic of the Latin *determinatio* and the German *Bestimmung*, or to its other sense of destination, purpose, end, etc. Undoubtedly, the empirical fact that two natural languages combine under one yoke two different meanings, for either etymological or conventional reasons, possesses no demonstrative power whatsoever. But, in contradistinction to such empirical coincidence, the linkage on the level of thought of the two aspects of determination, limitation and purpose, is no coincidence at all. It is a necessary relation whether or not there happens to be one word in a natural language to express that relation.

Indeed, all determining qualification and singularisation through limitation necessarily takes place in the perspective of an end, that is, of a unifying and equally individualising determination. What happens to be thought as such under the term 'determination' corresponds to a major necessity of thought. One may perhaps not want to go as far as Nikolai Hartmann in asserting that it represents a fundamental category of philosophical thought itself, but one cannot overlook the peculiar relevance that it has had in philosophical thought at least since the eighteenth century. The history of this concept of determination remains to be written. It is the history of a category which in Baumgarten is still limited to a merely historical and aesthetical status, but which, under the form of self-determination, becomes a dominating logical and philosophical concept in German Idealism's transformation of logic as it had existed since Leibniz and Wolff. In the philosophy of Hegel, the problematic of determination achieves its foremost elaboration. Its speculative perspective of self-determination has remained, together with the works of the Early Romantics whose theories were informed by the same problematic, the point of reference and the frame within which all major philosophy of history and art, as well as all forms of literary criticism, have operated. This dominating role of determination as a logical, aesthetic, and historical category becomes problematic for the first time with Heidegger, and in the type of philosophical interrogation that leads to the work of Derrida. And, thus, the history that we have been referring to would have to feature Heidegger's contention that determination as an essential category of philosophising has been involved in the forgetting of the essence of thought itself since philosophy's inception. Derrida's (provisionally) last major elaboration on that concept, however, does not criticise determination in the name of a more originary understanding of the task of thought. What Derrida is concerned with in his notion of *destinerrance*, on the contrary, allows a better understanding of the law that regulates the philosophical necessity according to which limitation and destination must combine in order to yield to the requirements of thought as such. Such a perspective, it seems to us, represents the appropriate frame in which a history of the concept of determination ought to be written.[14] Yet, for want of such a history that would establish the continued intertwining of history and aesthetics in the interlocked relation of the concepts of limitation and end, we will now turn to two examples in literary criticism to illustrate that essential congeniality even in contemporary thought.

The two examples that we choose represent types of criticism that seem as different and as alien as possible. Schematically speaking, one, the criticism associated with Wolfgang Iser, i.e., reader-oriented criticism, belongs, because of its indebtedness to Russian Formalism and the phenomenology of art of Roman Ingarden, to the more aesthetically-oriented text theories, whereas, the other, Mikhail Bakhtin's type of criticism, represents a paradigm of historical, sociologically oriented – at the limit, 'marxist' – literary theory.

In *The Act of Reading*, Iser follows Ingarden's distinction, in the wake of Husserlian phenomenology, between real and ideal objects, in order to reach a definition of the aesthetic object. Whereas ideal objects are said to be a function of acts of constitution that allow for their complete constitution, and thus autonomy, real objects are to be comprehended, and can in principle be completely comprehended. For what we are interested in, however, it is important to emphasise that comprehension of real objects proceeds through determination. An object is only fully comprehended if it is universally determinate, in short, if all its distinguishing traits (*Merkmale*) have been detailed in the only mode of cognition that objects call for, and that amounts to a determining compulsion. Aesthetic objects, in contrast to real and ideal objects, lack the autonomy of the first, and the complete determinacy of the second, class of objects. The aesthetic object is distinguished by what Ingarden designates as 'spots of indeterminacy'. The reason for this indeterminacy is that fictional texts draw up their own objects, and do not copy something already in existence as a scientific text would do. The intentional object that is the aesthetic object, according to Ingarden, is, for reasons of principle, incomplete. It would thus seem, at first, that everything that we have said concerning the constitutive function of determination regarding aesthetic objects does not pertain in the case of Ingarden's aesthetic theory. Yet what Ingarden's theory concerning an essential indeterminacy of the work of art serves to account for is the possibility of the work of art's communication with its beholder or reader. However, such participation of the beholder or reader in the production and the comprehension of the work's intention is viewed by Ingarden as, precisely, a series of acts of determination. Indeed, for this author, 'the never fully determinate intentional object is laid out as if it *were* determinate and must also pretend to be so'.[15] The aesthetic object becomes concretised by its participating beholder, who fills in the empty places, or even glosses them over, so as to produce an illusion of total determinacy.[16] In short, in spite of the inversion of accents put on determinacy, determination remains a central category in the attempt to define the nature of the work of art. The illusion of full determinacy remains a major criterion of the work of art which, for Ingarden, becomes complete in the beholder's or reader's interaction with the work.

Now, it is certainly the case that Iser finds fault with Ingarden's account of the construction of the work of art as a fully determined individuality by the participating subject. Yet Iser's objections basically concern the illusory nature of this determination alone, as a mere simulation of individual determinacy as far as the aesthetic object is concerned. He writes :

> This purpose of simulation is fulfilled both by the removal and the filling-in of the indeterminacies, because it is these that denote the openness of the intentional objects and must therefore be made to disappear in the act of concretization if a determinate aesthetic object is to be produced. If this is, indeed, the basic function, then 'places of indeterminacy' as a condition of communication are of very limited historical significance, for their removal simply means creating the illusion of a totality, and this is a principle typical of the period of the *trompe l'oeil* illusion in art.[17]

Iser, clearly, does not take issue with the need of filling in the aesthetic object's constitutive blanks and thus rendering it determinate. What he questions is the illusory and private nature of determination. Indeed, the whole of Iser's aesthetics is centred on the question of how the heterogeneous segments and blanks of the text can give rise to combinations and series that escape purely arbitrary subjectivity, without, however, turning the work of art into the fully completed objectivity characteristic of discursive representation. Determinacy remains an inescapable requirement. Iser shows it to be a function of the infrastructural laws that regulate the segments and blanks of the text, and the interaction of the beholder or reader. Neither merely of the order of the objective nor of the phantasmatic, determinacy is each time historically singular. As a careful analysis of *The Act of Reading* would demonstrate, the realised sense (*Sinn*) of a work of art is the result, for Iser, of a synthesis of the structural possibilities of determination on the level of the text's infrastructure and the determining historical agency of the reader. The sense engendered in the interaction between the text and its elements, on the one hand, and the reader, on the other, remains a unity brought about through limitation and purpose. The major difference, as opposed to the classical theories referred to, is only that the sense that constitutes the work of art is now shown to be a finite determined individuality, which, although it is not objectively determined, is not, for all that, subjective or private.

But let us now turn to Bakhtin's historical criticism, and in particular to his treatment of the work of Rabelais. Grotesque art for Bakhtin, art in close proximity to folk art, is the only art that truly counts, precisely because such art alone is intrinsically historical. At the beginning of his work on Rabelais, the author notes that the 'specific and radical popular character of Rabelais's images . . . explains their exceptional saturation with the future'.[18] In what follows, we intend to show that the identity of the radical, because popular, aesthetic of Rabelais's novel, and its equally radical historicity, can be explained only through reference to the double concept of determination. That which causes Rabelais's work, and all folk art as well, to be intrinsically historical is the artistic principle constitutive of grotesque realism, debasement, or degradation. In debasement everything complete, individual, autonomous, and thus abstract, according to Bakhtin, becomes folded back into the lower stratum principle, that is, into the particular materialised truth which, under the sensuous image of the double body of the immortal and indestructible people, represents the infinite source of all becoming. Debasement serves to relink everything that has torn itself away from the whole of 'the immortal people who create history' back to that generating force in order to rejuvenate it.[19] The movement of degradation is to be understood as a teleologically oriented movement, not toward an ideal end or purpose, but towards the material lower stratum principle of the image of the infinite history-producing force of the people. It thus realises the sense of destination characteristic of *Bestimmung* or *determinatio.* Degradation achieves the historicising reinvigoration of everything individual by deindividualising, delimiting it. Apropos of Rabelais, Bakhtin writes: 'All that was definite and completed within the epoch was in some way comic, insofar as it was limited. But laughter was gay, while all that was determined and finite was about to die and to open new possibilities.'[20] Debasement, by reaching back into the material source of all change, time, and history, thus definitises and delimits all that which through limiting determination had acquired an isolated individuality. By degrading everything definite and complete, debasement appears, consequently, as an operation negatively moulded on determination as identification through limitation. It attempts to undo the individualising limitation brought about by adding a *differentia* to an entity by which the latter becomes sharply set off, in its own identity, against that Other. Debasement undoes identification through determining negation, and, hence, appears to exclude the second sense of determination, the one by which objects are constituted as historical or aesthetic individualities. But if that is the case, one major characteristic of the aesthetic or historic object would be found lacking in Bakhtin's criticism. The question must, consequently, be whether debasement really is entirely critical of the individuality and singularity which we had found to be as important as the movement of destination insofar as the aesthetic and historical object is concerned. Indeed, if grotesque art is to be both radically aesthetic and historical, it cannot do without at least a variation on determination through limitation.

In the same way as debasement does not fully reproduce determination as destination (but keeps of it only the movement of teleological orientation, while giving up the ideal end for the lower stratum source of the material generating power of the body of the people), debasement, though critical of limitation, negation, and identification through *differentiae*, will save what Bakhtin himself refers to as the *principium individuationis.* Indeed, as his analysis of the three levels of data that make up the whole of Rabelais's work reveals, individuality and singularity prevail on all these levels. As far as the familiar foreground of Rabelais's presentation is concerned, 'everything is individual, historically unique. The general is minimized : each object is called by its own name.'[21] The second plane of the work – the actual events of historical importance – is equally 'concrete and historically individualized. There is absolutely no abstract generalization, no typification, but this individualized picture is presented in wider dimensions. From the minor we are transferred to the major individuality.' The third plane of all these images, writes Bakhtin, is constituted by 'the popular carnivalesque plane. . . . The third, popular dimension is also individualized and concrete, but this is the broadest, all-embracing, universal individuality.'[22] Yet, how are we to reconcile debasement's degradation of everything individual and autonomous with the all all-dominating presence in grotesque realism of individualities themselves comprised in the universal individuality of the carnivalesque representation of the people? Such reconciliation is possible only if individuality, in its positive sense, is not constituted by limitation. In fact, if Bakhtin can mention in the same breath individuality and historicity, it is not, as in the classical theories, because the fully determined, and, thus, limited, constitutes the historical, but because what he calls individual is so singular, unique, idiosyncratic, as to be, in its very instability, already in the process of changing, of turning into another singularity as idiosyncratic as the first. That is also true of the founding individuality, 'the broadest, all embracing, universal individuality', to which all the 'familiar objects and localities . . . which occupy the foreground, are related [as] to the major individual whole of the world, a two-bodied whole in the state of becoming'.[23] Precisely because that whole is the sensuous representation of the lower stratum principle of change, it is a principle so unique, so singular – a Romantic *individuelles Allgemeine*, so to speak – that there can be no generic, no universal name for it, and it can represent itself always only in a manner so idiosyncratic that it always already points to its ensuing representation. In what Bakhtin calls the 'individualising torrent' of grotesque art, 'the dividing lines between persons and objects are weakened', and all distinctions 'lose their absolute character, their one-sided and limited seriousness'.[24] In short, the grotesque individualities, instead of being constituted in sharp difference with respect to an Other, are, by virtue of their irreducible and unnamable idiosyncrasy, in the process of endlessly changing into that Other. Since this is the case with the founding image of the carnivalesque representation of the double body of the people as well, all determinate distinctions and, with them, all hierarchies vanish. Precisely because this last instance is said to penetrate all the images of the two other levels, which all receive their meaning in every detail from this 'final whole' which itself is singular and historical through and through, the distinction between that whole and its parts, the founding One and what is founded, vanishes, and with it, the possibility of foundation as well. All becomes One, or rather, one. Singularisation turns so extreme that the unifying ground of all singularities is itself so singular that it becomes indistinguishable from them. In grotesque art, time itself speaks in a historical manner. Because of its singularity, this art is historical itself. To sum up: although the two interlocked sides of determination are radically transformed by Bakhtin – determination as destination becomes debasement of everything completed through limitation in a downward thrust toward the lower stratum of the image of time under the form of the sensuous representation of the procreating body of the people; determination as limitation becomes a movement of freeing individualities into an extreme singularity so unique and pointlike that they are always already in the process of changing into the Other – their interplay is the condition of possibility of why folk art, the art of the people, can be beautiful and intrinsically historical at the same time.

In both types of criticism, the more aesthetically-oriented type of Iser, and the more historically-oriented type of Bakhtin, the category of determination continues to play the dominant role. It is determination by limitation which in Iser explains why the infrastructure of the work of art can also become the object of an historical and singular act of concretisation by a subject, that is, in an act of determination as destination. It is determination as destination that explains why the historicising movement of debasement in Bakhtin also produces aesthetic, and not only historical, singularities, that is, products that are a function of a (transformed) movement of determination as limitation. Because of the necessary interplay of the two sides of determination, the aesthetic criticism of Iser cannot but be historical as well. On the basis of that same necessity, the historical criticism of Bakhtin is also profoundly aesthetic. The constitutive role of the category of determination, instead of permitting a clear opposition of the two types of discourse, rather establishes a profound and fundamental complicity between both. This is not to say, of course, that the differences between the two types of approach are negligible. Yet they are derivative, and make sense only with respect to the underlying unity of history and aesthetics.

Before concluding, let us circle back to the question of the relation between structure and genesis from which we started out. If Husserl radically rethought that relation by centering on something like a structural opening of structures in a minor sense, and of genetic development too, the reason for this is to be found not least in his attempt to unground the dialectically conciliatory grounding of the two bipolar concepts. To a dialectical philosophy such as Hegel's, for instance, the telos of becoming coincides with the (static) structure of the infinite totality of all (material and logical) determinations. According to this most powerful model for thinking becoming, one that continues to inform most philosophies of history and forms of literary criticism, the historical ideal is more successfully achieved in the totalising structure in which history has come to an end. In it, genesis finds the realisation of its essence and can thus come in it to a rest, as the very telos of all becoming and development. As far as the relation between aesthetics and history is concerned, the situation is analogous. Within the tradition that we have been considering here, history and aesthetics are interlinked in such a manner as to make poetry, as the discourse in which concrete individuality is brought about by total determination, the very goal of the historiographic ideal. If history is not simply seen as a subgenre (however important) of poetry, as in Baumgarten, with the result that poetry becomes the ideal horizon of all historiography, the converse is true, and history as the discourse of all inclusive determinateness becomes the telos of poetry. These two possibilities are clearly a function of the constitutive category of determination. It is thus naive to believe that one could be played off against the other, because they both play into each other's hands in a speculative slide toward all-inclusive determinateness. But it would be equally naive to believe that such totalisation can be avoided in a non-naive manner. Bakhtin's criticism and aesthetic theory are a good case in point. His aesthetics continues to yield to the concept of totality and determinateness, the only difference being that such totalisation is achieved through delimitation, and by including in the totality the representation of the principle of change, time, and history as well.

If post-structuralism means anything at all, it does so not by its insistence on the necessity of rediscovering history, because history was never lost. If, by contrast, it does mean something, it does so by stressing the need to think towards the conditions of possibility and the law that rules the difference between such concepts as structure and genesis, or aesthetics and history. What is needed, indeed, is a better understanding of the structural complicity of both in order to reassess their difference. Though we intimated at the beginning of the essay that we were not to engage in a transcendental analysis regarding the difference between history and aesthetics – and if we did this, it was also because we believe that the type of opening of difference that we envision can no longer be simply termed transcendental – the following suggestions may serve to indicate the direction which such an inquiry might take. Since the concept of determination, of *Bestimmung*, is the constituting operator of the poetic and the historical as two different and complicitous modes of totalisation through limitation, the 'transcendental' structure of their difference would have to be sought in an analysis of the modes of agreement and correspondence (*Stimmigkeit*) that cause the determined always to be determined in the perspective of an end, purpose, fate, or destiny. Such a 'transcendental' structure governing the agreement between determination as destination and determination as limitation would itself necessarily fall outside the realm of what it makes possible. It would, thus, also represent the non-transgressable limit of determination as limitation enabling that structure also to account for disagreement, indetermination, and irrecuperable straying. The reinscription of that limit into the ineluctable thought of determination, so it seems to us, could lead post-structuralism not to *re*discover history, but to discover it altogether for the first time.

NOTES

1 Jacques Derrida, *Writing and Difference*, tr. A. Bass (Chicago: University of Chicago Press, 1978), p. 5.

2 Alexander Gottlieb Baumgarten, *Reflections on Poetry*, tr. K. Aschenbrenner and W. B. Holther (Berkeley: University of California Press, 1954). (Henceforth abbreviated in the text as *RP*, followed by the relevant page numbers.)

3 Helmut Kuhn, *Schriften zur Aesthetik* (Munchen: Kösel, 1966), p. 35.

4 Hans Robert Jauss, *Toward an Aesthetic of Reception* (Minneapolis: University of Minnesota Press, 1982), p. 49.

5 Gottfried Wilhelm Leibniz, *Discourse on Metaphysics*, tr. P. G. Lucas and L. Grint (Manchester: University of Manchester Press, 1953), p. 41.

6 Ernst Cassirer, *Philosophy of the Enlightenment* (Princeton: University of Princeton Press, 1968), p. 346.

7 Alfred Baeumler, *Das Irrationalitätsproblem in der Aesthetik und Logik des 18 Jahrhunderts bis zur Kritik der Urteilskraft* (Darmstadt: Wissenschaftliche Buchgesellschaft, 1981), p. 229.

8 Although Baumgarten did not invent the category of determination but received it from Spinoza, Leibniz and Wolff, this is not the place to demarcate his use of that concept from that of his predecessors.

9 Baeumler, *Das Irrationalitätsproblem* . . ., p. 15. In order to do justice to the relation between aesthetics and history as it develops in the eighteenth century, it is necessary to mention that it was not only the time at which aesthetics became the paradigm for history, but that, conversely, it was also the time at which the historical foundations of poetics were laid out in the writings of Schiller, Schlegel and Hölderlin.

10 Baeumler, *Das Irrationalitätsproblem* . . ., pp. 223–4.

11 See also pp. 29–31 of the preface by K. Aschenbrenner and W. B. Holther to their edition of Baumgarten's *Reflections*. The editors stress the indebtedness of Baumgarten's aesthetics to the principle of the imitation of nature, and the theological model of the process of creation.

12 See also the scholia to paragraph 28 on p. 48 of the *Reflections*.

13 The only dictionary to my knowledge that features an entry of importance on the concept of determination is the *Historisches Wörterbuch der Philosophie* (Darmstadt: Wissenschaftliche Buch-

gesellschaft, 1971). The entry is by V. Warnach and S. Körner.

14 The present essay is part of work in progress on that history and its implications for both philosophy and literary criticism.

15 Wolfgang Iser, *The Act of Reading. A Theory of Aesthetic Response* (Baltimore: Johns Hopkins University Press, 1978), p. 171.

16 Ibid., p. 175.

17 Ibid., p. 175.

18 Mikhail Bakhtin, *Rabelais and his World*, tr. H. Iswolsky (Bloomington: Indiana University Press, 1984), p. 2.

19 Ibid., p. 376.

20 Ibid., p. 454.

21 Ibid., p. 445.

22 Ibid., p. 447.

23 Ibid., p. 448.

24 Ibid., pp. 463 and 448.

The sign of history

JEAN-FRANÇOIS LYOTARD

Under the somewhat enigmatic title, 'The sign of history', I am going to suggest an introduction to a reconsideration of the historico-political reality of our time. In order to do this I shall appeal to the critical thought of Immanuel Kant. I hope that you will see why this detour is necessary as you follow it with me.

Anyone who tries to reflect on historico-political reality today (as always) comes up against names – proper names. These names form part of the treasure of phrases that he has received in his share of language and that he must continue by allowing new phrases. For we have all of us a sort of debt, or a sort of rivalry, with respect to names.

These proper names have the following remarkable property: they place modern historical or political commentary in abeyance. Adorno pointed out that Auschwitz is an abyss in which the philosophical genre of Hegelian speculative discourse seems to disappear, because the name 'Auschwitz' invalidates the presupposition of that genre, namely that all that is real is rational, and that all that is rational is real. Budapest '56 is another abyss in which the genre of (Marxist) historical materialist discourse seems to disappear, because this name invalidates the presupposition of that genre, namely that all that is proletarian is communist, and that all that is communist is proletarian. Nineteen sixty-eight is an abyss in which the genre of democratic liberal discourse (republican dialogue) seems to disappear, because this name invalidates the presupposition of that genre, namely that all that concerns the political community can be said within the rules of the game of parliamentary representation. The crisis of over-capitalisation that the world economy has been suffering since 1974 and will suffer for some time to come invalidates the presupposition of the discursive genre of post-Keynesian political economy, namely that a harmonious regulation of needs and the means to satisfy them in work and in capital, with a view to the greatest enjoyment of goods and services for all – that this regulation is possible and on the way to being achieved.

One is tempted to close these wounds as quickly as possible, to forget these names, to re-establish these genres in their respective pretensions to universal validity in terms of historico-political reality, and to carry through to completion the project of 'modernity', as Habermas puts it. From all sides we are being urged to restore confidence in one or other of these genres. The philosopher tries, rather, to take his inquiry further, although in fact these names show him no direction to take, but only directions not to take. He sees that he is dealing with a sort of *fission* affecting the unity of the great discourses of modernity.

At the same time, this fission affects the rules of philosophical discourse itself. The genres available to this discourse – the Treatise, the Manual, the Meditation, the Discourse, the Dialogue, the Lecture, the Manifesto, the Diary – which are so many ways of proceeding in thought, seem to the philosopher to damp the echo of this fission with the deafness of established forms. For these genres of philosophical discourse have their rules for the formation and linking of phrases, and their rules for the presentation of objects (examples) which can validate these phrases.

The philosopher who is willing to echo the shock associated with these names of history thus discovers or rediscovers that, whatever the genre involved, philosophical discourse obeys a fundamental rule, namely that it must be in search of its rule. Or, if you prefer: its rule is that what is at stake is its rule. How to form phrases and how to link them together is the question of literature too: philosophy adds to this question that of knowing what sort of presentation can validate those phrases and linkings. The philosopher discovers or rediscovers that his discourse takes place only in order to find out how it has the right to take place: and thus that it takes place *before* that finding-out, and that he therefore judges without any criterion (in the absence of established rules) that such and such a phrase is philosophical and that such and such a case permits it to be validated. Philosophical discourse is waiting for its criterion.

By describing the current situation of thought in this way, we cannot fail to encounter the critical reflexion of Kant. Indeed, we are already in his company. The name 'Kant' (it is not the only one) marks at once the prologue and the epilogue to modernity. And as epilogue to modernity, it is also a prologue to postmodernity. The historian assigns to this name a definite chronological place (the end of the eighteenth century), but the philosopher accords this name (and others) the status of a sign, a sign of thought, which is not only determined by its historical context, but which 'gives food for thought' with respect to many other historical contexts, with respect to the context which is ours.

The philosophical phrase according to Kant is an analogon of the political phrase according to Kant. It can be this analogon only insofar as it is critical, and not doctrinal. The doctrinal, or systematic, phrase must come after the critical phrase : the rule for it is to be found in the regulation implied by the idea of system, and is an organ of the organic body of doctrine – a legitimated phrase. In order to establish its legitimacy, it has been necessary to judge its pretension to validity : if it has the pretension of speaking the truth, this means judging if and how it manages to do so; if its pretension is that of speaking the just or the good, this means judging if and how it manages to do so; and so on. These judgements bearing on the respective pretensions of the various families of phrases (cognitive, ethical, juridical, etc.), and these verdicts which establish the respective validity of each of them in its field, territory or domain are the work of the critique. It is well known that Kant often symbolises the critical activity as that of a tribunal or a judge. But this judge cannot simply be a magistrate, for he has at his disposal no code of law, criminal or civil, nor even a collection of already-judged cases, for the conduct of his enquiry or the formulation of his verdict. He does not judge pretensions with the yardstick of an established, incontestable law. This law must in its turn come under his examination. From this point of view, critical philosophy is in the position of a juridical authority which must declare : 'this is the case, this phrase is the right one' (with respect to the true, the good, even the just) – in this position, rather than in that of an authority (in any case entirely illusory, and in the first place illusory for Kant himself) which would only have to apply, without further ceremony, an already established rule to a new piece of data. This does not mean that this authority has at its disposal no criterion by which to make its evaluations, but that the applicability of the criterion in the given case is itself subject to evaluation. And then either one must admit a regressive search for criteria of criteria *ad infinitum*, or else place one's faith in that 'gift of nature' called judgement, which allows us to say, 'here, it is the case'. Now, according to Kant, it is the case of philosophy, as critical philosophy, to say 'it is the case'.

Next, how does the critical philosopher judge that it is the case when there is no intuition to present for the case? In the *Critique of*

Judgement, Kant makes a distinction between two modes of presentation, or hypotyposes. For determinant judgements, that is when we are dealing with descriptive phrases, either these phrases are experience-phrases (empirical concepts), and intuition presents them with objects as *examples*, or else they are knowledge-phrases, and pure intuition presents them with objects as *schemata*. When we are dealing with Ideas (of the world, of the beginning, of the element, of the first cause or origin, of God and of course of historical totality), in which case intuition cannot, by definition, present anything as an object, presentation takes place indirectly by analogy : 'One submits an intuition such that with respect to it the procedure of the faculty of judgement is simply analogous with the procedure it follows when it schematises.' The form of presentation, that of the intuitive mode (the schema) is drawn out from the concept which can be intuited (since this latter is absent), and under this form is placed another intuition, 'equally empirical', which would, in sum, allow the validation of the Idea if it were a concept of the understanding. In other words, the non-cognitive phrase, which is descriptive but dialectical, is presented with an 'as if' referent, that is, one which would be its referent if the phrase were cognitive. This indirect presentation is called symbolic presentation, or presentation by symbols, and makes use of *analoga*.

In this way the critical philosopher can continue judging a phrase, even when there is no empirical case directly presentable for its validation. Through the analogy all properly philosophical (i.e. critical phrases) operate like an external critique, and *must* do so, at least if they are striving for conformity with their Idea. It is because it has to judge, and more particularly to find *analoga* (symbols or others) for its Ideas (including the Idea of itself) that philosophy cannot be learned : 'At most, one can learn to *philosophise*'.

It remains to argue the assertion that this reflecting condition is analogous with that of the political, as Kant sees it.

Kant's historico-political texts are, *grosso modo*, scattered through the three *Critiques* and a dozen or so opuscules. The Critique of Political Reason was not written. It is legitimate, within certain limits yet to be determined, to see in this dispersion, whatever its 'cause' (demanded too hastily by the phrase of understanding, the cognitive phrase), the sign of a particular heterogeneity of the political as an 'object' of phrases. This heterogeneity of the object is already noticeable in the third *Critique*. Here the faculty of judgement is provided not with one specific object, but with at least two – art and nature.

I say 'at least', because of the problem (which might be the whole problem) of knowing whether this faculty of judgement is indeed a faculty. Kant has previously given this word 'faculty' a precise meaning – a potential of phrases subject to a group of rules of formation and presentation (in the Kantian sense), when it was a matter of sensitivity, understanding and reason for theoretical matters, of reason alone for practical matters. But in fact judgement intervenes already and necessarily, every time one has to say that 'it is the case': in other words in order to establish presentation – in cognitive phrases under the rule of the schema, in dialectical argumentative phrases under that of the *symbol*, and in prescriptive phrases (in evaluation of responsibility and morality) under that of the *type*.

In the Introduction to the third *Critique*, the dispersion of families of phrases is not only recognised, but is dramatised to such an extent that the problem is that of finding 'transitions' (*Ubergänge*) between these heterogeneous types of phrases. And because of its very ubiquity which I have just recalled (that is, the fact that it is called on every time a phrase has to be validated by a presentation), the 'faculty' of judgement is seen as a potential of interfaculty 'transitions', to such an extent that it is given a major privilege over other faculties when it comes to unification, and simultaneously a major defect when it comes to knowing what object would be specific to it – this defect is that it *has* no determined object. This is why we might wonder if it is indeed a faculty of knowledge in Kant's sense. In all the families of phrases, however heterogeneous they are with respect to each other, what Kant obstinately calls the 'faculty of judgement' is the determination of the right mode of object-presentation for each of these families.

Suppose we had to present an object for the Idea of the proliferation of the faculties seen as capacities for having objects (as domains, territories or fields): this object with which to validate the dispersion or fission of the faculties can only be a symbol – I would suggest that of an archipelago. Each family of phrases would be like an island, and the faculty of judgement would be (at least in part) like a ship-fitter or an admiral, sending out expeditions with the job of presenting one island with what they had found ('invented', in the etymological sense) on the others. This task-force or venture-force has no object, but requires a *milieu*: the sea, the *Archepelagos*, the major sea as the Aegean used to be called. In the Introduction to the third *Critique*, this sea has a different name, that of the 'field', the *Feld*:

'To the extent that concepts are referred to objects without one's considering whether a knowledge of these objects is possible or not, they have their field, which is determined solely according to the relationship of their object to our faculty of knowing in general.' And the end of the same Introduction tells us that this faculty of knowing *in general* includes the understanding, the faculty of judgement, and reason. All these faculties find their objects in the field, some marking out a territory, others a domain : the faculty of judgement marks out neither, but looks after the transitions between those of the others. So this faculty is, rather, that of the *milieu* in which all marking-out of limits to legitimacy takes place. More still, it is what allowed territories and domains *to be* marked out, and what established each family's authority over its island. And it could do this only because of the commerce it keeps going between them.

At this point we ought to establish this on the basis of cases drawn from critical activity itself. We would examine how, and at the cost of what transitions, the beautiful can stand as a symbol of moral good, as explained in the third *Critique.* How, and at the cost of what transitions, the maxims of ethical action, the categorical imperative, as Kant writes in the second *Critique*, 'must withstand the test of the form of a natural law in general', i.e. how and at what cost the pure 'Act' is accompanied by the analogical '*so dass* (meaning "in such a way that" and/or "as if") the maxim of your will could be laid down as the principle of a universal legislation'. Here the transition is called a *type* : Kant writes, 'Natural law serves only as a *type* for a law of freedom'. Were it not for this *type*, which results from a transfer from nature to the will, the imperative would provide no guiding thread, but would simply prescribe action without suggesting any regulating Idea (that of a supersensible nature, of a community of practical, i.e. free, beings) to guide the judgement of what must be done. We would examine as further cases of transitions other strange objects of Kant's thought, such as the Ideas of the imagination, which result from a transition from Reason to imagination by inversion : these are intuitions without a concept, whereas the Ideas of Reason are concepts without a sensory intuition. Or again – and these are perhaps more paradoxical – we would examine the ideals of sensibility, which Kant calls 'monograms', and which are 'inimitable models of possible empirical intuitions', that is, 'floating designs', 'incommunicable phantoms' inscribed in the sensibility of painters (and physiognomists), which do not to be sure give them determined rules (of plasticity, for example), but which nonetheless direct their judgement in matters of sensibility.

The importance of the philosophy of the beautiful and the sublime in the first part of the third *Critique* lies both in the de-realisation of the object of aesthetic feelings, and in the absence of a real aesthetic faculty of knowing. The same thing holds, perhaps even more radically, for the historico-political object, which as such has no reality, and for any political faculty of knowing, which must remain inexistent. The only things that *are* real (i.e. that for the concept of which intuitions can be presented) are phenomena, all of them both conditioned and conditioning. The series of these phenomena, which makes up the history of humanity (and not even its natural history, only its cosmological history), is never itself given. This series is not given, but is the object of an Idea and, insofar as it is a human world, comes under the same antithetics as the cosmological series in general.

In general in Kant's work the cognitive phrase, with its double criterion of pertinence (with respect to negation or the principle of contradiction on the one hand, and to intuitive perception on the other), is opposed to vain hopes, false promises and prophecies. It is used to refute the right of insurrection and to condemn the violent substitution of a new authority for the old one. The argument runs as follows : the existence of the 'common being' (*das gemeine Wesen*) is the referent of a phrase which is either cognitive (of the understanding) or objective–teleological (finality in organised beings). This common being's proximity to the Good is judged in a subjective–teleological phrase (moral finality in rational beings). Revolution breaks open (*Abbruch*) an existing common being : another cannot fail to replace it (by natural law). The heterogeneity of the two families of phrases is not modified. Revolutionary politics is based on a transcendental illusion in the political domain, confusing what can be presented as an object for a cognitive phrase and what can be presented as an object for a speculative and/or ethical phrase – in other words it confuses schemata or examples with *analoga*. The progress of a common being for the better is not to be judged on the basis of empirical intuition, but on the basis of signs.

The expression 'sign of history' is an outstanding example of the complexity of the 'transitions' which have to be made in order to phrase the historico-political. The question posed (against the Faculty of Law) is whether it can be asserted that the human species is progressing continuously for the better, and if the answer is yes, *how* it can be asserted.

The first difficulty lies in the fact that such a phrase has as its referent a part of human history yet to come, and is thus a phrase of *Vorhersagung*, of anticipation, a prognostic. Kant immediately distinguishes it from the *Weissager*'s (fortune-teller's) phrase, by showing that, following the rule for cognitives, there can be no direct presentation of the object of this phrase when it bears on the future.

So we shall have to change our family of phrases in order to produce the required demonstration. We shall have to look in the experience of humanity, not for an intuitive *datum* (a *Gegebene*) (which can only validate the phrase describing it, and no more), but for what Kant calls a *Begebenheit*, an event, a deal (in the card-playing sense) – a *Begebenheit* which would only indicate (*hinweisen*) and not prove (*beweisen*) that humanity is capable of being not only the cause (*Ursache*) but also the author (*Urheber*) of its progress. More precisely, explains Kant, this *Begebenheit* delivered in human historical experience must indicate a cause the occurrence of which remains undetermined (*unbestimmt*) with respect to time (*in Ansehung der Zeit*) – and we recognise in this rule the clause stating the independence of causality by freedom from the diachronic series of the mechanical world. This is the price to be paid for being able to extend this cause's possibility of intervening to past and future too.

And this is still not all. The *Begebenheit* must not itself be the cause of progress, but only an index (*Hindeutend*) of progress – a *Geschichtszeichen.* Kant immediately makes clear what he means by sign of history: '*signum rememorativum, demonstrativum, prognosticum*'. The *Begebenheit* we are looking for will have the job of 'presenting' causality by freedom along the three temporal directions – past, present and future. What is this enigmatic, even contradictory 'fact of being delivered'? We might expect some heroic deed to be the looked-for 'deal' bearing witness to the power of free causality. But such a heroic deed is still only a *datum*. Certainly it can be given several readings (descriptive phrase, dialectical phrase), but this only means that it is an equivocal object which can be seized on by one or other of these phrases indifferently. Here the critical judge's requirements go further, to the extent of seeming paradoxical. He is not satisfied with letting the advocate of determinism and the advocate of freedom or finality be reconciled by an arrangement satisfying both, but leaving the decision whether to phrase one way rather than the other indeterminate (in the sense of contingent). The

Begebenheit, which is a *datum in* experience at least, if not *of* experience, must be the index of the Idea of free causality. With this *Begebenheit* we must get as close as possible to the abyss to be crossed between mechanism on the one hand and liberty or finality on the other, between the domain of the sensory world and the field of the supersensible – and we should be able to leap across it without suppressing it, by fixing the status of the historico-political – a status which may be inconsistent and indeterminate, but which can be spoken, and which is, even, irrefutable. This is the price to be paid for being able to prove that humanity has a natural inclination to use its reason, and for being able to anticipate with certainty a continuous progress of its history for the better.

At this point Kant goes off on what can seem to be an unexpected detour in order to present this *Begebenheit*, but this detour also allows the most minute location of this 'as if object', the historico-political, and the location most faithful to its complexity. We have, he writes, a *Begebenheit* satisfying the conditions of the problem, and which is not a great deed: 'We are here only concerned with the way of thinking [*Denkungsart*] of the spectators [*Zuschauer*] as it reveals itself [or betrays itself, *verrät*, as one betrays a secret] in public [*offentlich* : a public use of thought then, in the same sense as the article on the *Aufklärung* distinguishes a public use of reason] on the occasion of [this is how I translate *bei*, which does not mean *in*] this drama of great transmutations [*Umwandlungen*] [this drama, *dieser Spiel*: which drama? Kant will give the example of the French Revolution, the text dates from 1795], in which is expressed a taking of sides [a participation, a taking up, *eine Teilnehmung*] for one set of antagonists against their adversaries, a taking of sides so universal and yet so disinterested – even at the risk that this taking of sides can be of disadvantage to them (the spectators) – that it provides the proof [*beweist*] (because of its universality) that there is a character of mankind as a whole and (because of its disinterestedness) that this character is a moral one [*moralisch*] at least as a disposition [*Anlage*], and this character not only allows us to hope for human progress, it is already this progress, insofar as its scope is within reach of what is possible at present.' Kant adds that the recent Revolution of a people which is *geistreich*, rich in spirit, may well either fail or succeed, accumulate misery and atrocity, it nevertheless 'arouses in the heart [*in den Gemütern*, in the spirits] of all spectators (who are not themselves caught up in it) a taking of sides according to desires [*eine Teilnehmung dem Wunsche nach*] which borders on enthusiasm

[*Enthusiasm*] and which, since its very expression was not without danger, can only have been caused by a moral disposition within the human race'.

I will not give a detailed commentary on this text which contains in condensed form Kant's thought (maybe the whole of his thought) on the historico-political. I shall simply make three observations, the first on the nature of enthusiasm, the second on its value as a *Begebenheit* in the historical experience of humanity, and the third on its links with critical thought. All three observations will be made in accordance with the clause controlling the elaboration of the *sign of history*, that is, that the meaning of history (i.e. all phrases pertinent to the historico-political field) does not only show itself in the great deeds and misdeeds of the agents or actors who become famous in history, but also in the feeling of the obscure and distant spectators who see and hear them and who, in the sound and fury of the *res gestae*, distinguish between what is just and what is not.

The first observation is that according to Kant the enthusiasm they feel is a modality of the sublime feeling : *sublime feeling* rather than *feeling of the sublime* since, if we are to believe the third *Critique*, 'it is not the object which must be named sublime, but the disposition of the mind provoked by a certain representation which occupies the reflective faculty of judgement'. The imagination attempts to provide an object given as a totality in intuition, i.e. to provide a presentation for an Idea of reason (for the totality is the object of an Idea : for example, the totality of practical rational beings) – the imagination fails, and thus feels its impotence, but at the same time discovers its calling (*Bestimmung*, its destination), which is to realise its accord with Ideas of reason by providing a suitable presentation. The result of this inhibited accord is that instead of having a feeling for the object, we have on the occasion of this object a feeling, 'for the Idea of mankind in us as subjects'. In this text from paragraph 25, the feeling Kant comments on is that of respect. But the analysis works for any sublime feeling inasmuch as it involves a 'subreption' (*Subreption*) which substitutes a regulation (which is in fact a non-regulation) between the faculties of a subject, for a regulation between an object and a subject.

The regulation of the sublime is a non-regulation. By contrast with taste, the regulation of the sublime is good when it is bad. The sublime involves the finality of a non-finality and the pleasure of an unpleasure : 'We discover a certain finality in the unpleasure felt in proportion with the extension of the imagination necessary if it is to fit with what is without limit in our power of reason, i.e. the Idea of an absolute whole, and consequently also in the non-finality [*Unzweckmässigkeit*, the non-affinity, the incommensurability in terms of the goal] of the power of the imagination for the Ideas of reason, and the arousing [*Erweckung*] of these Ideas . . . The object is apprehended as sublime with a joy which is only made possible by the mediation of pain.'

Even the most extensive imagination cannot manage to present an object which could validate or 'realise' the Idea. Whence the pain: from the inability to present. What is the joy which, nonetheless, is grafted onto this pain? It comes from the discovery of an affinity in this discord: even what is presented as being very big in nature (including in human nature and in the natural history of man, such as a great revolution) is still and will always be 'small compared with the ideas of reason'. What is discovered is not only the infinite scope of Ideas, which are incommensurable with any presentation, but, also, the calling of the subject, 'our' calling, which is that of having to supply a presentation for the unpresentable and thus, in terms of Ideas, to go beyond anything that can be presented.

Enthusiasm itself is an extreme form of the sublime feeling: the attempt to provide a presentation not only fails, thus giving rise to the tension I have described, but also, so to speak, is reversed or inverted so as to provide a supremely paradoxical presentation, which Kant calls a 'simply negative presentation', and which he characterises with some audacity as a 'presentation of the infinite'. We have here the most inconsistent of all 'transitions' – a blind alley. Kant even ventures to give examples of it: 'There is perhaps no passage in the Old Testament more sublime than the commandment: Thou shalt not make graven images, nor any representation of the things on high in heaven, below on earth, and under the earth . . . Only this commandment can explain the enthusiasm that the Jewish people, in the period when it was flourishing, felt for its religion when it compared itself with other peoples, or the pride inspired by the Mahometan religion.' And he continues, 'It is the same with the representation of the moral law and the disposition to morality within us'.

What is required of the imagination, for this abstract presentation which presents nothingness, is that it should 'unlimit' itself. The fact remains that this extreme painful delight called enthusiasm is an *Affekt*, a powerful affection; and that as such it is blind and thus cannot, writes Kant, 'serve as a satisfaction for reason'. It is even a *dementia*, a *Wahnsinn*, in which the imagination is 'unleashed'. As such, it remains of course preferable to the *Schwärmerei*, to the tumult of exaltation, which is a *Wahnwitz*, an *insanitas*, a 'disorder' of the imagination, an 'illness deeply rooted in the soul', whereas enthusiasm is a 'passing accident which can affect the most healthy understanding'. The *Schwärmerei* gives rise to an illusion, to 'seeing something beyond all limits of sensibility', i.e. to thinking that there is a presentation when there is not. It makes a non-critical transition which is comparable to the transcendental illusion (the illusion of knowing something beyond all the limits of knowledge). Enthusiasm, on the other hand, sees nothing, or rather sees *the* nothing and refers it to the unpresentable. Although it is to be condemned ethically as pathological, 'it is aesthetically sublime since it is a tension of forces due to Ideas, which give the soul an *élan* which acts much more powerfully and durably than the impulsion given by sensory representations'.

Historico-political enthusiasm thus borders on *dementia*. It is a pathological attack and as such has in itself no ethical validity, since ethics requires one to be free of all motivating pathos, allowing only the apathetic pathos which accompanies obligation and which is called respect, and not the *Affektlosigkeit* which is still too sublime, and which Kant proceeds to discuss immediately in his study of the sublime. And yet the pathos of enthusiasm in its episodic outbursts retains an aesthetic validity; it is an energetical *sign*, a tensor of the *Wunsch*. The infinite nature of the Idea draws all other capacities (i.e. all the other faculties) to itself, and produces an *Affekt* 'of the vigorous type', which is characteristic of the sublime. The 'transition', then, does not take place; it is a 'transition' in transit, and its transiting, its movement, is a sort of agitation on the spot, in the blind alley of incommensurability, above the abyss, a 'shaking', writes Kant, 'that is the rapid succession of repulsion and attraction for the same object'. And this is the state of the *Gemüt* of the spectators of the French Revolution.

Second observation: this enthusiasm is the *Begebenheit* looked for in the historical experience of humanity in order to validate the phrase, 'Humanity is continually improving.' Great changes such as the French Revolution are not in principle sublime in themselves. As objects they are like those spectacles of physical nature on the occasion of which the spectator feels the sublime: 'It is rather in its chaos and its disorder (if grandeur and force manifest themselves) in its wildest and most unbridled devastation, that nature best provokes Ideas of the sublime.' What best determines the sublime is the indeterminate, the *Formlosigkeit* : 'the sublime of nature . . . can be as if without form or figure'; 'no particular form of nature is represented therein'. The same must be the case for the Revolution, and for all great historical upheavals – they are the formless and figureless in historical human nature. Ethically there is nothing valid about them: on the contrary they come in for critical judgement as we have seen; they are the result of a confusion (which is the political illusion itself) between the direct presentation of the *Gemeine Wesen* and the analogical presentation of the Idea of a Republican contract.

As an event in the historical nature of mankind, the Revolution belongs to the residue of data, the remainder made up of singularities and existences waiting for a phrase once the cognitive phrase has taken charge of what belongs to it in the intuitions it can subsume under regularities, in the mode of the presentation of examples. This remainder is waiting for the teleological phrase, and yet its lack of form looks as if it ought to cause the absolute failure of this phrase. But in the enthusiasm aroused in the *Gemüt* of the spectators by this formlessness, this failure of all possible finalisation is itself finalised. The *dementia* of enthusiasm for the Revolution and the revolutionary party bears witness to the extreme tension felt by spectating mankind – a tension between the 'nullity' of what is presented to it and the Ideas of reason – i.e. the Idea of the Republic which unites the Idea of autonomy, of the people and that of peace between States. What is given in this *Begebenheit* is thus a tension in the *Denkungsart* occasioned by an object which is almost pure disorder, which has no figure, which is however extremely big in historical nature and which is a sort of abstraction refractory to all functions of presentation – even by *analoga*. But because of these negative properties of the object which is the occasion of this tension, it proves all the more indubitably by the very form it imprints on feeling, that it is polarised, '*aufs Idealische*, towards something Ideal, *und zwar rein Moralische*, that is something purely moral, to which the concept of right is similar'.

Third observation : Kant writes in the third *Critique*, 'All that matters in the resolution of an antinomy is that two propositions which apparently contradict each other do not in fact do so, and can be maintained alongside each other even if the explanation of the possibility of their concept surpasses our faculty of knowing'. Let us call this solution *parathetical*.

What are, notably, involved in the parathetical solution of the Antimony are also the senders and addressees of the various families of phrases. In principle their situation is regulated, i.e. subject to determination, according to the way the referent is presented by the phrase. This is at least what was established by the *Analytic* of the first *Critique.* But in certain cases, and in the first place that of the ethical phrase, only the situation of the addressee is regulated – the sender of the moral law remaining indeterminable. (In fact the situation of the referent is regulated too, since one of the properties of the ethical phrase is that the sender must bring the referent into existence – the referent being the action prescribed by the imperative.) In other cases, and in the first place that of the aesthetic phrase, what is regulated is the fact that there *is* no rule, since there is no determinable presentation of the referent. And yet this rule of non-regulation nonetheless appeals to a possible agreement between sender and addressee of the ethical phrase about a referent which is, however, never directly presentable. There is thus a bond of 'communicability' between them, which is not subject to the rule of presentation which is valid for the cognitive phrase. This communicability is required 'as a duty, so to speak', and taste is the faculty which judges it a priori. The *sensus communis* is thus in the aesthetic field *like* the totality of rational practical beings in the ethical domain. It is an appeal to the community made a priori, judged without a rule of direct presentation : simply the ethical community is mediated by a concept of reason, the Idea of freedom, whilst the aesthetic community of the senders and addressees of the phrase on beauty is immediately situated in feeling, in that it is a priori to be shared between those senders and addressees.

Enthusiasm as a '*Begebenheit* of our time' is thus phrased according to the rule of the aesthetics of the most extreme mode of the sublime. Extreme firstly because the sublime is not only a disinterested pleasure and a universal without a concept, but also because it involves a purposiveness of anti-purposiveness and a pleasure by pain, as opposed to the feeling of the beautiful, the purposiveness of which is only without purpose, and the pleasure of which is left to the free accord of the faculties amongst themselves. With the sublime we go a long way into heterogeneity, so that the solution to the aesthetic antinomy appears to be more difficult for the sublime than for the beautiful.

A fortiori more difficult when we are dealing with enthusiasm, which is at the extreme limit of the sublime. Kant recognises that 'the disposition of the mind supposed by the feeling of the sublime requires *eine Empfanglichkeit* to Ideas [that the mind be susceptible to Ideas, sensitive to Ideas]'. And a little later, 'The judgement on the sublime in nature [of human nature too] needs a certain culture', which does not mean that it is produced by that culture, for 'it has its foundation in human nature'. Kant says no more on this subject in this paragraph. But this allusion to culture is cleared up in the critique of teleological judgement in the paragraph dealing with the ultimate aim of nature. Here (as in many of the political opuscules) Kant refutes the thesis that this goal could be the happiness of the human race, and shows that it can only be its culture. 'To produce in a rational being the general aptitude for the aims which please him (and consequently in his freedom), that is culture.' Culture is the ultimate aim pursued by nature in the human race because culture is what makes men more 'receptive to ideas', and is the condition which opens the door to thinking the unconditioned.

In the same paragraph Kant makes a distinction between the culture of skill and the culture of will : and in the former, between the material and the formal culture of skill. Now the formal developments of the culture of skill requires the neutralisation of conflicts of free beings on the individual scale, by means of a 'legal power in a totality called *bürgerlich Gesellschaft*, civil society'. And if men get ahead of the plans of natural providence, the development of the culture of skill requires the same neutralisation, but this time on the scale of the State, by means of a 'cosmopolitical totality, *ein weltbürgerliche Ganzes*', the federation of States. In this way the enthusiasm which is publicly revealed on the occasion of the French Revolution – firstly because it is an extreme sublime feeling, secondly because this feeling already requires a formal culture of skill, and finally because this culture in turn has as its horizon civil and perhaps international peace – this enthusiasm, then, in itself, 'not merely allows us to hope for human improvement, but *is* this improvement, insofar as its scope is within reach of what is possible at present'.

So not just any aesthetic phrase can provide the proof (*beweisen*) that humanity is in constant progress in improvement – but only the phrase of the extreme sublime. The beautiful will not do: it is only a symbol of the good. But because the sublime is the affective paradox, the paradox of feeling (of feeling publicly) in common a formlessness for which there is no image or sensory intuition – because of this, the sublime constitutes an 'as if' presentation of the Idea of civil and even cosmopolitical society, and therefore of the Idea of morality; where however there can be no such presentation in experience. This is how the sublime feeling is a sign. This sign does no more than indicate a free causality, but it nonetheless counts as proof for the phrase affirming progress: since spectating mankind must *already* have made progress in culture to be able to feel this feeling, or in other words to make this sign, by its 'way of thinking' the Revolution. This sign *is* progress in its present state, as far as can be, although civil societies are not, far from it, close to the Republican regime, nor States close to worldwide federation.

The faculty of judgement at work in critical philosophy (in Kant writing the *Contest of Faculties*) sees a sign of history in the enthusiasm of the people for the Revolution, because it is a proof of the progress of the faculty of judgement in mankind as a whole as a natural species. However, this faculty appeals to the anticipated bond of the *sensus communis* and, in feeling, mankind judges the Revolution to be sublime, despite its lack of form. This sign is indicative when it is evaluated against the rule of presentation of the phrases of historical knowledge: it is a simple *Begebenheit* among the *Gegebene* of historical data open to intuitions. But in the family of the strange phrases of judgement it is a proof for the Kantian phrase which judges that there is progress, since it is *itself* this phrase of the people, which is not 'spoken', to be sure, but which is publicly expressed as a feeling which can in principle be shared, on the occasion of an 'abstract' *datum*. Kant's reflecting phrase, 'there is progress' does no more than reflect the 'there is progress' of the people, which is necessarily implied in their enthusiasm.

This is why Kant can continue rather solemnly: 'Without the mind of a seer, I now maintain that I can predict [*vorhersagen*] from the aspects and precursor-signs [*Vorzeichen*] of our times, the achievement [*Erreichung*] of this end, and with it, at the same time, the progressive improvement of mankind, a progress which henceforth cannot be totally reversible.' For, adds Kant, 'a phenomenon of this kind in human history *can never be forgotten* [*vergisst sich nicht mehr*]'. No politician (the politician of politics, whom Kant calls the 'political moralist') would have been 'subtle enough to extract from the previous course of things' this capacity for improvement in human nature, discovered by enthusiasm. He adds, 'Only nature and freedom combined within mankind in accordance with principles of right, have enabled us to forecast [to promise, *verheissen*] it; but only in non-determined fashion in terms of time, and only as a chance *Begebenheit*.' The aspects of intemporality and fortuitousness remind us of the necessarily, determinedly indeterminate character of the 'transition' between nature (i.e. the Revolution and the pathological aspect of the feeling it arouses) and freedom (i.e. the tension towards the moral Idea of absolute Good which is the other, universal and disinterested, aspect of the same feeling).

'There is progress': the critical judge can legitimate this phrase every time he can present a sign to be a referent for this assertion. But he cannot say *when* such 'objects' will present themselves, because historical sequences forming a series only give data to the historian (data which are at best statistically regular) – and never signs. The historico-political only presents itself to assertions through *cases* which operate not as examples, still less as schemes, but as complex hypotyposes (perhaps what Adorno was asking for under the name *Modelle*); the most complex being the most certain. Popular enthusiasm for the Revolution is a highly validating case for the historico-political phrase, and thus permits a very certain hypotyposis, for the simple reason that it is itself a highly *improbable* hypotyposis (recognising the Idea of the republic in a 'formless' empirical *datum* in which 'grandeur and force' are revealed). As for the philosophy of history which cannot even be considered in critical thought, it is an illusion born of signs being a semblance of examples or schemes.

It seems to me that the *datum* (which can only be a *Begebenheit*) which we are dealing with, the *Begebenheit* which marks what has been called 'postmodernity' to designate our time, is (if you will allow me to use a symbol – but the critical judge *must* allow me to use it) – this *Begebenheit* is the feeling produced by the fission of the great discursive nuclei I mentioned at the beginning of this lecture.

As the *Begebenheit* Kant was faced with was occasioned by the French Revolution, the *Begebenheit* we shall have to think through as philosophers and moral politicians, and which is in no way homologous to the enthusiasm of 1789 (since it is not aroused by the Idea of one purpose, but by the Idea of several purposes or even by Ideas of heterogeneous purposes) – this *Begebenheit* for our time, then, would induce a new type of sublime, more paradoxical still than that of enthusiasm, a sublime in which we would feel not only the irremediable gap between an Idea and what presents itself to 'realise' that Idea, but also the gap between the various families of phrases and their respective legitimate presentations.

At the beginning of this lecture, I named certain events which provide a paradoxical, negative occasion for this highly cultivated community sense to reveal itself publicly : Auschwitz, Budapest 1956, May 1968 . . .

Each one of these abysses, and others, asks to be explored with precision in its specificity. The fact remains that all of them liberate judgement, that if they are to be felt, judgement must take place without a criterion, and that this feeling becomes in turn a sign of history. But however negative the signs to which most of the proper names of our political history give rise, we should nevertheless have to judge them *as if* they proved that this history had moved on a step in its progress; i.e. in the culture of skill and of will. This step would consist in the fact that it is not only the Idea of a *single* purpose which would be pointed to in our feeling, but already the Idea that this purpose consists in the formation and free exploration of Ideas *in the plural*, the Idea that this end is the beginning of the *infinity of heterogeneous finalities.* Everything that fails to satisfy this fission of the single purpose, everything that presents itself as the 'realisation' of a single purpose, as is the case with the phrase of politics, of the 'political moralist', is felt not to be up to (*angemenen*), not akin to (*abgezielt*) the infinite capacity of phrases given in the feeling aroused by this fission. And when I say : not commensurable, this is the least one can say. This pretension to realise a single purpose can, as we know, be threatening enough to embalm what is already dead, as is the case in Red Square, or to give life to a fable by terror and massacre, as under the Third Reich.

The idea of commensurability (in the sense of affinity with no rule to act as an established criterion) is of decisive importance in Kant's thought, and especially his thought about the historico-political. But for us today it moderates too strongly the event of fission. The exploding of language into families of heteronomous language-games is the theme that Wittgenstein, whether he knew it or not, took from Kant and which he took as far as he could towards rigorous description. For Kant's judge it is not enough to decide one way or the other; he must also admit at least the coexistence of heteronomous phrases. The obligation to compromise presupposes an attraction or general interaction of families of phrases, despite or because of their heteronomy.

Kant pulls the idea of this drive to commerce between phrases down onto that of a subject which otherwise would fall to pieces, and of a rationality which otherwise would be in conflict with itself and no longer worthy of its name. We today – and this is part of the *Begebenheit* of our time – feel that the fission given in this *Begeben-*

heit attacks that subject and that rationality too. Since Marx, we have learned that what presents itself as unity for the phrases of the postmodern Babel, as something that is capable of verifying them, at least in experience subject to concepts and direct presentation – we have learned that this is the imposter-subject and blindly calculating rationality called Capital, especially when it lays hold of phrases themselves in order to commercialise them and make surplus-value out of them in the new condition of the *Gemeinwesen* called 'computerised society'. But in the unnamed feeling I have suggested we make the *Begebenheit* of our time, we can easily find what we need to judge the pretension of Capital's phrase to validate all phrases according to its criterion of performativity, and the imposture which puts that phrase in the place of the critical judge – to judge this pretension and this imposture, to criticise them and to re-establish the rights of the critical tribunal – which will, however, not be the same as the tribunal of Kant's critical philosophy. For we cannot judge them according to the Idea of man and within a philosophy of the subject, but only according to the 'transitions' between heterogeneous phrases, and respecting their heterogeneity. This is why a philosophy of phrases is more 'akin' to this *Begebenheit* than a philosophy of the faculties of a subject. But then, what can *a* tribunal be? Is the only purpose of the reflective function which is ours to transform, as Kant thought, dispute [*différend*] into litigation, by substituting the law-court for the battle-field? Is not its aim also that of emphasising disputes, even at risk of aggravating them, of giving a language to what cannot be expressed in the language of the judge, even if he is a critical judge?

NOTE

'The Sign of History' was first delivered as the inaugural Michel Benamou memorial lecture at the Center for Twentieth-Century Studies, Milwaukee, in 1982.

Translated by Geoff Bennington.

History as text

Language as history/history as language: Saussure and the romance of etymology

DEREK ATTRIDGE

I

Once upon a time, in the realm of literary theory, 'history' stood as an unchallengeable reference-point, a solid and never-failing base for radical and conservative alike; now it has become a question difficult enough to generate a noisy debate with no obvious prospect of agreement or compromise. If it were possible to ask unproblematically: 'What is the historical origin of this disquieting state of affairs?' one answer would no doubt be: 'Saussure's influential distinction in the *Course in General Linguistics* between *diachrony* and *synchrony*, between language as an entity constantly changing through time, and language as a system existing at a given moment, and, more particularly, his privileging of the latter over the former'. From this source, the historian of our problem about history would trace the structuralist bracketing of temporality (and hence of social, economic and political change) in the interests of an undivided attention to system and structure, and would move from there to the post-structuralist inheritance of this unconcern with history (the name Foucault receiving honourable mention as a somewhat unaccountable exception). Thus, to take a representative example, Frank Lentricchia refers in *After the New Criticism* to the 'insistent charge that Saussure and his structuralist progeny suffer from a failure of historical consciousness that stems from the hierarchizing of synchrony and diachrony',[1] an accusation he finds in work by Fredric Jameson and Edward Said. And Lentricchia himself is in substantial agreement: 'It is clear that the recent structuralist inability to come to terms with the diachronic and executive dimensions of discourse has led to the Platonic pursuit of the taxonomy or model as transcendentals' (117). More recently, Terry Eagleton, in *Literary Theory: An Introduction*, has made a similar criticism, though without attempting to implicate Plato.[2]

Does Saussure really deserve the blame for our fallen condition? Is it accurate to portray his linguistic theory as profoundly and damagingly anti-historical, a portrayal which is a foundation-stone of Jameson's *Prison-House of Language* as well as a crucial staging-post in Lentricchia's *After the New Criticism*? Such a view, and it's a fairly widespread one, has first of all to come to terms with Saussure's own interest (and reputation) in the field of historical linguistics, evident in his *Mémoire* on the Indo-European vowel-system and in the fact that the *Course in General Linguistics*, though you would never guess this from most commentaries on it, devotes more space to diachronic than to synchronic language study. That the priority given in the *Course* to synchronic linguistics is a methodological one should be clear enough to any conscientious reader: diachrony simply does not exist for the ordinary language-user (even a feeling that certain words are older than others is a synchronic fact which may or may not have diachronic underpinning). To analyse language, therefore, as the knowledge and practice of the speaker and the community, diachronic facts must be ignored, however tempting they might be to the learned analyst. The continuing emphasis in the *Course* is on the necessary *separation* of diachronic and synchronic approaches, as different kinds of linguistics involving different procedures and different goals. And though this separation produces difficulties for diachronic (and indeed synchronic) linguistics which Saussure himself never overcomes and to which we shall return, it does not mean that he regards the historical study of language as uninteresting or unimportant.

Lentricchia is able to represent Saussure's careful distinction as a *rejection* of diachronic linguistics by assimilating it to a quite different distinction, that between *langue* and *parole*. In making the latter distinction, Saussure is indeed separating what he considers susceptible to systematic study (a language as a shared system) from what he feels is not (individual acts of uttering and understanding speech), but he makes it absolutely clear, using a diagram to reinforce his point, that synchrony and diachrony are both aspects of *langue*, and both are worthy of the linguist's attention (139/98).[3] Lentricchia blurs the two distinctions by leaping over a hundred pages of the *Course* in mid-quotation, and supplying his own causal connection: '"From the very outset we must put both feet on the ground of language (*langue*) and use language as the norm of all other manifestations of speech" [25/9] because language "is a system whose parts can and must be considered in their synchronic solidarity" [124/87]' (116). In the first statement, Saussure is fixing on *langue* as the object of study rather than *langage* (the general phenomenon of human language, misleadingly rendered in the translation used by Lentricchia as 'speech') precisely because it is amenable to analysis – both synchronic and diachronic; in the second he is giving methodological priority to the synchronic approach, for the reasons I've already touched on.[4]

Saussure's third famous distinction, between syntagmatic and associative (or paradigmatic) relations, is also conflated with the distinction between diachrony and synchrony. 'It is clear', states Jameson, 'that Saussure's bias is for the synchronic, for the associative or paradigmatic, as against the diachronic or the syntagmatic' (*Prison-House*, 38). It's not clear at all, in fact, that there is any privileging one way or the other in the paradigmatic/syntagmatic distinction; Saussure argues, quite rightly, that they function with complete interdependence in discourse (177–80/128–31). Nor is there any particular link between synchronic and paradigmatic, or between diachronic and syntagmatic; after all, it is the paradigmatic relations which connect the present utterance with the past via associations stored in the memory, and the syntagmatic relations which co-exist, as Saussure puts it, *in praesentia*.[5] The notion that syntagmatic relations occur in a temporal dimension (between the utterance of a verb and the utterance of its object, say), and therefore belong exclusively to diachrony, rests on mistaken conceptions of both syntagmatic relations and of diachrony: as rule-governed relationships enshrined in the language-system, syntagmatic connections (which would include morphological and syntactic rules) are as much part of the synchronic state as paradigmatic ones, and a diachronic description of language, far from being concerned with utterances as they are spoken in time, deals with changes in the system of paradigmatic and syntagmatic relations occurring *across* time (194–7/140–3).

All three distinctions are combined in order to accuse Saussure of a bias towards the transcendental as against the historical: thus Lentricchia summarises, and endorses, Jameson's view that 'the distinction between syntagm and paradigm is a disguised form of the enabling opposition between diachrony and synchrony, *parole* and *langue*, which generated Saussure's entire theory: the determinate syntagm is temporal whereas the indeterminate paradigm is transcendental' (*After the New Criticism*, 120).[6] One doubts whether even the maligned structuralists would have jettisoned so much in the way of content to collapse a series of oppositions into one. Lentricchia's conclusion could easily be reversed: one might argue that syntagmatic rules are transcendental in that they exist in a fixed form prior to and independent of the subject's employment of them, whereas the unlimited openness of the paradigm to individual associations and specific contexts – and thence to history, in one of its senses – is truly temporal. Indeed, such a reversal is implicit in Lentricchia's own citation of the New Critics' willingness to give Marvell's 'vegetable love' a mid-twentieth century meaning (121): here the syntagmatic relations have remained relatively stable, while the associations of the word 'vegetable' bear the imprint of three centuries of change.

Although both Jameson and Lentricchia cast Saussure in the role of original sinner, both tend to oscillate in their judgements, seeking a point of view from which his work can be redeemed as a necessary and positive stage in modern intellectual history. It's perhaps not surprising, then, that Lentricchia is prepared to excuse Saussure, for all his faults, and shift some of the responsibility for our current malaise onto his 'progeny', structuralists and post-structuralists (a characteristic strategy of the revisionist historian, of course, and one that Lentricchia also applies to Derrida and *his* 'progeny'). Thus he awards high marks to the notion of the arbitrariness of the sign, by which 'Saussure's linguistics situates discourse, literary or otherwise, in its true home in human history', since 'to designate the sign as arbitrary is simultaneously to call attention to it as a temporal and cultural production' (119). (Terry Eagleton makes a similar point about literary structuralism in *Literary Theory*, 107–8; and for a realisation of this potential, one need only turn to Barthes's *Mythologies.*[7]) But Lentricchia's willingness to mitigate the harshness of the charge against Saussure doesn't obscure the negative thrust of his general argument, which colours his entire reading of recent intellectual events: that the very notion of system and structure, so potent in modern literary theory, and so evidently derived from Saussurean linguistics, is fundamentally and inexcusably anti-historical. What I wish to argue, by examining one aspect of the interface between synchrony and diachrony, is that Saussure's achievement lay not in clarifying (as he hoped to do) but in *problematising* the notion of history and its relation to the present, and that if we want to escape the drift away from history that characterises so much literary theory today – and the writings of Jameson, Lentricchia, Said, and Eagleton have been of the utmost importance in warning us of the dangers of that drift – we need to work through the problematic with which Saussure confronts us. After Saussure, there's no going back to a simple notion of the explanatory force of history in any domain constituted, like language (and like literature), by systems of equivalence (what Saussure terms 'value').[8] And it's in this sense that one might after all posit the *Course in General*

Linguistics as the origin of our present debate – except that it's precisely such an unproblematised notion of origin as explanation that his work shows to be impossible, raising questions in advance about the thesis *and* methodology of a history of theory like *After the New Criticism*.

II

Probably the most familiar area of diachronic linguistics to the non-specialist is the history of words. Etymology is a field in which the productiveness of Saussure's sharp distinction between synchrony and diachrony can be clearly and convincingly shown, and he uses it illustratively at several points. The first example he gives to demonstrate that the distinction is 'absolute and does not admit of compromise' is the connection between two French phrases, *un mur décrépi* ('a peeling wall') and *un homme décrépit* ('a decrepit man') (119/83). For a contemporary speaker of French these homophones are related by more than mere coincidence of sound, and actually come together in an expression like *une façade décrépite* ('a dilapidated façade'). Yet their histories are quite distinct. *Décrépi*, etymologists tell us, comes from *dé+crépir*, *crépir* being to 'rough-render', a descendant of Latin *crispus*, 'wavy'; *décrépir* is therefore 'to remove the plaster from', and *se décrépir* 'to peel'. *Décrépit*, on the other hand, is derived from the Latin adjective *decrepitus* ('worn out with age'). A comparable English example would be the connection perceived by most speakers between the words *rage* and *outrage*, where the former comes from the French *rage* and the Latin *rabies* ('madness'), and the latter is a noun formed from *ultra* ('beyond') and the suffix *-age*, so that an outrage is a 'going beyond the bounds', and has no historical connection with *rage*.[9]

Saussure's position here is, in its own terms, unassailable; if such coincidences of sound become meaningful parts of the linguistic system for the speakers of the language, they cannot be dismissed as 'illegitimate' or 'historically unfounded'; they simply become facts of language. 'Outrage' and 'rage' *are* synchronically related, no matter what counterpressures the etymological dictionary and the learned philologist bring to bear. What is under attack here is the common assumption that a speaker who has a knowledge of etymological history is in some sense a 'better' speaker of English.[10] Miss Jean Brodie's faith in etymology is as ill-founded as her belief in her own 'prime' when she tells her girls: 'The word "education" comes from the root *e* from *ex*, out, and *duco*, I lead. It means a leading out.'[11] Such a view of etymology implies the belief that the earlier a meaning the better, which must depend on a diagnosis of cultural decline (Miss Brodie, we remember, is an admirer of Franco, Mussolini and Hitler) or a faith in a lost Golden Age of lexical purity and precision. The word *etymology* itself derives from such an assumption, and offers its own self-confirmation : its Greek root means 'discourse on true meaning'; while the Book of Genesis offers a different version of the same myth. This view of etymology is one version of the widespread notion that words have *authentic meanings*, a notion instilled early in formal education and powerfully upheld by the ubiquity and status of the dictionary as a cultural institution.[12] Although it flirts with history, it's a deeply anti-historical attitude, replacing the social and historical determination of meaning (operating upon the arbitrary sign) by a transcendent 'true' meaning. Just as some literary theorists cling to the notion of authentic meaning for a text, not because this notion is consistent with itself or with the facts of literary history, but because they assume that to give it up is to invite unbridled relativism (and perhaps even revolution), so there's a common assumption that every word must have its authentic meaning, or else meaning could not exist at all. And just as the literary theorist may turn to authorial intention, or to the original readership, as the only source (however inaccessible) of an authentic meaning, so the theorist of language turns to etymological origin. It's worth noting how often cheaper dictionaries prefer to dispense with obsolete meanings, which are of real value in reading the texts of the past, rather than with etymologies which are of no practical use whatever but appear to guarantee the identity and authenticity of the words they claim to 'explain'. Saussure's insistence on the separation of synchrony and diachrony, replacing 'authentic' meaning by the meanings possessed for a specific group at a specific time, opens the door to history, while a naive view of the historicity of language completely closes it.[13]

The faith in 'authentic meaning', and in etymology as the key to it, is a popular survival of a theory that remained influential in Western thinking about language for a long period. It was propounded by the followers of Heraclitus (Plato's Cratylus among them) and was a central strand in medieval thought, as indicated by the extensive use made by Aquinas of the collection of bizarre etymologies by Isidore of Seville.[14] Its heyday was in the late eighteenth century, when, spurred by Condillac's arguments to trace in the forms of language the lineaments of the human mind, linguistic students devoted a great deal of ingenuity and energy to the search for primary meanings, unhampered by the constraints of rigid principles or consistent methodology. The massive – and massively influential – work of men like Charles de Brosses in France (*Traité de la formation méchanique des langues*, 1765) and John Horne Tooke in England (*The Diversions of Purley*, 1786–1805) made full use of the freedom offered by the etymological method,[15] at times almost justifying Voltaire's famous jibe: 'Etymology is the science in which the vowels count for nothing and the consonants for very little' (outdone a century or so later by Mark Twain's derivation of 'Middletown' from 'Moses' by dropping '-oses' and adding '-iddletown').

In the nineteenth century, however, the belief in authentic original meaning waned (who after Darwin – himself influenced by the study of etymology – could claim that the origin of an evolutionary process revealed the true nature of an existing specimen?); and the unconstrained free-for-all that characterised late eighteenth-century etymology was countered by the introduction of rigid principles, primarily with reference to the laws of sound-change enunciated in the new positivistic science of philology. A derivation which involved a phonetic change could only be accepted if that change was in accordance with the established laws; and this seemed to provide a new and trustworthy foundation for an objective science of etymology. It rested, in fact, on nothing more stable than a vicious circle: as Saussure observes, to say that the identity of Latin *mare* and French *mer* is guaranteed by the fact that their relationship observes a recognised law is to put the cart before the horse, since such 'identities' between words in different languages or periods have to be postulated before any law can be formulated (249/182). Nevertheless, etymology became accepted as a reliable and important branch of linguistics, and the work of scholars like Skeat, Partridge, Onions, and the compilers of the New (later Oxford) English Dictionary entrenched it firmly in the public's image of the language-specialist, where it still remains.

What kind of history was represented in the new etymology, no longer conceived of as the search for authentic meaning in the sands of time? Let us pause on a characteristic example from the early twentieth century: Ernest Weekley's much reprinted collection of etymological divertissements, *The Romance of Words* (first published in 1912)[16] (a companion volume to *The Romance of Names*, *Adjectives and Other Words*, *Words Ancient and Modern*, and

More Words Ancient and Modern). In a section devoted to the names of high functionaries, to take a typical discussion, Weekley traces *chancellor* back to 'a kind of door-keeper in charge of a *chancel*, a latticed barrier'; *constable* and *marshal* back to the names for servants who tended horses; and *steward* (as well as the Royal House of Stuart) to the *sty-ward* who 'looked after his master's pigs' (87–90). But what does it mean to say that *steward* and *sty-ward* (or *stigweard*) are really the 'same word', as etymology invites us to do? They can only be so from a completely transhistorical viewpoint; as Jameson points out (*Prison-House*, 6), they were never the same word for a speaker in history. (Indeed, the word 'word' is given a wholly new sense in etymology: *steward* and *sty-ward,* like many an etymologically-connected pair, differ in both form and meaning.) It is evident that, far from reinforcing the presence and pressure of history, philological etymology drains it of its heterogeneity and materiality: substituting the myth of Progress for the myth of the Golden Age, it adopts a teleological orientation, and takes as its guide-rope through the welter of the past a present crystallisation of signifier and signified, oblivious of the fact that the past had no knowledge of or use for the present unit. It assumes an unproblematic notion of 'identity' across time; it claims to stand outside the history it relates; and it finds its rewards in 'explanations' that are neat, ingenious, or ideologically satisfying – and therefore 'convincing'. The analogy with certain other kinds of history need not be spelled out.[17]

Not surprisingly, the rise of the more rigorous enterprise of modern structural linguistics effectively put paid to the scientific pretensions of etymology – partly, no doubt, when the Saussurean divorce between synchrony and diachrony left no room for even the most attenuated hope that etymology could illuminate current meanings. Saussure's own comments on etymology in the *Course*, in a brief Appendix to the section on diachronic linguistics (259–60/189–90), are dismissive: etymology mixes descriptions of sound-change and meaning-change, it draws indiscriminately on phonetics, morphology, semantics, and other branches of linguistics, it lacks a coherent methodology, and it fails to scrutinise its own procedures. Text-books on language and linguistics now seldom have sections on 'Etymology', and although the fascination with the origins of words persists, it's more likely to manifest itself in the pages of the Sunday newspaper. The occasional linguist who champions etymology today has to do so in defensive terms; thus Yakov Malkiel writes in 1962 of etymology's 'temporarily forfeited controlling position within linguistics',[18] as if it were a King Arthur whose time will come again. And Ernest Weekley is less well remembered as the author of *The Romance of Words* than as the Nottingham professor who, in the year in which that volume was first published, introduced his wife Frieda to an ex-student of his called D. H. Lawrence.

III

Saussure's exposure of the fallacy of assimilating current meaning to etymological derivation, then, is only anti-historical in so far as it attacks a simplistic view of history and its relation to present structures of signification. In his distinction between a synchronic and a diachronic approach, Saussure poses two meanings of 'history' against each other: history as the complex of social and material forces which modify the individual and the community in a succession of experienced presents, and history as a supra-individual, supra-communal, transtemporal continuum, genetically or teleologically oriented. Jameson, although he portrays Saussure's distinction as a rejection of history, spells out very clearly the implications for historiography of the two kinds of linguistics, synchronic and diachronic: 'The former lies in the immediate lived experience of the native speaker; the latter rests on a kind of intellectual construction, the result of comparisons between one moment of lived time and another by someone who stands outside, who has thus substituted a purely intellectual continuity for a lived one' (*Prison-House*, 6).[19] Thus in the act of freeing synchronic linguistics from the yoke of a naive and essentialist conception of history, Saussure places diachronic linguistics, and the mode of historiography it represents, in a very difficult position. In particular, the historian of value-systems (cultural, political, economic) who wishes to make the past bear fruitfully upon the present is denied a simple notion of origin as explanation, a straightforward appeal to the way things were in order to change the way they are. To take a somewhat generalised example, the ideological system of values which helps to maintain the class-structure in Britain today is obviously the product of history, but it functions in the present, synchronically, in ignorance of history (or, more accurately, by virtue of a particular myth of history). Just as a word cannot be revealed in its authenticity by the production of an etymological origin, so this structure cannot be justified, as Burkean conservatism would seek to do, by referring to its history; but by the same token it cannot be discredited by its history either, any more than a linguistic usage we may wish to see disappear because of its sexist or racist connotations can be dislodged by an appeal to earlier forms.

In attempting to escape the damaging effects of this distinction between past and present, with its enfeeblement of diachronic historiography, there would seem to be little point in returning to the discredited notion of etymology. Yet there remains something we haven't accounted for, something compelling in the revelation of an unexpected etymological origin that isn't quite negated by the Saussurean dismissal. Even Saussure's own discussion of *décrépi(t)* has an interest beyond its usefulness as an example : we can't simply disregard the connection between peeling walls and the impotence of old age once our attention has been drawn to it, and if we take Saussure's hint and trace the words further back the picture grows even more interesting. Latin *crispus*, the source of *crépir*, referred to curly hair, an attribute of youth rather than age among the Romans; while *decripitus* divides etymologically into *de+crepitus*, in which *de* could be an intensifier of the symptoms of age suggested by *crepitus* – 'rattling, clattering, chattering or noisily breaking wind' – or an indication of a *reversal* of meaning, in which case *decripitus* presents old people not as garrulous and flatulent, but, in the words of Lewis and Short (trying by a dab of poetic colour to enforce their choice of derivation), 'creeping about like shadows'. (One amateur etymologist who was fascinated by these tracings that yield opposite meanings within the same word was, of course, Freud.[20]) Saussure himself can't escape the lure of etymology, however difficult it is to say what it illuminates : he asserts, surprisingly, that 'the [diachronic] conditions which have produced a [synchronic] state throw light upon its true nature [*véritable nature*] and guard us from certain misconceptions' (128/90). Yet his argument has been that there's no such thing as a synchronic misconception : *décrépi* and *décrépit are* related, however much the etymologist may protest, and a word's 'true nature' is not a matter of history but of its present systematic relations. He even argues etymologically himself, justifying the usefulness of the idea of 'language articulation' by a reference to the meaning of *articulus* in Latin (26/10), and, as Derrida has pointed out in *Glas*,[21] appealing to etymology to defend the arbitrariness of the sign against the encroachments of onomatopoeia (102/69). And he becomes prescriptive in just the way that is elsewhere the object of his attack when he compares the alternative pronunciations of the French word for 'wager' : *gažür* and *gažör*. 'The real question', he insists, 'is etymological: *gageure* was formed from *gager*, like *turnure* from *tourner*... Only *gažür* can be justified' (53/31).

The temptation to turn for support to etymology isn't peculiar to Saussure: indeed, it occurs throughout the Western philosophical tradition, and for many writers it's provided an important mode of argument: among the more obvious texts one could cite are Plato's *Cratylus*, Nietzsche's *Genealogy of Morals*, Freud's essay on 'The Uncanny', and the many etymological tracings of Heidegger and Derrida. Philip Sidney, in a gesture typical of Renaissance humanism, offers as a proof of poetry's importance the supposed derivation of Roman and Greek words for 'poet'; Vico founds an epistemology and a historical method upon etymology; and post-structuralist writing seems to find the etymological turn irresistible. If this practice has no 'truth' to offer about the language we speak, what is its function? Why is the appeal of etymology so powerful and so enduring? What is the status of etymology after Saussure?

Here we can call upon *La preuve par l'étymologie*, a brilliant little book by Jean Paulhan which is concerned with just this topic.[22] Paulhan provides a forceful statement of the Saussurean position: he remarks, for instance, that we may learn something about the history of cooking when we find that *foie* comes from Latin *ficus* because the Romans ate liver stuffed with figs, but we learn nothing about the current meaning of *foie* (47).[23] Indeed, Paulhan points out, etymology is more likely to mislead us as to current meaning – *sou* comes from *soldus*, piece of gold: *chrétien* and *crétin* come from the same root (49). But having banished etymology from the realms of logic and science, he welcomes it instead in a different realm (and one which perhaps subsumes those of logic and science): the realm of rhetoric, where it has a subtle and scintillating role to play. Its rhetorical partner, from which it's sometimes indistinguishable, is the *calembour* or *paranomasia*, the play on words. In both devices, the same process occurs: two similar-sounding but distinct signifiers are brought together, and the surface relationship between them invested with meaning through the inventiveness and rhetorical skill of the writer. If that meaning is in the form of a postulated connection between present and past, what we have is etymology; if it's in the form of a postulated connection within the present, the result is word-play.[24] Word-play, in other words, is to etymology as synchrony is to diachrony. Thus it's an etymological move to write that *steward* and *sty-ward* are related through the historical rise in status of the swineherd, but a play on words to write: 'I'll gild the faces of the grooms withal,/For it must seem their guilt' (*Macbeth*, II. ii. 53–4). It's not hard to imagine the etymology and the paranomasia exchanged, and a poet exploiting the echo between *sty-ward* and *steward* while an etymologist derives *guilt* from *gild* and *gold* (no doubt finding a useful stepping-stone in German *Geld*). (The *OED* in fact regards what for Weekley is etymology as no more than word-play, though not without a suspicion of relishing it in the act of discarding it: 'There is no ground for the assumption that *stigweard* originally meant "keeper of the pig-sties".') Edmund in *King Lear* may seem to be playing the etymologist when he exclaims: 'Why brand they us/With base? with baseness? bastardy?' (I. ii. 9–10) but he is in fact playing the poet: the words *base* and *bastard*, the etymologists tell us, are historically unrelated. Saussure himself is on the way to enunciating the connection between etymology and word-play when he insists that 'Etymology is before everything the explanation of words by research into their connections with other words', and the example he gives of what he calls 'the most important part of etymological research' is, in fact, not etymology at all in the normal sense but the synchronic investigation of verbal relationships (259).[25]

That the etymologist is more of a poet than a scientist is by no means a new idea – Socrates, as he begins his etymological outpouring in the *Cratylus*, describes himself as one who is inspired and possessed (and the witty and ironic quality of his etymologies is certainly more literary than scientific); Sidney's glorification of the poet as God-like creator is a rhetorical rather than a logical formulation, and loses nothing of its power when Paulhan tells us that *poetes* is better translated as *librettist* than maker (60); and Vico's frequent use of etymology is related to his privileging of rhetoric, poetry and the imagination over logic and reason. Modern etymologists seem quite prepared to accept the 'poetic' aspect of their activity; thus Malkiel compares the etymologist to a pool-player 'who, through a skilful and, above all, imaginative succession of shots . . . eventually succeeds in landing all the balls in the pockets',[26] while Raimo Anttila asserts that 'the ingenuity of the etymologist and the power of his invention and combination cannot be replaced by mechanical rules'.[27] It was principally the etymologists of the late 19th and early 20th centuries who modelled their work on the natural sciences, and vigorously rejected the imaginative element: thus Skeat, in the Preface to his *Etymological Dictionary of the English Language*, deplores 'those unscrupulous inventions with which English "etymology" abounds, and which many people admire because they are "so clever" '.[28] He adds 'The number of those who literally prefer a story about a word to a more prosaic account of it, is only too large.' But, we may ask, what are etymologies if not stories? What *is* the model for the history of the word if not the biographical narrative? And what *are* Weekley's accounts of the fortunes of *steward*, *chancellor*, *constable*, and *marshal* if not versions of the Cinderella myth, that comforting fiction in a society where sty-wards tend to remain sty-wards?[29] He himself refers to his etymologies on more than one occasion as 'short stories'[30] – and it's not for nothing that his book is called *The Romance of Words.*

If, then, the etymologist is neither a tracker-down of authentic meanings buried in history, nor a detached scientist presenting an objective truth about the past, but a manipulator of words, a story-teller, a rhetorician, is etymology to be relegated once and for all to the realm of the secondary and the superfluous, in comparison with the truth-revealing synchronic analysis of the language system, or the diachronic account confined modestly to observable material changes in sound and spelling, with no importance for the present? And by analogy, is the historian of literature (or literary theory, or any aspect of the world of human discourse and signification) a mere entertainer, telling us stories which have no bearing on the present, a present given to us as a self-sufficient system whose origins are as unknowable as they are irrelevant? If this were so, it would substantiate entirely the charge that the Saussurean linguistic model leads to a rejection of history, and there would seem to be no way of retrieving history without reintroducing the confusions which Saussure so effectively exposed. Although the notion of the arbitrary sign within a synchronic system of differences valuably demonstrates that language is a product of historical forces, as Lentricchia and others have observed, we seem to be effectively prevented from making anything of that history by the very same notion.

IV

The question we're posing itself hints at the possibility of a different way of reading Saussure's *Course* which may lead to more positive answers than those we've been able to give so far: a reading which treats it not as a scientific study (couched, *faute de mieux*, in words) to be judged correct or incorrect, consistent or inconsistent, but as a verbal text, a discursive production, perhaps even as a story. And in such a reading we would need to ask where the narrative falters, where the tone betrays a struggle, where the rhetoric protests too much, since these are the points at which the strains of Saussure's enterprise, and therefore the possibilities of moving beyond it (and beyond the structuralist tradition which stems from it), will be most evident.

There *are* times – we've already noted one of them – when the serene descriptive surface of the *Course* is ruffled by the kind of prescriptive attitude that Saussure, and with him the whole tradition of modern scientific linguistics, professes to abhor. Derrida has subjected *one* of these moments to a revealing analysis in his well-known discussion of writing and speech in the *Course*, but by isolating it has given only a partial picture of the tensions at work in Saussure's text. If we return to the example of *décrépi(t)*, we may observe – indeed, it's implicit in Saussure's account – that the meanings of the two words (as of the words *rage* and *outrage* in English) have in fact been *modified* by the false (and unconscious) etymological theorising of native speakers, who assume connections between signifiers on the ground of their similarity in sound; the synchronic state of the language is thus affected not by a 'blind' external force, on which Saussure places all his emphasis, but by *the community's own interpretation of its language's history.* Pronunciation, too, can be affected by such native-speaker theorising; most of us probably pronounce the noun *outrage* with the same vowel-sound as *rage*, and not, as the 'correct' etymology would suggest, and as the *OED* stipulates, *outrij* (as in *bondage* or *breakage*). This kind of language-change is a phenomenon known as 'folk' or 'popular' etymology,[31] and it provides many a colourful passage in the annals of lexical history. Thus we are told that the word *renegade*, one who *renegues*, became as a result of a vivid image of a refugee in flight, *runagate*; or the Dutch phrase *verloren hoop*, the 'lost heap' of soldiers in the vanguard of an attack, became naturalised – and generalised – as *forlorn hope.* The 'scientific' etymologist is often to be found taking quiet pleasure in a quaint misunderstanding of the ill-educated but imaginative 'folk' that has resulted in the introduction of a new pronunciation, meaning, word, or phrase into the language. Ernest Weekley, as one might imagine, has a field-day with folk etymology.

Such changes form part of the readily observable diachronic mutation of language, and Saussure accordingly devotes a brief chapter of the section on 'Diachronic Linguistics' to 'Etymologie populaire'. But instead of merely recording the operation of folk etymology, for which his separation of synchrony from diachrony would seem to provide the perfect framework, he reveals an unexpected animus against it. It begins when we 'mangle' words ('estropier' can mean to 'cripple' or 'mutilate'), producing 'bizarre innovations', and it results in what Saussure calls 'des coq-à-l'âne' (238/173–4) (which his translators render as 'absurdities' or 'howlers'; it means arbitrary changes of direction, literally 'from cock to ass'). Folk etymology 'maltreats' words (240/174) and like onomatopoeia (itself a kind of folk etymology which derives words from non-linguistic sounds) and words created *ex nihilo* by individuals (another example of the language-user's intervention in language change), it 'is not to be taken seriously into account' and has 'only minimal importance or none at all' (242/176). And in a sentence excluded by the editors from the final version of the *Course*, Saussure uses the terms 'vicieux' ('erroneous', but with a hint of 'perverse') and 'pathologiques', ('pathological') to describe the effects of folk etymology on the language.[32]

The other kind of change which Saussure resists, and the one on which Derrida has commented in *Grammatology*,[33] is known as 'spelling pronunciation', where a phonetic alteration occurs because speakers are influenced by the way a word is spelt (thus in English it's becoming normal to give spelling-pronunciations to *often* and *forehead* instead of saying *offen* and *forrid*). Saussure's hostility to this perfectly ordinary process is again palpable, revealing itself at times in exactly the same terms he uses for, or rather against, folk etymology: 'the visual image leads to the creation of erroneous pronunciations ("*prononciations vicieuses*"); this is in a strict sense a pathological phenomenon' (53/31). Spelling pronunciations are 'des cas tératologiques' ('monstrosities'), which the linguist should 'place under observation in a special compartment' (54/32). It will be recalled that the threat of the spelling pronunciation of *gageure* (as *gažör*) is so great that, as in the case of claims for onomatopoeic derivation, Saussure is prepared to call upon the discredited testimony of etymology to reinforce his attack on it.

What is it that produces this highly emotive and ethically-coloured language, so at odds with the claim to be neutrally concerned with scientific observation? Why are folk etymology and spelling pronunciation not merely registered among the common types of language change whose effects are observable in the synchronic state of the system? (We should note that the argument that Saussure's hostility is primarily towards *writing* fails when we bring folk etymology into the picture, since here it's precisely speech unsupported by writing that is often the culprit.) Before we attempt to answer this question, we can add to these two kinds of change the effects of prescriptive intervention, the existence of which Saussure simply denies: 'Not only would an individual who wished to do so be unable to modify in any way a choice that has been made [within the language], but the community itself cannot exercise control over a single word: it is bound to the language as it exists' (104/71).[34] There is, in fact, plenty of evidence that languages *do* change as a result of prescriptive intervention: one example is the existence of spellings and often pronunciations which reflect 'reforms' carried out in the name of classical etymology. Thus the deliberately-introduced 'b' in *debt* or 'd' in *adventure* are as firmly entrenched as their more 'natural' brethren. Saussure himself cites a French example: the *d* in *poids* inserted because of a 'false etymology' (50/28). He also argues fiercely against the spelling pronunciations he hears around him, clearly hoping that he will produce an effect on the language in contradiction of his own rule.[35] Here the learned etymologist plays a role exactly equivalent to that of his popular namesake; when the former derives *aventure* from *ad-venire* and the latter derives *renegade* from *run-a-gate* they aren't doing anything essentially dissimilar – both are engaged in the kind of word-play we've discussed; both are telling stories about their language. It's not the 'correctness' or 'incorrectness' of the derivation that's at issue; what unsettles Saussure is the fact that the language undergoes a change arising directly from the intrusion of a diachronic interpretation into the synchronic system. It could be called a problem of *feedback*: the rigid insulation of synchrony from diachrony is threatened by a short-circuit, whereby history is reinscribed in the present – not as a series of 'real events' (which, having passed, can no longer intrude) but as the only way in which history *can* intervene in the present, as a theory or story of the past.[36] The chapter on folk etymology in the *Course* is largely devoted to differentiating between it and *analogy*, which is the process whereby language-users create new forms on the model of familiar ones (as when the plural *cows* came to displace the old plural *kine* by analogy with most other English plurals). Although this is also a process whereby the language-user reinterprets the language according to an 'incorrect' theory, Saussure is perfectly happy with it, regarding it as part of what he calls the 'normal functioning of language'. The crucial difference, he insists, is that analogy results from the 'forgetting' of the language's history, while folk etymology, a 'diametrically opposed process', results from a 'confused memory' of that history (240–1/175–6). The effacement of the past is 'natural', the re-activation of the past, as memory, story, or history, is 'pathological'.[37]

Saussure's hostility towards spelling pronunciation now appears in a different light from that shed on it by Derrida's reading : it's not just the hostility of the phonocentrist towards writing, but a reluctance to accept that a word's spelling, a record (accurate or not) of its past, should modify its present state.[38] Spelling pronunciation joins folk etymology and learned prescriptivism as a means whereby the language user and the language community intervene, whether consciously or unconsciously, to alter the language system, on the basis of a diachronic model completely at odds with Saussure's own. Saussure's emphasis, we recall, is entirely on language's openness to external modification by material and humanly uncontrollable forces (and it's in this sense that it situates discourse, to use Lentricchia's phrase, 'in its true home in human history'). What he regards as secondary is history as intellectual construct, the history of the etymologist and the theorist of language (academic or popular), and when history in *this* sense interferes it threatens the whole distinction between synchrony and diachrony, and therefore the stability and self-consistency of the system, and has to be excluded.[39] The stories we tell about the past are all very well in their place, but they have no right to change the way we live. Saussure's failed attempts to control folk etymology, spelling pronunciation, and prescriptive modification point the way towards a different view of history, one which will not simply reverse his privileging of synchrony over diachrony, but will encourage what Saussure tried to forbid: the entry of diachrony *into* synchrony – the entry of history into our current experience and current struggles.

V

One could, no doubt, trace similar uneasy spots produced by the phenomenon of feedback in much structuralist literary theory, moments when the claim to theorise from a point outside the history of texts and readers comes up against the effects that precisely such theorising has upon that history, or when the denial of the validity of authorial intention or historical meaning confronts the fact that reading is inescapably affected by conceptions of authorial intention or historical meaing (just as language is affected by its users' belief in etymological and onomatopoeic motivation, however 'erroneous'). Bearing the wider implications of our linguistic model in mind, let us ask how we might build into a theory of language the effects of popular and learned etymology, and of spelling and prescriptive arguments, instead of attempting, like Saussure, to exclude them; how we might acknowledge the feedback of history into the here and now, and the determination of language not by 'blind' forces but by human, social, and political agency, both conscious and unconscious. To do so would mean regarding language as *inherently* unstable, internally (and eternally) shifting between synchrony and diachrony – not in the sense that the past can itself reach forward and affect the present, but that the present is always inhabited and modified by theories (or stories) of the past, popular and scholarly. Synchrony is an impossible fiction, not because language is always changing – Saussure knew that better than most – but because even as a methodological hypostatisation it's not consistent with itself. Folk etymology and spelling pronunciation are only points at which language's difference from itself becomes obvious; if the way I pronounce *outrage* implies an etymological theory, isn't this the case with every word I utter, using *this* rather than *that* pronunciation? Am I not, as a literate English speaker, *always* suspended between written and spoken forms, modifying each by its relation to, and difference from, the other? Doesn't my knowledge of past forms of the language (whether accurate or not) necessarily affect my present use and understanding of it? And aren't the coincidences of sound upon which word-play is based continually subverting the dictionary's attempt to keep words (and meanings) in separate compartments?[40] Language and theories about language (popular even more than academic) must be seen as constantly in a condition of mutual interchange, and for this reason a neutral descriptive linguistics is impossible; and the same goes for literature and theories about literature. The way people speak has been modified in this century by supposedly nonprescriptive linguists; the way people read has been modified by supposedly metacritical literary structuralists; the way people act has been modified by supposedly objective historians.[41] And more than that: those self-proclaimed 'objective' theories have always been formulated in the service of certain goals, usually concealed but occasionally emerging with disarming clarity, as in the following sentence from Weekley's preface to the third (1917) edition of the book already mentioned: 'In the interval since the last edition of *The Romance of Words* the greatest *Romance of*

Deeds in our story has been written in the blood of our noblest and best' (ix).

Weekley's comment is interesting not just because of the overt political rhetoric, but because he succeeds in accommodating even the First World War to the same narrative model that serves him so well in his etymological derivations. This brings us back to the question of etymology's status as imaginative story-telling (and, by implication, the similar status of all historical writing). It's from their success as stories with good plots and ingenious word-play that folk etymologies (and for that matter learned etymologies) derive their power to change the language, not from their accuracy;[42] thus Greek *alcuon* 'kingfisher' became Latin (and English) *halcyon* through the charming but mistaken belief that the Greek word was made up of *hals* (sea) and *kyon* (conceiving), with reference to the fable that the halcyon broods on her nest floating on the calm sea. Similarly, the power possessed by history, whether that of the professional historian, the journalist, or the man-in-the-street, to sustain or to alter prevailing value-systems depends on the success of the stories it tells. (Etymology and word-play tell us, in fact, a story about the interchangeability of *history* and *story*, even more striking in the doubleness of *histoire* and *Geschichte*.) Hayden White and Fredric Jameson have argued, in different ways, for the centrality of narrative in historiography, and Jonathan Culler has portrayed theories of reading as stories themselves.[43] As I tried to show in the first part of this essay, the version of Saussure's theory produced by Jameson and Lentricchia conforms less to the 'objective reality' of Saussure's text than to the demands of the story they wish to tell about twentieth-century literary theory.[44]

Not only do historical and theoretical narratives, if they are convincing enough, change the way we think and act, but the theories *about* them can do the same: thus the story that the etymologists tell about the 'folk' and their picturesque wit, their resourceful ingenuity, their quaint misapprehensions, has itself had an effect on our understanding of language change, thanks to its conformity to a certain romantic class-stereotype.[45] (The *OED* itself half admits that its etymology for *halcyon* is only a fable about a fable: 'The spelling *halcyon*,' it begins, 'is supposed to have arisen out of the fancy that . . .') One of the most compelling stories about history (which is also told about literary theory and about linguistics) is the one about the importance and achievability of strict objectivity – of history *without* story – and Saussure remains one of the most persuasive tellers of it. (The vigorous rhetoric of *After the New Criticism* relates the same story, and, in this respect at least, Lentricchia must be numbered among Saussure's 'progeny'.)[46] We may agree that the point, as always, is not to interpret the world but to change it; the problem, however, is that to interpret it convincingly *is* to change it – and there are few more powerful stances from which to effect such change than the one which disclaims any intent or even any capacity to do so.[47] The really effective story is the one that is understood as anything but a story.

In order to challenge this position without simply replacing it by another authoritarian assertion of 'objective truth', it is necessary to have recourse to other kinds of reading and writing, which follow through the traces of narrative, of rhetoric, of ideological pressure, in supposedly neutral theory or history (as we have done with Saussure), but which remain aware of their own fictionality and provisionality. One of the methods of achieving this kind of reading is to exploit the power of etymology. Etymology *can* be used, as we've seen, to confirm a dominant ideology, to deny the possibility of purposeful change, to reinforce the myth of objective and transcendent truth; but it can also be used to unsettle ideology, to uncover opportunities for change, to undermine absolutes and authority – and to do so without setting up an alternative truth-claim.[48] The etymological content of such arguments may be erroneous, but their effect on the reader does not depend on correctness. ('Correctness' is not, in any case, a concept which can be rigorously utilised in etymology; the question mark that etymologists sometimes place before a particularly dubious derivation should, strictly speaking, be placed in front of all derivations, since they are all finally untestable.) It depends on the way in which words we regularly encounter, and treat as solid, simple wholes (representing solid, simple concepts), can be made to break apart, melt into one another, reveal themselves as divided and lacking in self-identity, with no clear boundaries and no evident centre. When Vico informs us that ' "logic" derives from the word *logos*, which first and properly meant *favola* [fable] which became the Italian *favella* [language]'; when Nietzsche traces words for 'good' back to words associated with a conquering race; when Freud explores the history of *heimlich* in Grimm's dictionary; when Heidegger argues that the common source of *bauen* ('build') and *bin* ('am') reveals their true meaning as 'dwell'; when Barthes makes much of the derivation of *text* from *textus* ('woven'); when Derrida turns to Littré to show that *hymen* and *hymn* might be etymologically related:[49] none of them is simply deploying the etymological argument favoured by Miss Brodie, and ruled out of court by Saussure. Rather, they're turning the etymological dictionary against itself by using the power of etymology to undermine the easy mastery of language implied in much of our literary and philosophical tradition, and to shake our assurance in fixed and immediately knowable meanings.

They are also, it seems to me, denying that the speaker and the community are simply helpless in the face of a language system which is always already in position. For Saussure has his own highly influential myth of authentic and single meaning, not based on etymological origin but determined and guaranteed by the synchronic system, held in joint ownership by the linguistic community, codified and enforced by the dictionary and the grammar of current usage – and impervious to the self-reflexivity of folk etymology or linguistic theorising. In order to initiate a science of linguistics, he needs to constitute a stable and knowable object of this sort,[50] and he has to resist, as we've seen, the language user's reintroduction of the history he has so deliberately excluded. But this is precisely what the writers I've mentioned are doing: recognising the impossibility of a detached and objective science of language, which observes and describes without altering the object of its attention, in a metalanguage wholly independent of the language it is discussing, they intervene – they offer, if you like, their own folk etymologies – to make manifest the instability of language, to demonstrate the diachronic density within any synchronic state, to present language as always open to reinterpretation and change. They vary, of course, in the degree to which they openly invite such a reading: Vico and Heidegger may sound more like de Brosses and Tooke in their earnest search for 'authentic' meanings, while Plato's and Derrida's ironies play freely through their writing. Derrida observes of his own procedure at one point: 'We turn again to Littré, from whom we have never, of course, been asking for the *truth*'.[51] (In Plato's case the irony is not at the expense of the notion of an absolute and transcendent truth, of course, but of language as a guide to that truth.) But in every case, the use of etymology fissures the synchronic surface of the text, introducing diachronic shadows and echoes, opening the language to shifts of meaning that can never be closed off. Even when the etymological argument is explicitly offered in the service of the doctrine of original authentic meaning, as in Horne Tooke's unearthing of a single Anglo-Saxon origin for a whole series of similar-sounding modern words, or in the service of a bourgeois ideological position, as in the case of Weekley's discussion of *steward*, it sets going a movement which cannot be arrested at a single point of truth or origin.

In thus employing etymology, writers are, in their different ways, exploiting its affinity with word-play – or, what amounts to the same thing, we are exploiting this affinity in thus reading etymological accounts. And the connection between etymology and word-play can be generalised to a connection between etymology and literature. Literature, too, can be read for or against absolutes, transcendence, closure, authentic and original meaning; and it too varies in the degree to which it invites a reading that opens rather than closes. But where etymology uses the tools of the tradition whose hierarchies it deconstructs – the tools of logic, empiricism, scientific method – and is thereby granted by our culture the right to be read in, and against, that tradition, the word-play of literature is all too easily partitioned off as another pathological development of the language to be kept under observation. This is one reason why the deconstructive etymological argument, and post-structuralist theory more generally, has an important role in the cultural and political arena, where the notions of 'authentic meaning' and 'true history', and the stories in which they are embedded, exercise a powerful ideological function, and where any challenge literature and its readers might mount against these notions is disabled by their prior marginalisation.

Saussure, as I've tried to show, can be read in support of both sides in this struggle – as spokesman for and illustration of an essentialist and conservative account of human cultural productions and as a story-teller whose narrative opens possibilities for cultural – and political – praxis precisely at the points where it betrays its own rhetoricity. And the very existence of these two antithetical readings invalidates the view of history, and of reading, implied in one of them. That, at least, is *my* story.

NOTES

1 Frank Lentricchia, *After the New Criticism* (Chicago: Chicago University Press, 1980), p. 117. Lentricchia refers in particular to Fredric Jameson, *The Prison-House of Language: A Critical Account of Structuralist and Russian Formalism* (Princeton: Princeton University Press, 1972), and Edward Said, 'Abecedarium Culturae: Structuralism, Absence, Writing', in *Modern French Criticism: From Proust and Valéry to Structuralism*, ed. John K. Simon (Chicago: University of Chicago Press, 1972). Further references to these works will be given in the text.

2 Terry Eagleton, *Literary Theory: An Introduction* (Oxford: Blackwell, 1983), pp. 110–11.

3 In quoting from Saussure, I give page references first to the standard French edition of the *Cours* (Paris: Payot, 1960), which are unchanged in the Critical Edition, ed. Tullio de Mauro (Paris: Payot, 1972), then to the translation by Wade Baskin (New York: McGraw-Hill, 1966, and London: Fontana, 1974). The translations I cite are my own, but I have found the versions of both Baskin and Roy Harris (London: Duckworth, 1983) useful.

4 The frequent conflation of the opposition synchrony/diachrony with the opposition system/systemlessness may derive from a misunderstanding of Saussure's claim that language change is the product of external, 'blind', historical forces, unanalysable and unpredictable (see n. 34 below). Saussure is here describing the non-linguistic pressures which the language system suffers at particular points, but it must be stressed that *within* the system, all change (occurring in response to this arbitrary external modification) is, of necessity, systematic and analysable. Such changes first manifest themselves in the actual speech of a few people before spreading to become part of the system; hence Saussure observes that '*everything that is diachronic in language* [*langue*] *is only so through speech* [*parole*]' (138/98) – a remark which is sometimes wrongly taken to reinforce the misidentification of diachrony and *parole*. Even David Carroll's valuable reconsideration of the synchrony/diachrony distinction (in *The Subject in Question: The Languages of Theory and the Strategies of Fiction* (Chicago: University of Chicago Press, 1982), Ch. 6) tends to conflate these categories (pp. 141–4).

5 Jameson's use of a spatial metaphor is revealing: the diachronic, for him, is the 'temporally successive, horizontal dimension', while the synchronic is 'the simultaneous and systematically organised vertical one' (*Prison-House*, p. 37). Since this spatialisation is entirely arbitrary, it suggests that the model Jameson has in mind is not the passage of history so much as the time elapsed in an utterance, which in the West tends to be symbolised as horizontal and left-to-right because of the influence of writing. But Saussure's spatialisation is *vertical* for diachronic and *horizontal* for synchronic (see his diagrams in Part 1, Ch. 3, and the illustration of the cuts in a plant stem (125/88)). Jameson is followed in his conflation of Saussure's oppositions and in his spatialisation by Terence Hawkes (*Structuralism and Semiotics* (London: Methuen, 1977), p. 78).

6 There is some justification for the notion that syntagmatic relations have a connection with *parole*, in that Saussure regards the sentence as the free combination of units in the act of speaking; it is not until Chomsky that the sentence is fully incorporated in the system of *langue* by means of rules that allow, especially through the property of recursivity, for creativeness on the part of the speaker. But Saussure's discussion of syntagmatic relations (172–3/124–5) makes it clear that as systematic connections between units they are an

aspect of *langue*. See also the Critical Edition of the *Cours*, ed. Tullio de Mauro, n. 251; Robert Godel, 'F. de Saussure's Theory of Language', in *Current Trends in Linguistics*, 3, 'Theoretical Foundations', ed. Thomas A. Sebeok (The Hague: Mouton, 1966), pp. 490–2; and Roland Barthes's discussion of syntagmatic relations in *Elements of Semiology*, tr. Annette Lavers and Colin Smith (London: Cape, 1967), pp. 59–71.

7 Roland Barthes, *Mythologies*, tr. Annette Lavers (London: Cape, 1972).

8 It should be noted that the extension of the Saussurean distinction between synchrony and diachrony beyond such systems of equivalence to wider domains of history and historical discourse (as in the work of Althusser) removes much of the original point of Saussure's categorisation, and involves a set of problems quite distinct from those discussed here.

9 Other commonly-associated pairs cited in etymological studies as having no historical connection are *isle/island*, *ear* (of corn)/*ear* (of body), *reign/sovereign*, *noise/noisome*, *school* (of pupils)/*school* (of fish).

10 Thus George. H. McKnight writes in the Preface to his *English Words and Their Background* (New York: Appleton, 1923): 'In order to operate an instrument efficiently one must be acquainted with the nature of its mechanism. In the same way in order to have an effective command of the resources of the English vocabulary, one must know about the materials of which the vocabulary is composed and the process by which its words have reached their present meanings' (p. v). A more convincing point is that such a speaker speaks a somewhat *different* language – see John Lyons, *Introduction to Theoretical Linguistics* (Cambridge: Cambridge University Press, 1968), p. 407.

11 Muriel Spark, *The Prime of Miss Jean Brodie* (Harmondsworth: Penguin, 1969), p. 36.

12 On the ideological function of the dictionary, see Roy Harris, *The Language Makers* (London: Duckworth, 1980), Ch. 6; Richard A. Rand, 'Geraldine', in *Untying the Text: A Post-Structuralist Reader*, ed. Robert Young (London: Routledge and Kegan Paul, 1981), pp. 295–9; and Allon White, 'The Dismal Sacred Word', *Literature Teaching Politics* No. 2 (1983), 4–15.

13 Freud tells of an objection to his theory of masculine hysteria on the grounds that *hysteria* is etymologically descended from the Greek for 'womb' – and Derrida cites this anecdote in replying to conservative objections to *his* work (*Dissemination*, tr. Barbara Johnson (Chicago: Chicago University Press, 1981), p. 182.

14 For brief accounts, see Etienne Gilson, *Les idées et les lettres* (Paris: J. Vrin, 1932), pp. 159–69; E. R. Curtius, 'Etymology as a Category of Thought', in *European Literature and the Latin Middle Ages*, tr. Willard R. Trask (Princeton: Princeton University Press, 1967), pp. 495–500; William T. Noon, *Joyce and Aquinas* (New Haven: Yale University Press, 1957), pp. 144–60. Curtius calls Isidore's

Etymologiarium libri 'the basic book of the entire Middle Ages' (p. 496).

15 There are useful discussions of the work of de Brosses in Gérard Genette, *Mimologiques: Voyage en Cratylie* (Paris: Seuil, 1976), pp. 85–118, and of Horne Tooke in Hans Aarsleff, *The Study of Language in England, 1780–1860* (Princeton: Princeton University Press, 1967), Chs. 2–3.

16 Ernest Weekley, *The Romance of Words* (London: John Murray (1912), 2nd rev. edn, 1913). Further references are given in the text.

17 An example may be found close at hand, however: the history of language-study, as Murray Cohen complains, tends to regard as important only those studies which can be said to lead to the 'true' linguistics of the nineteenth century (*Sensible Words: Linguistic Practice in England 1640–1785* (Baltimore: Johns Hopkins University Press, 1977), p. xv); the whole introduction is valuable for its discussion of intellectual history. See also note 44 below.

18 Yakov Malkiel, 'Etymology and General Linguistics', *Word* 18 (1962), 219.

19 Saussure's notion of a synchronic state as a complete and homogeneous system cannot, in fact, be as easily derived from the individual language-user's experience as he implies, and I shall argue later for a representation of that experience which does more justice to its heterogeneity. See also Roy Harris, *The Language Myth* (London: Duckworth, 1981), pp. 49–53.

20 See Freud's review of Karl Abel's 'The Antithetical Sense of Primal Words', in *On Creativity and the Unconscious* (New York: Harper and Row, 1958), pp. 55–63.

21 Jacques Derrida, *Glas* (Paris: Galilée, 1974), pp. 105–9, right-hand column.

22 Jean Paulhan, *La preuve par l'étymologie* (Paris: Minuit, 1953). (Page references will be given in the text.)

23 My concern in this essay is not with the use of etymology, or rather semantic change, as an index of social or ideological shifts; this is a mode of argument with its own difficulties and its own rewards. It has been employed in the service of many views of history – one might compare Raymond Williams's demonstration of the historical production of culture in *Keywords* (New York: Oxford University Press, 1976) with the following statement from the Preface to Ernest Klein's *Comparative Etymological Dictionary of the English Language*, 2 vols. (Amsterdam: Elsevier, 1966–7): 'Language is a mirror in which the whole spiritual development of mankind reflects itself. Therefore, in tracing words to their origin, we are tracing simultaneously civilization and culture to their real roots' (p. x).

24 Sometimes jokes work by pretending to be etymologies, as in the (untranslatable) example discussed by Freud: '*Eifersucht* [jealousy] is a *Leidenschaft* [passion] which *mit Eifer sucht* [with eagerness seeks] what *Leiden schafft* [causes pain]' (*Jokes and Their Relation to the Unconscious* (Harmondsworth: Penguin, 1976)), p. 68.

25 Saussure's defence of the pronunciation of *gageure* with the same vowel as *tournure*, mentioned earlier, might have been put not as an etymological argument but as a matter of relationships entirely within the synchronic system – which makes his appeal to etymology all the more surprising.

26 Yakov Malkiel, 'Each Word has a History of Its Own', *Glossa* 1 (1967), 137–49.

27 Raimo Anttila, *An Introduction to Historical and Comparative Linguistics* (New York: Macmillan, 1972), p. 331.

28 W. W. Skeat, *An Etymological Dictionary of The English Language*, 4th edn (Oxford: Clarendon Press, 1910), p. xxviii.

29 When Max Müller, in his *Lectures on the Science of Language*, wishes to give picturesque examples of etymology to his audience, he chooses a set of words of exactly the same type: *palace, court, government, minister, lord, lady, earl, king*, etc. – and shows how each one has 'risen in rank' (Second Series (London: Longman, 1864), pp. 251–6). Richard Chevenix Trench, however, manages to draw an ethical and religious lesson from both rises *and* falls in English words, the former revealing 'the influences of a Divine faith working in the world', the latter being something 'which men have dragged downwards with themselves' (*On the Study of Words* (New York: W. J. Widdleton, 1878), pp. 72–9; see also pp. 160–1).

30 See the Prefaces to *Words Ancient and Modern* (London: John Murray, 1926) and *More Words Ancient and Modern* (London: John Murray, 1927).

31 Some linguists make a distinction between 'popular etymology', denoting the widespread but erroneous assumptions about the history of words, and 'folk etymology' (*Volksetymologie*), denoting language changes brought about by such assumptions.

32 See the Critical Edition of the *Cours*, ed. Tullio de Mauro, n. 286.

33 Jacques Derrida, *Of Grammatology*, tr. Gayatri Chakravorty Spivak (Baltimore: Johns Hopkins University Press, 1976), pp. 41–2.

34 Anti-prescriptivism is a regular feature of both nineteenth-century philology and twentieth-century structural linguistics: it is part and parcel of the claim to an objective, descriptive, scientific status for language-study, which must not be suspected of meddling with ethics, or politics, or subjective judgements. Saussure insists that language change can come only from *outside* the system, and is in that sense 'blind' (127/89; 209/152); and it is the *social* character of language, its existence within the domain of material human history, that makes it vulnerable to these historical forces (112–3/77–8). (The illusion of purposeful change results from the diacritical nature of the system, so that an alteration at one point can have widespread and regular effects.) The impossibility of prescriptively-induced change is presented as a result of the arbitrariness of the sign: no *linguistic* reasons can be adduced for preferring one form to another. (Other reasons, such as moral or political ones, can be adduced and can be effective: but for Saussure, wishing to constitute

an object for study as close as possible to the objects of natural science, these would be external to the language system as such.)

35 In fact, the rule proved the stronger: no-one today would share Saussure's horror at the pronunciation of the *t* in *sept femmes.*

36 Barry Hindess and Paul Q. Hirst state most forcefully the impotence of history understood as that which existed in the past: 'The study of history is not only scientifically but also politically valueless. The object of history, the past, no matter how it is conceived, cannot affect present conditions. Historical events do not exist and can have no material effectivity in the present' (*Pre-Capitalist Modes of Production* (London: Routledge and Kegan Paul, 1975), p. 312. This is not to say, however, that history understood as a *representation in the present* of past events (or of past representations of events), however unscientific, is ineffectual; its power is only too evident.

37 Other etymologists see no important distinction between popular etymology and analogy: thus McKnight ends his chapter on 'folk-etymology' thus: 'The process of folk-etymology is, then, only a popular form of a tendency, prevailing among the lettered as well as the unlettered, to attempt to bring about uniformity and system into speech . . . Strange appearing words, native as well as foreign, are recast in familiar molds. Attempt is made, on the part of scholars, to restore distorted forms of classical derivations to their original form' (p. 190). For a more recent assertion that popular etymology is a normal and significant part of language change, see John Orr, 'L'étymologie populaire', in his *Essais d'étymologie et de philologie française* (Paris: Klinksieck, 1963), pp. 3–15.

38 Derrida's demonstration of the consistent privileging of speech over writing in Western philosophy needs to be balanced by an awareness of the reverse prioritisation in many areas of thought, produced by the fixity and permanence of writing – especially when, as was the case with Latin for several centuries, a common orthography contrasted with national variations in pronunciation (see Derek Attridge, *Well-weighed Syllables: Elizabethan Verse in Classical Metres* (Cambridge: Cambridge University Press, 1974), pp. 54–7). Saussure's hostility towards writing is in part directed against this privileging of a fixed form of language, and he argues always for a view of language as inherently and unpredictably changeable, infinitely open to the accidents of history (though entirely closed to the intentions of man). 'It is impossible', he writes of sound changes, 'to foresee where they will stop. It is childish to think that a word can change only up to a certain point, as if it had something in it which could prevent it' (208/151). It ought to be noted, however, that in a spelling pronunciation it is not strictly spelling as an immutable form untouched by history that inhibits or reverses changes in speech but *interpretations* of that spelling according to current practice, which may have little relation to any actual pronunciation of the past.

39 Saussure is here following in the footsteps of those who founded the

study of language as a science in the nineteenth century on the model of natural history; thus Max Müller, in his enormously influential lectures on language, emphasised that though language is constantly changing, 'it is not in the power of any man either to produce or change it' – and as a result 'language is independent of political history' (see Hans Aarsleff, *From Locke to Saussure* (Minneapolis: University of Minnesota Press, 1982), p. 36).

40 This subversion operates even on the boundaries between proper and common nouns: see Jacques Derrida, *Signéponge/Signsponge*, tr. Richard Rand (New York: Columbia University Press, 1984).

41 Note also the way in which the psychoanalyst's interpretation can affect the analysand's dreams: Freud, *The Interpretation of Dreams* (Harmondsworth: Penguin, 1976), p. 516.

42 John Orr, in the essay referred to in n. 37 above, argues that there is a kind of 'unconscious poetry' in folk etymology, which he relates to rhyme and punning – and which, he asserts, 'ne diffère pas essentiellement de sa soeur savante, l'étymologie des philologues' (p. 14).

43 Hayden White, *Metahistory: The Historical Imagination in Nineteenth-Century Europe* (Baltimore: Johns Hopkins University Press, 1973), and *Tropics of Discourse: Essays in Cultural Criticism* (Baltimore: Johns Hopkins University Press, 1978); Fredric Jameson, *The Political Unconscious: Narrative as a Socially Symbolic Act* (Ithaca: Cornell University Press, 1981); Jonathan Culler, *On Deconstruction* (Ithaca: Cornell University Press, 1983). White makes the interesting point that the historian, by turning a chronicle of events (in mere succession) into a story, transforms them 'into a *completed* diachronic process, about which one can ask questions as if he were dealing with a *synchronic structure* of relationships' (*Metahistory*, p. 6). See also White's 'The Value of Narrativity in the Representation of Reality' and 'The Narrativization of Real Events', in *On Narrative*, ed. W. J. T. Mitchell (Chicago: Chicago University Press, 1981), pp. 1–24, 249–54. John Frow's 'Annus Mirabilis: Synchrony and Diachrony', in *The Politics of Theory*, ed. Francis Barker *et al.* (Colchester: University of Essex, 1983), pp. 220–33, is a valuable discussion of the literary historian's dilemma, while Jean-François Lyotard extends the category of 'narrative' to cover a variety of non-scientific modes of knowledge in *The Postmodern Condition*, tr. Geoff Bennington and Brian Massumi (Minneapolis: University of Minnesota Press, 1984).

44 The history of the study of etymology, and of linguistics more generally, is not exempt from the need for narrative: thus Chomsky tells a story about the importance of Descartes and the Port-Royal grammar which is unabashedly designed to establish an ancestry for his own linguistic theory (*Cartesian Linguistics* (New York: Harper and Row, 1966)), while Hans Aarsleff counters with a story about the importance of Locke and Condillac (*From Locke to Saussure*); both are challenging an older story about the negligibility of language study before 1800, and neither acknowledges the degree to which

'importance' is retroactively constituted by just such narratives and their success in meeting the needs of their time. For a more complex notion of 'anticipation' in the history of linguistics, see Jacques Derrida, 'The Linguistic Circle of Geneva', *Margins of Philosophy*, tr. Alan Bass (Chicago: University of Chicago Press, 1982), pp. 137–53.

45 This is exemplified, for instance, in the Rev. A. Smythe Palmer's massive *Folk-Etymology: A Dictionary of Verbal Corruptions or Words Perverted in Form or Meaning, by False Derivation or Mistaken Analogy* (London: Bell, 1882), and its companion volume, *The Folk and their Word-Lore: An Essay on Popular Etymologies* (London: Routledge, 1904).

46 A characteristic of the rhetoric that promotes 'objectivity', of course, is blindness to its own rhetoricity; thus Lentricchia can complain, apparently without any awareness of the further irony involved in his own statement: 'The irony of many of these texts is that they attempt to demonstrate their theories not so much by the power of their arguments, but by the posture of their various rhetorics' (*After the New Criticism*, p. 216).

47 It is interesting to note that one of the charges brought against any argument which seeks to undermine the notion of an attainable objective truth is that it is a *dangerous* argument – an appeal to pragmatic effects of precisely the kind that undermines the notion of objectivity. On the ideological function of claims to historical objectivity, see Hayden White, 'The Politics of Historical Interpretation: Discipline and De-Sublimation', *Critical Inquiry* 9 (1982), 113–38.

48 The use of etymology for ideological ends is nothing new; Noon notes of Aquinas's use of Isidore: 'In general one might say that Aquinas appeals to the etymological argument whenever it favors his own, and that he disputes it whenever his own argument has anything to lose thereby' (*Joyce and Aquinas*, p. 146). It is, of course, the unprovability of etymology that makes it such a versatile ideological weapon.

49 Giambattista Vico, *The New Science*, tr. T. G. Bergin and M. H. Frisch (Ithaca: Cornell University Press, 1970), pp. 85–6 (para. 401); Friedrich Nietzsche, *The Genealogy of Morals*, tr. Francis Golffing (New York: Doubleday, 1956), pp. 162–4; Sigmund Freud, 'The Uncanny', *On Creativity and the Unconscious*, pp. 122–61; Martin Heidegger, 'Building Dwelling Thinking', in *Poetry, Language, Thought*, tr. A. Hofstadter (New York: Harper and Row, 1975), pp. 146–7; Roland Barthes, 'From Work to Text', in *Image Music Text*, tr. Stephen Heath (London: Fontana, 1977), p. 159 and 'Theory of the Text', in Robert Young, ed., *Untying the Text*, p. 32; Jacques Derrida, 'The Double Session', *Dissemination*, p. 213.

50 See Samuel Weber, 'Saussure and the Apparition of Language: The Critical Perspective', *MLN* 91 (1976), 913–38.

51 'The Double Session', *Dissemination*, p. 271. Derrida criticises the naive use of etymology as a key to true meaning (which he calls 'etymologism') in 'White Mythology: Metaphor in the Text of Philosophy' (*Margins of Philosophy*, pp. 253–5).

Fallen differences, phallogocentric discourses: losing *Paradise Lost* to history

MARY NYQUIST

Milton may be what Virginia Woolf said he was, the first of the masculinists, but he is certainly not the last. And in the case of the simile that is this essay's point of departure, Milton's misogyny would seem actually to be exceeded by that of his ostensibly more enlightened twentieth-century commentators. The simile, to be found in lines 1059–63 of Book 9 of *Paradise Lost*, elaborates Eve and Adam's awakening after their first fallen love-making :

> So rose the *Danite* strong,
> *Herculean Samson,* from the harlot-lap
> Of *Philistean Dalilah,* and wakd
> Shorn of his strength, They destitute and bare
> Of all thir virtue.[1]

With only one or two not very clearly developed exceptions, modern critics and editors alike are determined to find in this simile an analogy between Samson's betrayal by Dalilah and Adam's by Eve, in spite of the fact that on the level of syntax alone it is perfectly clear that both Adam and Eve are being compared with Samson. The *anagnorisis* that Milton here dramatises is a literary enactment of Genesis iii.7, 'And the eyes of them both were opened, and they knew that they were naked'[2]; and biblical commentators on this verse have always used the plural pronoun in discussing this stage of the Fall. Yet even Northrop Frye, our century's most influential theorist of the relations between the Bible and literature, can claim that the simile associates Samson with the fallen Adam.[3] In what follows, I shall both enact and analyse a variety of readings – all ideologically charged – of this simile and its textual context. In doing so I'll be entering current debates about the relations of post-structuralism, feminism and Marxism by raising, among others, the following issues: the institutional and hermeneutical status to be given this misogynistic reading (whether, for example, it is appropriate simply to refer to it as a misreading); the theoretical and ideological implications of an attempt to correct it by an appeal to history and to an historically-inflected notion of authorial self-consciousness; and, finally, the possibility of regarding the text both as historical product of the critical acts that mediate its reception and as the product of determinate social forces at work in the historical moment of its inception.

I would like to start by asking how the misconstruing of this simile is to be accounted for. As has long been noted, the lines immediately preceding the simile are somewhat problematical, textually.[4] But since editors and commentators who do not point to these textual matters perpetuate the misreading, there is obviously more at work here than faulty or misleading pointing. It's hard to avoid the suspicion that one thing behind this misreading is the figure of Milton the injured husband, who here as elsewhere – most memorably in *Samson Agonistes* – uses a poetic occasion of his own devising to pay off old scores and give voice to his own misogynistic feelings. Indeed, one wonders whether the very existence of *Samson Agonistes* as a text signed and authored by Milton does not provide the necessary cultural condition for the production of the Samson simile's misreading. Commentators on Milton have long been accustomed to comparing Adam and Samson as heroes whose relations with the paternal order are ruptured when they submit to their wives. And both heroes have been assumed to stand in an expressive relationship with the biographical Milton; or, to be more precise, with the Milton whose presence in both *Paradise Lost* and *Samson Agonistes* has ever since the eighteenth century been made to communicate his own unhappy marital experiences. That the model of authorship this frequently assumes is not in any straigthforward or simple sense expressive can be seen in Thomas Newton's annotative remarks on the antifeminist diatribe delivered by the chorus in *Samson Agonistes*. Newton (who does not, incidentally, misconstrue the Samson simile) states that the reflections of the chorus 'are the more severe, as they are not spoken by Samson, who might be supposed to utter them out of pique and resentment, but are deliver'd by the Chorus as serious and important truths. But by all accounts Milton himself had suffer'd some uneasiness through the temper and behaviour of two of his wives; and no wonder therefore that upon so tempting an occasion as this he indulges his spleen a little, depreciates the qualifications of the women, and asserts the superiority of the men, and to give these sentiments the greater weight puts them into the mouth of the Chorus.'[5] Besides relying on a view of the chorus that today's scholars would no longer accept, this piece of biographical criticism draws on two interestingly different views of authorship. Like the fictional Adam in *Paradise Lost* and Samson in *Samson Agonistes*, Milton is here presented by Newton as succumbing himself, irrationally and as a result of private emotion (feeling interpreted from a masculinist perspective as justified), to a 'tempting' occasion involving women. But as author of occasion as well as of text, Milton is also regarded as the conscious and ideologically motivated manipulator of his readers' responses – as an author who indulges his spleen, but who cannily manages to do so with a calculated view to the authority of his fictionally displaced utterances.

As the very form of Newton's remark – the editorial annotation – indicates, the figure of Milton the injured husband is both a biographical and institutional construct, a construct that contributes in its own way to our culture's reifying of the author of *Paradise Lost*. More than two centuries later, it may be virtually impossible to disentangle the figure of the powerful and influential author, Milton, from the figure of the harsh and authoritative patriarch, the patriarch being just as determined not to forgive and forget as Milton the author is determined not to die – Roland Barthes's announcement of 'The Death of the Author' notwithstanding. In his essay 'What is an Author?' Michel Foucault analyses what he calls the 'author-function', the way in which the circulation and functioning of certain discourses within a society are governed by the figure of the author. His analysis produces, among other things, the following aphoristic remark: 'The author is the principle of thrift in the proliferation of meaning.'[6] Although this principle is only implicitly at work in comments on our simile such as Fowler's annotative 'See Judges xvi for the story of Samson's betrayal by Dalilah', it is clearly operative in the more crudely explicit reading given it by John Knott, who states that in this simile 'Milton confirmed Eve's abrupt descent from graceful innocence to guilt by comparing her with Dalilah', which he develops by saying: 'And as any reader of *Samson Agonistes* knows, Milton's insult is worse than calling Eve "whore", since it implies that her treachery is directed against God as well as Adam.'[7] Besides positing the figure of the author as patriarch, whose stern voice (actually the critic's) is heard insulting and berating Eve, this too-zealous reading definitely illustrates the principle of thrift at work, for it establishes a neat and unproblematical homology between epic simile and closet drama, an homology that assumes Milton is in both works engaged in *representing* a betrayal.

One could argue that by referring the Samson simile in *Paradise*

Lost back to the Samson-identified author, author of *Samson Agonistes*, modern commentators obscure the heterogeneous uses to which Milton puts the Samson story by privileging the personal and domestic. After all, the story is alluded to in a number of political tracts; and in *The Reason of Church Government*, where it receives an allegorical elaboration, Milton has the prelates (male to a man) playing Dalilah to the King's Samson. John Hollander remarks in *The Figure of Echo* that Miltonic simile 'is now generally understood as a form which likens A to B *in that* X is palpably true of them both, but with no mention of W, Y, and Z, which are also true of them both'.[8] The reading that has been given our Samson simile by modern critics not only links the wrong A (Adam, rather than both Adam and Eve) to B (Samson), but also seems to be incapable of getting beyond sex, or the 'X' that is palpably true of them both, oblivious, entirely, of the significance of W, Y, Z. In this, it undoubtedly illustrates a quintessentially modern form of bourgeois thriftiness.

II

If the modern reading of the Samson simile is to be regarded, unequivocally, as a *mis*reading, however, it must be set against a reading which is correct not only in the narrow sense of being responsive to the allusive import of the plural 'they' but also by virtue of being conceptually coherent. Such a reading I should now like to attempt, yet before doing so want to stress that its coherence (as well, perhaps, as any authority it might possess) derives in part from an appeal to historical documents, in particular to Protestant commentaries on Genesis. Two historically specific features of Milton's Reformed interpretation of the Genesis story are relevant to the Samson simile's interpretation. The first is a consequence of Renaissance humanism and Protestantism's tendency to dissociate evil from Eve or woman. As Roberta Hamilton and others have argued, this dissociation should be regarded as part and parcel of the development of a specifically bourgeois view of marriage.[9] But it also informs the Reformers' reading of the Genesis exchange between the serpent and Eve, which for the first time in its exegetical history is regarded as an exchange positioning Eve as a responsible, theologically informed speaking subject. The second feature, which is of more direct relevance to the Samson simile, concerns the view of the Fall developed by Protestant exegetes, who regard it as a linear and sequential dramatic process, with the result that what is taken to be the active and progressive experience of transgression precedes the moment of conscious discovery.[10]

Especially as formulated by Augustine, the Christian doctrines of the Fall and of Original sin have always insisted that the loss of innocence, immortality and other original goods occurred as a result of the penalty imposed by the paternal deity for the act of transgression; but they also want to suggest that the penalty is not so much vengefully exacted as it is implicit in the very act of disobedience or of wilful human agency itself. While this theologico-juridical schema is formulated in an outrageously dry, propositional discourse at many points in *Paradise Lost*, in the Samson simile's immediate context it is articulated with an action that is vividly represented. Although the representation takes place in the medium of narrative, it becomes clear that many of its salient features are generically dramatic when the speeches by Adam that precede and follow the passage I cite in full here are taken into account:

So said he, and forbore not glance or toy
Of amorous intent, well understood
Of *Eve*, whose Eye darted contagious Fire.
Her hand he seiz'd, and to a shady bank
Thick overhead with verdant roof imbowr'd
He led her nothing loath; Flow'rs were the Couch,
Pansies, and Violets, and Asphodel,
And Hyacinth, Earth's freshest softest lap.
There they thir fill of Love and Love's disport
Took largely, of thir mutual guilt the Seal,
The solace of thir sin, till dewy sleep
Oppress'd them, wearied with thir amorous play.
Soon as the force of that fallacious Fruit,
That with exhilarating vapor bland
About thir spirits had play'd, and inmost powers
Made err, was now exhal'd, and grosser sleep
Bred of unkindly fumes, with conscious dreams
Encumber'd, now had left them, up they rose
As from unrest, and each the other viewing,
Soon found thir Eyes how op'n'd, and thir minds
How dark'n'd; innocence, that as a veil
Had shadow'd them from knowing ill, was gone,
Just confidence, and native righteousness,
And honour from about them, naked left
To guilty shame: hee cover'd, but his Robe
Uncover'd more. So rose the *Danite* strong
Herculean Samson from the Harlot-lap
Of *Philistean Dalilah*, and wak'd
Shorn of his strength, They destitute and bare
Of all thir virtue: silent, and in face

> Confounded long they sat, as struck'n mute,
> Till *Adam*, though not less than *Eve* abasht,
> At length gave utterance to these words constrain'd.
>
> (9.1034–66)

The theologico-juridical schema makes its presence felt in this passage when the Genesis opening of the eyes is explicated by an emphasis on a mental loss or nakedness that marshals in a whole troop of abstract virtues: innocence, confidence, righteousness, honour, shame. Yet the emphasis falls also, dramatically, on the actors' discovery that the change has already, unbeknownst to them, occurred; that against expectation, innocence and her virtuous partners have simply disappeared.

Another way of putting this is that because the Protestant Fall is a finely articulated temporal process, *Paradise Lost* cannot conform to the model implicitly recommended by the *Poetics*, where Aristotle, using *Oedipus Tyrannus* as his example, states that the best kind of *anagnorisis* coincides with the *peripeteia.*[11] In *Paradise Lost* the central reversal and recognition occur in a sequential rather than simultaneous order. The text dramatises the dynamic linearity of the Fall when the emotionally charged scenario Adam and Eve histrionically create for Adam's transgression goes on to shape their intoxicated experience of the fruit's effects. This linearity continues dynamically to unfold when the intense pleasure got from this experience of 'true relish' brings forth its psychological offspring, the violent pleasures of sexual desire. The love-making that follows is said to be 'of thir mutual guilt the Seal, / The solace of thir sin'. Although as 'solace' it is notoriously short-lived, its ineffectiveness is the very dramatic vehicle of the *anagnorisis.* Eve and Adam awaken from their troubled sleep to discover their *mutatio in contrarium.* Thus the recognition, though it does not coincide with the reversal, is produced by an ingeniously dramatic mimesis, one that obviously respects Aristotle's suggestion in a later section of the *Poetics* that the discovery should use 'probable means', the love-making here being, precisely, the probable means.[12] If this is so, then the simile actually serves to explicate the intimate and discursively motivated temporal relationship between *Paradise Lost*'s central *peripeteia* and *anagnorisis.* It establishes an analogy between Samson arising from the 'harlot-*lap* / Of Philistean Dalilah' to discover that he is 'Shorn of his strength', and Eve and Adam arising from 'Earth's freshest softest *lap*' (9.1041) – no-one in the history of Milton criticism seems to have noticed the carefully plotted parellelism here – to discover that they are 'destitute and bare / Of all thir virtue'. Informing the simile's concern with a retrospective discovery of loss is Protestantism's theology of the Word, a theology so logocentric as to be able to align Samson, who has unknowingly been shorn of his strength as a result of breaking his Nazarite vow, with Adam and Eve, who have unknowingly lost their original innocence as a result of denying the Father's Word. Within the logocentric framework established by the epic's dominant discourse, the discovery or *anagnorisis* is ultimately supposed to be of greater importance than the reversal. The discovery of loss is more important than the loss – of strength in Samson's case or of sexual innocence in that of Eve and Adam – itself, since the discovery is supposed to make possible a conscious recognition of the ideal value of that which is no longer possessed. This privileging of discovery over reversal also cleverly draws attention away from the role played by the external agents of loss; neither Dalilah's shearing of Samson's hair nor the Father's withdrawal of Eve and Adam's native virtues is to be dwelt on by the reader. Instead, the simile asks that Samson in the act of discovering he has lost his strength be compared with Eve and Adam, who in becoming conscious of their loss of sexual innocence experience sensuously and immediately the loss of that most immaterial of theological goods, divine grace. In short, the simile suggests Eve and Adam awaken into what the epic takes to be human history by discovering that history has already, in a lap(se) of time, been made.

Against this reading, the modern misreading's pairing of Samson and Adam seems fixated on an atemporal form of proportional analogy. But while this interpretative thriftiness is certainly modern and bourgeois, it also probably draws on features of an archaic and self-universalising patriarchal symbolic order, according to which the representation of lack or loss can only but affirm the hierarchically ordered polarity of the sexes. As my reading would suggest, the signifier 'Shorn of his strength' is associated metaphorically with the signifier 'destitute and bare / Of all thir virtue'. Both mark the existential basis of change ('Shorn of his strength' suggesting precisely the way Samson's unshorn hair functions as a metonymy for his strength, itself a metonymy for his spiritual integrity, and 'destitute and bare' suggesting the way Eve and Adam's unselfconscious nakedness functions as a metaphor for innocence); and both signifiers, joined by 'wakd', appear to have been generated by a prior action. But read as modern commentators misread the simile, the signifier 'Shorn of his strength' would appear unconsciously to efface itself by collapsing into its presumed signified, Samson's experience of sexual depletion, the detumescence or, symbolically, the castration, Dalilah is guilty of bringing about. And since Eve cannot be represented as sharing *that* experience, the entire simile is without more ado taken to compare its two male subjects. It is of course only – to use Derrida's coinage – in a phallogocentric discourse governed by an economy of the same, where the phallus as privileged signifier dictates that differences be produced only and always as difference from the same, that is, from the unitary male subject who is able always to represent his own oneness, that such a slippage – from a Samson who lacks to a post-coital 'they' not capable of including Eve – can take place. It might at this point be thought that this critical unconscious is largely a fiction fabricated to fulfil the needs of a feminist theory of the text's consumption. But the phallocentric determinants of the Samson simile's misreading are revealed in a surprisingly literal manner by J. M. Evans in his edition of Books 9 and 10 of *Paradise Lost* for the *Cambridge Milton for Schools and Colleges* series. In his commentary on Book 9, Evans refers to the *anagnorisis* by saying 'Adam's eyes are opened', omitting reference to either Eve or the Genesis 'they'.[13] His introduction to the volume concludes with a chart on which are mapped the differences between 'pre-Fall', 'Fall', and 'post-Fall' states, the final entry of which opposes 'erect penis' on the unfallen side to 'flaccid' on the fallen. Claude Lévi-Strauss is mentioned in the words prefacing the chart.[14] Later, in the concluding 'Topics for Book 9', a specific myth reported in *The Raw and the Cooked is* cited, a myth linking sexual intercourse, reproduction and death. The myth tells the tale of a first man who, created in a state of perpetual tumescence, was taught by the first woman how to soften his penis in copulation; when the demiurge saw the limp penis, he cursed the man, consigning him to the reproductive cycle and therefore to death.[15] While Evans nowhere explicitly develops a coherent misogynistic misreading of the Samson simile, the textual apparatus he provides clearly more than enables such a reading. By the time a student of the Cambridge Milton series gets to Book 11 of *Paradise Lost*, where Michael says to Adam that 'Man's woe' begins from 'Man's effeminate slackness', a fairly graphic understanding of that slackness will have been shaped.

An historicised grasp of Milton's presentation of the Fall would, in contrast, stress the way in which the simile operates in a typically Protestant manner to direct attention away from the naked body *per se* (whatever that might be) to a recognition of the inward significance of the bodily signs of a changed sexuality. Adam and Eve, 'each the other viewing', see in one another the visible signs of an inward change or fall; as Adam puts it, their eyes are opened to see 'in our Faces evident the signs / Of foul concupiscence' (9.1077–8). It is almost as if Milton has constructed an *anagnorisis* that would avoid some of the embarrassments of Augustine's discussion in *The City of God*, where the Genesis opening of the eyes is explicated by the notion that what Adam and Eve's eyes are opened to is the novel disobedience, or involuntary movement of, their bodily members.[16] Since the various contexts in this work, the *De Genesi ad Litteram* and the *Confessions* in which Augustine speaks of unruly motions, disobedient members and so forth make it abundantly clear that his viewpoint is quite literally phallocentric and that he is concerned, not to say obsessed, with the phallus as privileged signifier, the awakening presented in *Paradise Lost* would seem deliberately to transform Augustine's scene of recognition so that what Eve and Adam see is not the involuntary action of the male member but rather the signs of a post-orgasmic desire inscribed in each of their faces. If this is the case, then modern misreadings of this simile, with their implicit or explicit primitivising of the specular gaze, are curiously and significantly anachronistic and ahistorical.

The misreading also completely obscures the novelty or historical specificity of *Paradise Lost*'s situating of the *anagnorisis* on the other side of an act of love-making. The Genesis opening of the eyes has of course traditionally been associated with an awakening of conscience. I have suggested that in *Paradise Lost* this awakening is mediated by Eve and Adam's visual recognition in one another of the lineaments of gratified desire. The sexualised body – rather specifically, and significantly, the face – therefore plays a role in producing a new form of subjectivity. Yet this new and fallen subjectivity would seem to have as the condition of its possibility a sexual experience inaccessible to consciousness. Although 'foul concupiscence' has always in the Occidental tradition been antithetical to rational awareness of the good, in this passage in *Paradise Lost* it makes its appearance in a way that suggests there is something in sexuality which by virtue of its being 'fallen' might be beyond the reach of the subject's consciousness. In the first volume of his *History of Sexuality*, Foucault discusses what he calls 'the principle of a latency intrinsic to sexuality' as one of the principles ensuring the modern deployment of sexuality. This principle is concerned, he argues, not as in earlier periods with what the subject her- or himself wishes to hide, but with what seems by definition hidden from the subject.[17] That *Paradise Lost* portrays the emergence of something very like this principle at the moment of the epic's pivotal scene of recognition suggests that the scene might be registering – or, more accurately, given the history of its reception, perhaps unconsciously acknowledging – its own role in the production of a new form of subjectivity. Since this historically new subjectivity deploys sexuality in a way that intensifies the affective bonds of the heterosexual couple, the Samson simile – if read correctly – can itself be regarded as a literary marker of historical change.

Modern misreadings which associate Eve with the harlot Dalilah are blind not only to the simile's stress on a mutual discovery of subjective change but also to the evidence of significant gender-crossing suggested by the frequently remarked allusion in lines 1042–4 to Proverbs vii.18, where a figure the King James Bible identifies as a 'whore' entices a young 'wanton' with 'Come, let us take our fill of love until the morning: let us solace ourselves with loves'. That Adam's 'But come, so well refresh't, now let us play' (1027) echoes this verse, as does the phrase 'The solace of thir sin' (1044), certainly points to the possible irrelevance of gender to this scene of mutual guilt. Further extrinsic support for the reading I am proposing here can be found in *The Westminster Confession of Faith*, which in a unique departure from an androcentric tradition uses the plural pronoun so consistently in the opening sections of its chapter on the Fall that it indicates the generic 'Man' of its heading is to be equated with 'our first parents' rather than with Adam, humankind's patriarchal representative.[18] Milton's heading for his chapter on the Fall in *De Doctrina* also stresses the potentially non-hierarchical oneness of Adam and Eve: 'Of the Fall of Our First Parents, and of Sin.'[19] But to continue marshalling support in this way is to continue forging a somewhat troublesome because positivistic link between an historicised and a 'correct' reading. It is also, at the same time, to ignore what eighteenth-century commentators on *Paradise Lost* considered the most noteworthy feature of the entire passage, beginning with line 1029, Adam's 'For never did thy beauty', and extending through the post-awakening lines of Adam's 'O Eve, in evil hour' speech.

III

Writing in the *Spectator* in 1712, Addison was the first to draw attention to the intertextual relation between the scene of Adam and Eve's love-making and the scene in Book 14 of the *Iliad* in which Hera, adorned with the enchanting zone of Aphrodite, comes upon Zeus, who greets her by proposing they make love and by declaring that he has never before so intensely desired any goddess or woman, including Hera herself. Adam's 'converse' with Eve after he has eaten of the forbidden fruit – in lines immediately preceding the lengthy passage quoted above – is said by Addison to be an 'exact Copy' of Zeus's passionate declaration to Hera:[20]

> But come, so well refresh't, now let us play,
> As meet is, after such delicious Fare;
> For never did thy Beauty since the day
> I saw thee first and wedded thee, adorn'd
> With all perfections, so inflame my sense
> With ardor to enjoy thee, fairer now
> Than ever, bounty of this virtuous Tree. (9.1027–33)

Although a similar invitation to love-making is uttered by Paris in Book 3 of the *Iliad*, the scene in Book 14 in which Zeus responds sexually to Hera's artificially heightened attractiveness is clearly the principal source of Milton's 'copying', which in this instance takes the form of what we would now call an overt allusion. That the allusion is unquestionably overt is established by Milton's imitation of other features of Homer's scene, such as the way the lovers' verbal exchanges come to an end when Zeus takes Hera in his arms and they make love on a peak of mount Ida which, as Addison notes, produces underneath them a bed of flowers they fall asleep on when sexually satisfied.

It is not only Zeus's invitation and the love-making itself that Milton imitates, however. As Thomas Newton points out in his 1749 edition of *Paradise Lost*, in an annotation modern editors pass on to their readers, Adam's post-discovery speech, 'O Eve, in evil hour', is based on the passage in Book 15 of the *Iliad* in which Zeus lashes out verbally at Hera upon awakening from a post-coital slumber to discover that he has, through her, lost control of the battle. As has already been mentioned, Newton construes the Samson simile correctly: 'As Samson wak'd shorn of his strength, they wak'd destitute and bare of all their virtue'.[21] Yet the awakening he is really interested in is Adam's post-coital verbal awakening to an outrage that resembles Jupiter's. The intertextual reading Newton produces tells the story of the progress in the two patriarchs of an emasculating or effeminate desire: 'As this whole transaction between Adam and Eve is manifestly copied from the episode of Jupiter and Juno on mount Ida, has many of the same circumstances, and often the very words translated, so it concludes exactly after the same manner in a quarrel. Adam awakes much in the same humour as Jupiter, and their cases are somewhat parallel; they are both overcome by their fondness for their wives, and are sensible of their error too late, and then their love turns to resentment, and they grow angry with their wives; when they should rather have been angry with themselves for their weakness in hearkening to them'.[22] By suggesting an ironic dimension, Newton here modifies Pope's openly misogynistic comments in his edition of this book of the *Iliad*, where he states that both Adam and Zeus, whose 'Circumstance is very parallel', awaken 'full of that Resentment natural to a Superior, who is imposed upon by one of less Worth and Sense than himself, and imposed upon in the worst manner by Shews of Tenderness and Love'.[23] Newton's reading is less stridently masculinist, for he implies that far from being the legitimate expression of patriarchal self-righteousness, the anger verbalised by Zeus and Adam merely indicates, ironically, the defensive self-deception that results when patriarchal superiority becomes unsettled. Where the emphasis of Pope's discussion falls on the evil consequences of female duplicity, Newton's stresses the instability of male superiority. But in spite of this, by concentrating, like Pope, on the similarities or parallels between Adam and Zeus, Newton contributes to a masculinist reading of the passage in *Paradise Lost* we are here considering. Granted, Newton generously remarks that the positions of the two patriarchs are 'somewhat' rather than 'very' (Pope's choice) parallel. Yet even a qualified parallelism seems the product of a decidedly phallogocentric structure of thought. For it tends to obliterate the difference between the scene of sexual seduction which Hera consciously designs, with an intent to deceive Zeus, and the scene of Adam's transgression against the Father's Word, a scene in which *Paradise Lost* has Eve participate only ambiguously since she is herself deceived. The critics' parallelism also erases the narrative or temporal difference between Book 9's two scenes of temptation against the Word and the scene of the fallen Eve and Adam's love-making on 'Earth's freshest softest lap'. That even Newton's modest parallelism ends up conflating verbal or intellectual temptation and sexual seduction can be seen in his statement that both Jupiter and Adam 'should rather have been angry with themselves for their weakness in hearkening to them', a statement which unmistakably, even if unintentionally, echoes the patriarchal Lord's judgement of Adam; the phrase echoed appears both in Genesis iii.17,

'Because thou hast hearkened unto the voice of thy wife', and in *Paradise Lost*, 10.198.

But is this difference-denying parallelism generated solely by masculinist commentators or is it implied by *Paradise Lost*'s overt illusion to the *Iliad*? It is of course impossible to imagine on what grounds such a question might be given a definitive answer. One could argue, against the neo-classical commentators cited above, that the allusion functions ironically and that it intends to mark the *difference* between Zeus's anger at his seductress Hera and Adam's, which is 'fallen' or inherently and therefore illegitimately self-exculpating. Yet *Paradise Lost* makes any rigorous pursuit of this line of thought rather difficult, since the narrator has already, officially, remarked that Adam was 'not deceiv'd, / But fondly overcome with Female charm' (9.998–9). If in referring to the parallel weakness of Zeus and Adam in 'hearkening' to their wives Newton echoes both Genesis and Milton's epic, in stating that 'they are both overcome by their fondness for their wives' he echoes these very lines from *Paradise Lost*. Newton's echo therefore draws attention to the way the narrator's interpretative intervention itself conflates spiritual fall and sexual seduction, thereby sanctioning a reading of the overt allusion to the *Iliad* which concentrates on the parallels between Zeus and Adam.

If parallelism, thus overcoming difference, can be seen to inform both commentaries and text, then it is necessary to conclude that the allusive context *Paradise Lost* creates for Eve and Adam's post-coital awakening clearly complicates matters considerably, perhaps to the extent of calling into question the notion that the Samson simile has been misogynistically *misread*. To safeguard the reading of the simile I earlier proposed, it would seem necessary either to suppress or to make light of this context, for it forcibly reintroduces the very hierarchical polarisation of the sexes that that reading has shown to be basically irrelevant. Instead of illustrating, unequivocally, Adam and Eve's mutual recognition of a mutual change, the simile now appears significantly and inescapably expressive of the deeply sexist attitudes that its context, with its exclusively patriarchal spokesmen (Book 9's narrator, Adam, Zeus, and then Addison, Pope, Newton), makes explicit. If Hera is to Zeus what Eve is to Adam, then the Samson simile suggests, in spite of itself, that Eve has the same relation to Adam as her temptress daughter, Dalilah, has to Samson. The sexes become related just as our phallocentric cultural tradition would lead us to expect they would be: the (either 'somewhat' or 'very') righteously aggrieved Zeus, Adam and Samson are aligned against the beguiling and deceitful Hera, Eve and Dalilah.

But what are we to make of the contradictory possibilities for meaning our discussion has so far opened up? The question is tricky precisely because the contradictions have not before been exposed. Dwelling only on Milton's copying of the *Iliad*, eighteenth-century commentators registered no difficulties with the passage. More recently, J. M. Evans simply posits a noncontradictory relationship between allusive context and simile. Referring to Milton's allusive use of the *Iliad*'s scene of immortal love-making in Book 9 of *Paradise Lost* and in its innocent counterpart in Book 4, Evans says: 'The point of the allusion is that Hera had deliberately set out to distract Zeus's attention while his rival, Poseidon, assisted the Greeks. The love-making was a political manoeuvre on the wife's part; the husband was the dupe. Hence the balancing allusion to the biblical story of Samson's betrayal by Dalilah, the "harlot" who sold her body for his secret . . . The combined effect of these references, internal (to Book 4) and external (to the *Iliad* and Judges), is to make Adam and Eve's erotic siesta seem guilty and to confirm Eve's role as seductress.'[24] Evans, author of *Paradise Lost and the Genesis Tradition*, the major and most comprehensive scholarly treatment of this subject, here suppresses altogether *Paradise Lost*'s allusion to Genesis, which the Samson simile explicates; and it is obviously suppressed precisely because far from 'balancing', the Genesis allusion, with its unequivocal 'they', topples the whole structure. Aligning Hera, Dalilah and Eve, Evans thus mediates a decidedly patriarchal construction of the text, while by minimising its contradictions he also, simultaneously, produces a stabilising, or phallogocentric, discourse.

Setting aside previous attempts to master this passage's allusive meanings, however, let us ask again what we're to make of the way the Samson simile's allusive context undermines its ostensible meaning. We could, if we wished to use New Critical terms, talk about the 'tension' between the 'correct' reading of the Samson simile and its error-inducing context. Invoking the figure of the author, and the psychological determinants the use of this figure sanctions, we could then refer this tension back to Milton's own ambivalence about the relations of the sexes. But we could also, much more appropriately, see in this remarkable instance of intertextuality the signs of an historically, not psychologically, determined ambivalence. In this case, the text would testify to the success with which a dominant patriarchal ideology, here represented by the overt allusion to the

Iliad, is able to contain and defuse egalitarian sentiments, the limited expression of which might be encouraged, historically, by an emerging bourgeois family structure. To put this another way, the allusive context exposes what will increasingly become the merely formal status of the equality of the sexes in bourgeois society, an equality here elaborated in the Samson simile. The simile therefore uses the theologico-juridical schema to acknowledge that both Adam and Eve are, technically, guilty; it defers to Genesis, signifying, according to the letter of the text, that the eyes of them both have been opened. But it does so in a context that indicates clearly that this does not really matter; that what *really* counts is what has happened to Adam, father of mankind, Man. Indeed, the simile could be said to work in the way the title of Milton's first divorce tract does, *The Doctrine and Discipline of Divorce; Restored to the Good of Both Sexes, From the Bondage of Canon Law . . . to the True Meaning of Scripture . . .* The title promises, boldly, an enlightenment that its androcentric values tend repeatedly to withhold. That in *Paradise Lost* it is a patriarchal figure, Samson, to whom both Adam and Eve are compared is thus of crucial importance, ideologically; the syntactical priority of Samson to the 'they' for whom he is a figure suggests that 'Samson' functions in the slippery and misleading way the generic masculine still continues to do in our culture.[25] *Paradise Lost* would thus seem to generate the counterpart in poetic discourse of the sexist linguistic practice which codes the word 'man' equivocally to mean the generic humankind at the same time that, in context, it most often means exclusively the representative or exemplary male being. If we focus on the context that the allusion to the *Iliad* seems to provide, we find the ostensibly generic 'man', as it were, being cancelled by the masculine pronoun 'he', which thereby undoes the equality *Paradise Lost* appeared, in the briefly enlightened simile, to endorse. This cancellation finds itself, in turn, anticipating Milton's cancelling of his use of 'originals' to refer to Adam and Eve in the first edition of *Paradise Lost* to make 'original', meaning Adam, in the second (11.375).

IV

So far, I have followed eighteenth-century commentators in regarding Book 9's allusive use of the *Iliad*'s scene of immortal love-making in a way that suggests *Paradise Lost* simply re-represents specific features of Homer's representation. I have also limited the discussion to the imitation of basically dramatic features, such as Zeus's invitation to make love and his angry awakening, undeceived. But as Pope points out, in observations modern editors transmit, Milton also makes use of the passage in Book 14 of the *Iliad* in which the earth is presented as responding sympathetically to the sexual embrace of the two gods :

> So speaking, the son of Kronos caught his wife in his arms. There
> underneath them the divine earth broke into young, fresh
> grass, and into dewy clover, crocus and hyacinth
> so thick and soft it held the hard ground deep away from them.
> There they lay down together and drew about them a golden
> wonderful cloud, and from it the glimmering dew descended.[26]

In his notes on this passage Pope points to two places in *Paradise Lost* where it has been imitated. Citing lines 510–17 of Adam's narrative in Book 8, Pope remarks : 'The Creation is made to give the same Tokens of Joy at the Performance of the nuptial Rites of our first Parents, as she does here at the Congress of Jupiter and Juno'.[27] Adam there says :

> To the nuptial Bow'r
> I led her blushing like the Morn, all Heav'n
> And happy Constellations on that Hour
> Shed their selectest Influence; the Earth
> Gave sign of Gratulation, and each Hill;
> Joyous the Birds; fresh Gales and gentle Airs
> Whisper'd it to the Woods, and from their Wings
> Flung Rose, flung Odours from the spicy Shrub.

Closely related, though not so vividly linked to the moment of sexual intercourse – which, significantly, does not actually get represented – is the following passage from the narrator's description of the 'blissful bower' in Book 4 :

> each beauteous flow'r,
> *Iris* all hues, Roses and Jessamin
> Rear'd high their flourisht heads between, and wrought
> Mosaic, underfoot the Violet,
> Crocus, and Hyacinth with rich Inlay
> Broider'd the Ground, more color'd than with stone
> Of costliest Emblem . . . (4.697–703)

Of these lines Pope says that they 'are manifestly from the same Original'; and that 'the very Turn of *Homer*'s Verses is observed, and the Cadence, and almost the Words, finely translated'.[28] Finally, turning to the invitation and the love-making reproduced in Book 9, but without commenting at all on Milton's use of natural vegetation there, Pope shifts into an openly evaluative, not to say quintessentially moralistic, vein: 'But it is with wonderful Judgment and Decency he has used that exceptionable Passage of the Dalliance, Ardour, and Enjoyment: That which seems in Homer an impious Fiction, becomes a moral Lesson in Milton; since he makes that lascivious Rage of the Passions the immediate Effect of the Sin of our first Parents after the Fall'.[29]

Here the notion of imitation clearly implies transformation and appropriation. But it is possible that Homer's scene of immortal love-making has been transformed more radically than Pope's comfortable moralising of Milton's supposed moralisation of Homer supposes. Although Pope elsewhere in his annotations refers to Plato, in commenting on the story of Hera and Zeus he does not; nor, for that matter, does any more recent critic, so far as I know (Tillyard, for example, regards Book 9's 'dulcet description of the flowery bank' as 'strangely inept').[30] Yet it would certainly not be merely fanciful to suggest that the most influential and moralistic of commentators on Homer has mediated Milton's own appropriation. In Plato's critique of imitation in Book III of the *Republic*, Socrates, as is well known, takes Homer to task for representing the gods falsely, in ways unworthy of them and potentially dangerous to his audience. Among the numerous passages from Homer that Socrates singles out for censure is the sexual scene in Book 14 of the *Iliad*, of which he asks, is it really appropriate for young people to hear 'how Zeus lightly forgot all the designs which he devised, awake while the other gods and men slept, because of the excitement of his passions, and was so overcome by the sight of Hera that he is not even willing to go to their chamber, but wants to lie with her there on the ground and says that he is possessed by a fiercer desire than when they first consorted with one another'.[31] What Plato is referring to here is that specific moment in the exchange between Hera and Zeus preceding their love-making in which Hera pretends to be reluctant to sleep openly on the peaks of Ida and proposes that they go to the 'chamber' Hephaistos has built. In response, Zeus assures her they will not be seen where they are, for he will gather a 'golden cloud' about them. It is at this point that he embraces her and that the earth reacts by breaking forth in floral vegetation. In the passage just quoted from the *Republic*, Plato gives the content of this exchange-as-foreplay (and, on Hera's part, as-cunning) a definite moral significance, yet one that does not save Homer's text, constructing an ethically coded contrast between making love in an enclosure or 'chamber' and casually, 'on the ground', in order to stress the shameful shamelessness Homer has here, casually, depicted.

If Plato's moralisation indeed structures Milton's allusive use of the *Iliad* in the passage from *Paradise Lost* we are here examining, then its intertextual complexity is even greater than our discussion has so far suggested. Critics have frequently commented on the carefully structured opposition between prelapsarian eroticism and Book 9's post-lapsarian lust, and it has also been noted that in Book 9 Adam and Eve do not make it into their 'blissful bower'. As Fowler has remarked, the indefinite article 'a' in 'a shady bank' (9.1037) underlines the casual randomness of their choice of place.[32] Further, although this has not ever specifically been remarked, the passages in Books 4 and 8 that can be referred back to their 'Original' in Homer both have specific reference to the 'blissful bower'. The passage in Book 8 spiritualises Homer's scene by having the Earth give 'sign of Gratulation' at the nuptial union of Adam and Eve in their 'nuptial Bow'r'; the passage in Book 4 describes, specifically, the floor of the bower that the 'Sovran Planter' has set apart for his creatures: 'underfoot the violet, / Crocus and Hyacinth with rich Inlay / Broider'd the Ground'. In Book 9, however, the earth *neither* ceremonially participates in the love-making *nor* displays the signs of the artistically arranged naturalness making the floor of the blissful bower a different kind of 'Couch'. Although nature has participated sympathetically in the falls of both Eve and Adam, it is as if nature here is losing its capacity for response; rather than spontaneously gratulating their sexuality, nature is somehow, seductively, in a potentially ensnaring manner, simply there: 'Flow'rs were the Couch, Pansies, and Violets, and Asphodel, / And Hyacinth, Earth's freshest softest lap'.

Read in this way through Plato's mediating commentary, the main point of the Homeric allusions in Book 9 of *Paradise Lost* would now seem to be not the patriarchally structured polarity of male and female but the spiritually structured opposition between the sacred and the profane. The blissful bower, consecrated by the 'Sovran Planter' for prelapsarian love-making, is the polar opposite of 'a shady bank, / Thick overlaid with verdant roof embow'red'. Making love on the 'Broider'd' floor of the blissful bower is thus also the polar opposite of Adam and Eve's *al fresco* love-making on 'Earth's freshest softest lap'. Indeed, it is tempting to think that the figures of Samson and Dalilah with her 'harlot-lap' were initially generated by the profane role played in this structure of oppositions by 'Earth's freshest softest lap', the 'lap' – rather the two laps – here clearly signalling a lapse, *lapsus*, a fall, the Fall.

If 'lap(s)(e)' can be freed up as signifiers in this way, then the passage would seem to demonstrate in a pointed manner Johnson's remark that Milton saw nature 'through the spectacles of books'. But if it shows us Milton reading Homer through Plato's eyes, it probably also suggests a set of oppositions overlapping with that of the sacred and the profane. For Plato the sacred is of course associated with the realm of ideas, with the originals of which the realm of appearances and, *a fortiori*, artistic products are the profane and debased copies. Appropriated by *Paradise Lost*'s Christian Platonism, this becomes the opposition between a created or original sexual innocence and its fallen imitation, represented in Book 9. But the difference between original and copy, between Book 4's prelapsarian sexuality and its fallen counterpart in Book 9, is a difference produced in Book 9 by Milton's imitation of Homer's *Iliad.* This imitation would seem to insist that the Homeric scene is the literary site of a sexual act that is simply and unquestionably just that. The representational literality of these scenes of love-making is a literality that Plato himself associates with drama and that Book 9 would also seem to mark as essentially dramatic, since it presents its generically tragic central *peripeteia* and *anagnorisis* in the context of an overt allusion which relies, for its overtness, on the likeness of dramatic situation and speech in the cases of Adam and Zeus. Yet, as we have seen, Milton's imitation of the scene of immortal love-making in the *Iliad* is ultimately mediated by Plato's critique of representation. What Book 9 of *Paradise Lost* would therefore appear to give us is an imitation of a scene in the *Iliad*, which, subjected by Plato to an attack on its shameful debasing of its divine originals, is itself presented as a debased or fallen version, bringing forth shame in its actors, of its original in Book 4. To say, as eighteenth-century commentators do, that Milton here imitates or copies Homer, is thus entirely to miss the kind of logocentric critique of imitation that the scene, in this context, seems to constitute. Book 9's profane and self-implicated dramatic mimesis is radically dialectical, in that, by casting a Platonic doubt on the appropriateness of its own mimesis, it attempts to preserve its moralising discursive distance from the Fall.

The dramatic imitation's two laps, by acknowledging their status as the fallen mimetic ground of the action represented, could really both be considered harlot-laps, since in the only two instances in

Milton's poetic works besides this one where the term 'harlot' is used, it is firmly associated, in good anti-theatrical fashion, with a fallen and imitative status. (Obviously relevant here is the derivation of 'meretricious' from 'meretrix', prostitute or harlot.) In Book 4 in the hymn to 'wedded love' sung when Adam and Eve enter their blissful bower to make love, the narrator contrasts this sacred original – an original which, as the narrator's very presence in phrases such as 'I ween' reminds us, is *not* represented – with its profane and fallen copies:

Here Love his golden shafts imploys, here lights
His constant lamp, and waves his purple wings,
Reigns here and revels; not in the bought smile
Of Harlots, loveless, joyless, unindear'd,
Casual fruition, nor in Court Amours,
Mixt Dance, or wanton Mask, or Midnight Ball . . . (4.763–8)

Even more suggestively, in *Paradise Regained* the Son defends himself against Satan's temptation to devote himself to learning the wisdom of the Greeks by declaring:

That rather Greece from us these Arts deriv'd;
Ill imitated, while they loudest sing
The vices of thir Deities, and thir own
In Fable, Hymn, or Song, so personating
Thir Gods ridiculous, and themselves past shame.
Remove thir swelling Epithets thick laid
As varnish on a Harlot's cheek, the rest,
Thin sown with ought of profit or delight,
Will far be found unworthy to compare
With Sion's songs . . . (4.338–47)

We are apparently not to notice that the Son articulates this Judaic version of the opposition between original and copy by drawing on Plato's critique of Homer, just as *Paradise Lost* does in representing, against its better knowledge, not deceived, Adam and Eve's lapse into a merely mortal lust.

But what do we do with the Samson simile now? This Platonic turn suggests a way of reading *Paradise Lost*'s allusions to the *Iliad* that leaves intact a non-sexist reading of the simile. If the *Republic* mediates Milton's use of Homer, then it would seem to provide us with a genuine *tertium quid*, one that permits us to acknowledge the presence of the potentially sexist allusive context but does not require that it signify as it has been thought to do. It could even be argued that Genesis and the *Republic* – or rather theology and philosophy – work together to effect a transformation (or *Aufhebung*) of the phallocentric intertext established by the *Iliad*, Judges and our fallen symbolic order, emptying the allusions of their representational and patriarchal content, and raising from the representational laps(e) a complex of abstract and spiritual significations.

V

Such a transformation or *Aufhebung*, by relying on Milton's Platonic and therefore logocentric critique of representation, would neatly illustrate Derrida's view that the Hegelian *Aufhebung* dramatises the capacity of logocentrism to recuperate itself. For that reason alone, the reading I have produced by means of this Platonic turn is open to interrogation. The reading's attractiveness is in part the result of its capacity to stake out stable grounds for the Samson simile's intelligibility. It can claim these grounds, however, only by suggesting that theological, philosophical and poetic discourses join forces in this passage from *Paradise Lost* to carve out a space in which abstract meanings appear as if in their original or unfallen transparency. And since the only possible guarantor of such a neutral, non-sexist transparency is the textual or authorial self-consciousness posited by critical discourse, it is really critical discourse itself that would finally have to be the unacknowledged fourth partner in the work of saving the text. Both textual self-consciousness and the critical discourse that seeks to posit such consciousness by effacing itself are, of course, idealist and ultimately phallogocentric constructs. So while it might be tempting to argue that *Paradise Lost* is not only fully awake to the implications of its masculinist codes but knowingly and subtly transforms them, to do so would be to posit a textual self-consciousness as transhistorically vigilant as the Father's all-seeing eye.

There are other, institutional grounds for turning against this Platonic turn, as well. It could easily be argued that to save Milton's text by means of idealist constructs is to make use of the dominant discourse of Milton criticism in the academy. But to save this particular text is also to come to the defence of Milton the author, who can be made to appear in the light of this reading if not a proto-feminist, then at least a liberal humanist in the process of becoming one. There can be little doubt that the Milton establishment, perhaps especially in North America, the best-defended stronghold of liberal humanism, would heartily support such a defence. The rise in recent years of attacks on Milton by feminist literary critics has triggered a number of well-received apologies, which characteristically celebrate the egalitarian features of Milton's presentation of the marriage relationship in *Paradise Lost*, together with his representation of Eve as a character whose responsibility for her actions equals Adam's.[33] Yet as this brief account suggests, not only the defenders of the faith but the feminist 'opposition' (Joan Webber's term) as well have tended to conduct the debate without submitting its terms to any kind of ideological or historical analysis. As a consequence, the debate on Milton and sexual politics as it has taken shape over the last decade and a half has been severely restricted, both parties having been equally engaged with a highly individualised and ideologically charged figure of the author. The Milton of this debate is either appealed to as the patron saint of the companionate marriage and of the delicately imagined feminine sensibility or stands darkly towering over us, the prototypical patriarch, the bad father of us all, and all our woe.

On such a battleground, to take up arms against a misogynistic misreading is clearly to risk becoming conscripted, willy nilly, to the cause of the father's defence. The risk obviously has to be taken, since the powerful and historically long-lived hold that sexist values have had on critical discourse on Milton has to be contested – whether that hold is exemplified in the case of the Samson simile's modern misreading, in that of the masculinist appropriations of Book 9's allusive use of the *Iliad*, or elsewhere. Yet because there are other determinations at work in the field of Milton and literary criticism, it is clear that a feminist discourse also wishing to contest the academy's dominant discourses cannot simply put a polemically inspired feminist interpretation in the place of a misogynistic misreading, and leave it at that.

I would therefore like to argue that the diverse elements of the passage as a whole the readings here produced have brought into focus should not – even if they could – be fused into a single and unproblematical reading. Not because indeterminacy is everywhere and at all times characteristic of linguistic or literary acts; nor because the endless proliferation of meaning better befits our late capitalist economy than does thriftiness. But on the grounds that the history of the reception of *Paradise Lost* is a history that cannot merely be transcended by the fresh production of new, definitive readings, being a history in which, institutionally and culturally, we still participate, as the contemporary debate on Milton and feminist issues clearly indicates. My analysis has indicated that in the past various critical discourses have sought to stabilise the passage in question by producing only those allusions or intertextual relations which can be mastered. Yet if the various discourses that have, historically, sought mastery over the text were themselves to be placed in intertextual relation with it, *and* in conflictual relation with any feminist counter-readings, as I have tried to do here, then *Paradise Lost* as a text whose meaning is somehow pre-given or authoritatively present would be lost to history by being given up to it. Intervening in that history, a feminist reading of the text we have been looking at would refuse to stabilise or recuperate it, thereby appropriating *Paradise Lost* by happily letting it go.

One question remains, however, and that is, does losing *Paradise Lost* in this way to the history of its reception necessarily mean losing its contact with the historical moment of its production? A recent symposium on 'The "Text in Itself"' reveals a deeply felt suspicion that one loss necessarily entails the other; that to relinquish the idealist notion that the text is the source of its own meanings is basically to give up on the attempt to ground critical practice in a responsiveness to and an analysis of the material and social forces at work in the text's production.[34] I would like to suggest, tentatively, in conclusion, that the critique of historicism associated with post-structuralism need not issue in a reckless abandonment of this attempt. Although it is probably not yet possible to formulate a satisfactory programmatic statement on this issue, it would seem that the alliance between post-structuralist strategies and Marxism being proposed, most persuasively, by Tony Bennett, might *in certain instances* actually facilitate a kind of access to the text's participation in the economic and social formations of its time. With specific reference to the passage discussed in this essay, this would involve suggesting that one of the reasons it becomes, under analysis, the site of conflicting and historically variable readings is because it is an overdetermined site – perhaps *the* overdetermined site – of the conflicting and shifting views of the relations of the sexes in *Paradise Lost*. Or to put this another way, if this passage's allusive complexity seems actively to resist phallogocentrism's mastery, it could be because it thereby communicates the contradictory pressures exerted by the bourgeois family structure emerging in the mid-seventeenth century on female and male stereotypes, as well as on legal and symbolic forms of the marital relation. Yet of course this resistance has here been articulated by means of an analysis deploying deconstructive strategies.

One of the difficulties lying in the way of formulating this is the tendency, inherited along with the strain of modern formalisms, to think of the determinations associated with history as being located somehow *outside* of 'literary' texts. According to this legacy, the 'non-literary' character of historical discourse is integrally connected with history's existence outside the truly 'literary' text, which contains its meanings within it. Returning, for the last time, to the literary text under analysis here, we can see there is an interesting affinity between the literary text conceived in this way as sacred icon and the sacred bower framed by Milton's deity in *Paradise Lost.* Like the modern literary icon, the bower is a delimited sacred space within which an author-sanctioned generative activity takes place. Like the literary icon it is a highly wrought artifact, one which claims to use organic or natural materials. And, perhaps most importantly, its identity as sacred space is achieved by naming and excluding the other, keeping it outside : 'other Creature here / Beast, Bird, Insect, or Worm durst enter none; / Such was thir awe of Man' (9.703–5).

As I earlier suggested, when in Book 9 Eve and Adam make love outside the bower, they are entering what *Paradise Lost* takes to be human history, which is projected from Book 9 forwards in the form of a relentless and ineluctable linearity. Yet in a way it seems curious that this Protestant epic should construct the opposition between the sacred and the profane by means of such a seemingly literal insistence on designated ritual space. The deity of the New Testament is said to be no respecter of persons; in *Paradise Lost* he is also clearly no respecter of place. Michael, foretelling the (exegetically innovative and deeply Protestant) dissolution of Paradise in the flood, explains to Adam that it will be done to this purpose : 'To teach thee that God attributes to place / No sanctity, if none be thither brought / By Men who there frequent, or therein dwell' (11.836–8). This would suggest, what to any anthropologically informed reading would in any case be self-evident, that in *Paradise Lost* the opposition between the sacred bower and the unconsecrated ground is in the service of yet another opposition, namely, that between licit and illicit sexuality. And *that* is an opposition which both within *Paradise Lost* and without it, in the divorce as well as in other of Milton's polemical tracts, has meaning solely in reference to the institution of marriage – an institution which for Milton's radical Protestantism is, ambiguously, both sacred and profane.

To explore further the significance of this institutionally inflected opposition between licit and illicit sexual behaviour, we will have to return, briefly, to Plato's reading of the *Iliad*. What Plato seems especially to object to in Homer's immoral scene of immortal love-making is the presentation of the supreme god, Zeus, in the act of surrendering his rational consciousness as well as his interest in directing and controlling human affairs. Plato for this reason uses the contrast between making love in an enclosure and on the ground to encode the values he associates with the possession or loss of conscious control. While this same encoding obviously appears in *Paradise Lost*, its context is an emphasis on and valuation of heterosexual marital union which marks an important and historically shaped difference between Milton's epic and the *Republic*. Plato's reading of Homer may reveal sensitivities that are in some way class-based, but Milton seizes on just those details of Plato's reading that permit him to transform his epic into a bourgeois proto-novel that is distinctively modern. From the outset in Book 4 of *Paradise Lost*, human sexuality is imagined in relation to the institution of marriage, itself conceived unambiguously as a patriarchal institution. The narrator's famous hymn in praise of this well-regulated sexuality, a section of which has already been quoted, occurs after the blissful bower has first been described :

> Hail wedded Love, mysterious Law, true source
> Of human offspring, sole propriety
> In Paradise of all things common else.
> By thee adulterous lust was driv'n from men
> Among the bestial herds to range, by thee
> Founded in Reason, Loyal, Just, and Pure,
> Relations dear, and all the Charities
> Of Father, Son, and Brother first were known.
> Far be it, that I should write thee sin or blame,
> Or think thee unbefitting holiest place,
> Perpetual Fountain of Domestic sweets,
> Whose bed is undefil'd and chaste pronounc't,
> Present, or past, as Saints and Patriarchs us'd. (4.750–62)

Because the fictive present of a prelapsarian time is here temporarily forgotten, the hymn's polemical and historical character is vividly inscribed. A certain historical specificity necessarily accrues, therefore, to the two exclusions this passage performs : 'adulterous lust' and women – Mother, Daughter, Sister.[35] These two mutually dependent exclusions, working together to control female sexuality, form the basis of a patriarchal sexual economy which here openly associates the institution of marriage with 'propriety' or property.

It is no accident, then, that in *Paradise Lost*, the institution of marriage, which is here said to oppose human sexuality to animal, is given a home or sacred space which other creatures dare not enter. The propriety – in the sense of fittingness – of making love inside a domestic enclosure is thereby systematically associated with the 'propriety' of the marriage relation itself, which the hymn to 'wedded love' reveals to be an economic and social relation in which women have no real share. Nor therefore is it an accident that in Book 9, when Eve and Adam make love outside their marital home, the figures of the 'harlot' and the female 'lap' appear. Fallen or illicit sexuality is in this reading not merely imitative or meretricious and therefore, for that reason, figuratively a harlot. It is symbolically female because unwedded female sexuality is particularly threatening to the patriarchal order of pre-industrial capitalism, with its increasingly sharp separation of public and domestic spheres.

If we accept Foucault's argument in the *History of Sexuality* that a new, discursively shaped, relationship between subjectivity and sexuality emerges in the seventeenth century, then Book 9's scene of illicit sexuality also works to give shape to that patriarchal order's historically specific subjectivity. Read theologically, nature's simple there-ness in 'Earth's freshest softest lap' might signal the falling movement into a new and emergent maternality, now associated with death. But it is also possible to read this movement as revealing that the subjectivity emerging in *Paradise Lost*'s central scene of recognition is specifically and unambiguously a male, Oedipally structured, subjectivity.[36] In his lengthy soliloquy in Book 10, Adam protests the deferring of the death penalty, associated with the Father's thunderous Word, by crying:

> why do I overlive,
> Why am I mockt with death, and length'n'd out
> To deathless pain? How gladly would I meet
> Mortality my sentence, and be Earth
> Insensible, how glad would lay me down
> As in my Mother's lap! There I should rest
> And sleep secure; his dreadful voice no more
> Would Thunder in my ears, no fear of worse
> To mee and to my offspring would torment me
> With cruel expectation. (10.773–82)

Initially we might think we are to take this extraordinary desire for his Mother's lap and its accompanying construction of an Oedipal past to be merely a sign of Adam's fallen warpedness of mind. But in Book 11 Michael describes the process of dying naturally in exactly the same symbolic terms: 'So may'st thou live, till like ripe Fruit thou drop / Into thy Mother's lap, or be with ease / Gather'd, not harshly pluckt, for death mature' (11.535–7). Together these remarkable passages suggest that in *Paradise Lost*, when Eve and Adam, in a lapse of propriety, fall into 'earth's freshest softest lap', not just death but the now-paradigmatically-masculine subject's desire itself becomes associated inescapably with nature, mothers' harlots, their laps.

Foucault suggests that the production of our society's *scientia sexualis* depends both upon the establishment of the principle of a latency intrinsic to sexuality, discussed earlier, and on new methods of interpreting the truth concerning its hiddenness. As he puts it: 'The truth did not reside solely in the subject who, by confessing, would reveal it wholly formed. It was constituted in two stages: present but incomplete, blind to itself, in the one who spoke, it could only reach completion in the one who assimilated and recorded it. It was the latter's function to verify this obscure truth : the revelation of confession had to be coupled with the decipherment of what it said.'[37] In an attempt to establish a connection between *Paradise Lost*'s construction of a private sphere, represented by the bower, and the emergence of a newly ordered subjectivity, I have had to place myself in the position of an Other deciphering what neither Adam nor the text would seem to know. Yet *Paradise Lost* represents both Eve and Adam as becoming conscious of something their sexual activity had hidden within it. Book 9's *anagnorisis* is classically logocentric in that the awakening is represented as occurring without benefit of the revelation of confession; we are to understand that the eyes of them both are simply opened, even to the new darkness and blindness of their minds. For the reader of this *anagnorisis*, however, recognition or discovery of the truth is obviously not such a simple or straightforward matter. The work of interpretation generally presents itself as the natural partner of the self-revelations of the text. But as the various and conflicting readings enacted here would indicate, the knowing Other this scene of recognition would seem to demand is definitely not constituted by the text itself. To lose *Paradise Lost* to the history of its reception would be to acknowledge the absence of this assimilating Other, or rather to acknowledge the Other's presence as a matter of institutional and historical record. Yet who would want to deny that if the text fails to generate a stable position for the knowing Other it so attentively assumes, it might be because *Paradise Lost* is marked by a fall into the history of its inception as well.

NOTES

1 Quotations from Milton's poetry are from John Milton, *Complete Poems and Major Prose*, ed. Merritt Y. Hughes (New York: Odyssey, 1957).
2 Biblical quotations are from the King James version.
3 Northrop Frye, *Fearful Symmetry* (Princeton, N.J.: Princeton Univ. Press, 1942), p. 362. To the best of my knowledge, B. Rajan is the only modern critic to provide anything like a reading that compares both Eve and Adam with Samson; but he does so by stressing a common, newly acquired 'blindness to the things of the spirit', *'Paradise Lost' and the Seventeenth Century Reader* (1947; rpt Ann Arbor, Michigan, 1967), p. 73. Typically incoherent in its unacknowledged shifts from plural to (androcentric) singular is Harry Blamires's commentary in *Milton's Creation* (London: Methuen, 1971), p. 237: 'They find their *eyes* indeed *opened* (1053), but not in the way anticipated (cf. 706–8, 985). They are opened to the recognition of their own darkened minds, to the disappearance of that "veile" (1054) of innocence that has "shadow'd" them from knowledge of evil . . . Adam's waking to guilt is like Samson's waking from the lap of Dalilah, who, in his sleep, had cut off his hair and thereby deprived him of his strength. The correspondence underlines the concept of innocence as positive power, which it is important for the modern reader to sense. The loss of innocence is a virtual emasculation. "Shorn of strength . . . destitute and bare / Of all their vertue" (1062–3); this is their new condition'. E. M. W. Tillyard, in an edition of Books 9 and 10 for the *Harrap's English Classics* (London: Harrap Ltd, 1960), glosses the simile correctly, 'As Samson of the tribe of Dan woke to find his strength gone, so Adam and Eve woke to find their innocence gone', p. 141. But editions published since that time stubbornly persist in the masculinist reading. In addition to the texts cited below, R. E. C. Houghton's 1969 edition of Books 9 and 10 for Oxford University Press, for example, annotates lines 1059–63 with 'As Samson lost his physical strength when his hair was cut off (Judg. 16: 4–20), so Adam lost his original virtue, his moral strength, through sin and the ensuing sensuality', p. 172. In developing her view that Milton's post-lapsarian Eve significantly resembles Mary Magdalene, Louise Schleiner produces a more recent version of this reading in *The Living Lyre in English Verse* (Columbia, Missouri: Univ. of Missouri Press, 1984), p. 154. Stating that in both Book 4's dream and Book 9's fall Eve's 'sin with Satan' has 'taken the form of a sexual experience', she says of the simile: 'They arise from the nap like Samson and the harlot Delilah, the narrator concludes, with Adam "shorn of his strength". Since Eve has "played the harlot", as it were, what better model can there be for her penitence lyric than songs of Mary Magdalene?' I am grateful to Derek Attridge for providing this example.

4

> innocence, that as a veil
> Had shadow'd them from knowing ill, was gone,
> Just confidence, and native righteousness
> And honor from about them, naked left
> To guilty shame: hee cover'd, but his Robe
> Uncover'd more.

There is no stop after 'shame' in either of the original editions of *Paradise Lost*. Editors since Newton customarily provide one, however, often associating this personified 'shame' with Psalm cix, 29, 'Let mine adversaries be clothed with shame, and let them cover themselves with their own confusion, as with a mantle', and with *Samson Agonistes*, lines 841–2. Alastair Fowler, introducing a baroque variation on the misogynistic misreading, omits any stop after 'shame', offering among other explanations that 'Adam covers in response to Eve's guilty shame', *The Poems of John Milton*, ed. John Carey and Alastair Fowler (London: Longman, 1968), p. 917.

5 Thomas Newton, ed., *Paradise Regained and Samson Agonistes* (London, 1753), p. 277.

6 Michel Foucault, 'What is an Author?' *Textual Strategies*, trans. and ed. Josué V. Harari (Ithaca, N.Y.: Cornell Univ. Press, 1979), p. 159. It should be said here that while making use of Foucault in this essay I do so accepting the Marxist critique frequently made of his work. The most acute and suggestive to my mind is Peter Dews's 'Power and Subjectivity in Foucault', *New Left Review*, 44 (1984), 72–94.

7 *Poems of John Milton*, ed. Carey and Fowler, p. 918. John R. Knott, Jr, *Milton's Pastoral Vision* (Chicago: Univ. of Chicago Press, 1971), p. 124.

8 John Hollander, *The Figure of Echo* (Berkeley: Univ. of California Press, 1981), pp. 115, 116.

9 Roberta Hamilton, *The Liberation of Women* (London: Allen and Unwin, 1978), pp. 22, 64–8. For a discussion of the distinctively Puritan development of this ideology see William Haller's influential 'Hail Wedded Love', *ELH*, 13 (1947), 79–97, and 'The Puritan Art of Love' by Malleville and William Haller, *HLQ*, 5 (1942), 235–72. Margo Todd argues convincingly for the importance of situating Protestant views in the context of humanist thought in 'Humanists, Puritans and the Spiritualized Household', *Church History* 49 (1980), 18–34.

10 For a reading, relying on these commentaries, of Eve's temptation in Book 9 of *Paradise Lost* and of the dramatic linearity of that book's action, see my 'Reading the Fall: Discourse and Drama in *Paradise Lost*', *ELR*, 14 (1984), 199–229.

11 Aristotle, *The Poetics*, trans. G. M. A. Grube, *On Poetry and Style* (Indianapolis: Bobbs Merrill, 1958), Ch. 11, p. 22. The narrative in Judges seems itself to suggest that reversal and discovery are temporally ordered: 'And she made him sleep upon her knees; and she

called for a man, and she caused him to shave off the seven locks of his head; and she began to afflict him, and his strength went from him. And she said, The Philistines be upon thee, Samson. And he awoke out of his sleep, and said, I will go out as at other times before, and shake myself. And he wist not that the Lord was departed from him. But the Philistines took him, and put out his eyes . . .' For a psychoanalytical reading of the temporal gap between loss of strength and awakening here, see Mieke Bal, 'The Rhetoric of Subjectivity', *Poetics Today*, 5 (1984), 363–75.

12 Aristotle, *The Poetics*, trans. Grube, Ch. 16, p. 33.

13 J. Martin Evans, ed. *John Milton, 'Paradise Lost': Books IX–X* for the *Cambridge Milton for Schools and Colleges*, gen. ed., J. B. Broadbent (Cambridge: Cambridge Univ. Press, 1973), p. 33.

14 Ibid., pp. 9–10.

15 Ibid., pp. 167–8.

16 See St Augustine, *The City of God Against the Pagans*, Loeb Classical library, Vol. 4, trans. Philip Levine (London and Cambridge, Mass.: Harvard Univ. Press, 1966), Book XIV, Ch. 16 and 17, pp. 352–60. See also Chs. 3 and 15 of Book XIII. Ruether includes a discussion of Augustine's phallocentrism in 'Misogynism and Virginal Feminism in the Fathers of the Church', *Religion and Sexism*, ed. Rosemary Ruether (New York: Simon and Schuster, 1974), pp. 150–83.

17 Michel Foucault, *The History of Sexuality*, Vol. I, trans. Robert Hurley (New York: Random House, 1978), p. 66.

18 *The Westminster Confession of Faith*, in *The Creed of Christendom*, ed. Philip Schaff (New York: Harper and Brothers, 1877), III, 615–17.

19 Milton, *De Doctrina Christiana*, trans. John Carey, ed. Maurice Kelley, *Complete Prose Works of John Milton*, VI (London and New Haven, Conn.: Yale University Press, 1973), Bk I, Ch. XI, 382.

20 Joseph Addison, *The Spectator*, no. 351 (12 April, 1712), ed. Gregory Smith (London: Oxford University Press, 1945; rpt 1973), 100–12.

21 Thomas Newton, ed., *Paradise Lost* (London, 1749), II, p. 201.

22 Ibid., 202.

23 Alexander Pope, *The Iliad of Homer*, ed. Maynard Mack, Vol. VII of *The Poems of Alexander Pope*, gen. ed., John Butt (London and New Haven, Conn.: Yale Univ. Press, 1967), p. 193.

24 Evans, *Cambridge Milton*, 173.

25 That among the upper classes an increasing emphasis upon the 'conjugal core' was accompanied by a strengthening of patriarchal powers is the influential thesis of Lawrence Stone in 'Part Three: The Restricted Patriarchal Nuclear Family 1550–1700', *The Family, Sex and Marriage in England 1500–1800* (London: Weidenfeld and Nicolson, 1977), pp. 123–218. See also Ruth Perry, *Women, Letters and the Novel* (New York: AMS Press, 1978), pp. 27–62.

26 *Iliad*, trans. Richmond Lattimore (Chicago and London: Harper and Row, 1951), p. 303. All further quotations from the *Iliad* are from this edition.

27 Pope, *Iliad*, p. 181.
28 Ibid., p. 182.
29 Ibid., p. 182.
30 Tillyard, *Milton*, p. 140.
31 Plato, *The Republic*, III, 390, B-C, trans. Paul Shorey, Loeb Classical Library (London and Cambridge, Mass.: Harvard Univ. Press, 1953), pp. 216–17.
32 Fowler, *Milton*, p. 916.
33 Although this is not the place for a full bibliography, the following would qualify for membership in the feminist 'opposition': Marcia Landy, 'Kinship and the Role of Women in *Paradise Lost*', *Milton Studies*, 4 (1972), 3–18; Sandra Gilbert, 'Patriarchal Poetry and Women Readers: Reflections on Milton's Bogey', *PMLA*, 93 (1978), 368–82; Christine Froula, 'When Eve Reads Milton: Undoing the Canonical Economy', *Critical Inquiry*, 10 (1983), 321–47. Among the defences are Barbara Lewalski's 'Milton and Women – Yet Once More', *Milton Studies*, 6 (1974), 3–20; Joan Malory Webber's 'The Politics of Poetry: Feminism and *Paradise Lost*', *Milton Studies*, 14 (1980), p. 21; and Diane Kelsey McColley's *Milton's Eve* (Urbana: Univ. of Illinois Press, 1983). Although it, too, is engaged with the ideologically charged figure, the patriarch Milton, '"Rational Burning": Milton on Sex and Marriage' by David Aers and Bob Hodge is an interesting attempt to deal with some of the contradictions articulated in Milton's writings, *Milton Studies*, 13 (1979), 3–34.
34 See 'The "Text in Itself": A Symposium', in *Southern Review*, 17 (July 1984), 115–46. Participants include Terry Eagleton, Tony Bennett, Noel King, Ian Hunter, Peter Hulme, Catherine Belsey, and John Frow. As I should hope the present essay indicates, I am entirely in agreement with Bennett's view, formulated in the paper in this volume (see above, p. 73), and re-formulated for the symposium, that 'there is no fixed boundary between the extra-textual and the intra-textual which prevents the former from pressing in upon the latter and re-organizing it'. But Belsey points to a problematical feature of Bennett's position, that is, its tendency to distinguish 'theory, or the analysis of reading formations, the discursive conditions of the possibility of the producton of meanings; and criticism, the installation of the text in a new (and radical) reading formation'. As Belsey puts it, 'Existing readings come under "theory", while "the text" is the province of criticism' ('The "Text in Itself", p. 138).
35 For a related reading of this passage, see Jackie Disalvo, 'Blake Encountering Milton: Politics and the Family in *Paradise Lost* and *The Four Zoas*', in *Milton and the Line of Vision*, ed. Joseph Anthony Wittreich, Jr (Milwaukee, Wisc.: Univ. of Wisconsin Press, 1975), p. 155.
36 Francis Barker also uses Foucault in an attempt to specify the rise of a subject both bourgeois and Oedipal in his densely argued *The Tremulous Private Body: Essays on Subjection* (London: Methuen, 1984). For an extended discussion of the Renaissance *topos* of the

seductive female lap and its relevance to the Samson simile, see an essay of mine related to the present one, 'Textual Overlapping and Dalilah's Harlot-Lap', forthcoming in *Literary Theory/Renaissance Texts,* ed. Patricia Parker and David Quint (Baltimore: Johns Hopkins Univ. Press, 1986). I'd like to say here that I am indebted to conversation with my colleague Eleanor Cook for this play on 'lap(se)'.

37 Foucault, *Sexuality,* 66–7.

Ezra Pound: the erasure of history

MAUD ELLMANN

for this stone giveth sleep
staria senza piũ scosse
and eucalyptus that is for memory
Ezra Pound, Canto LXXIV

I AN ADDRESS IN TIME

Pound defines the epic as 'a poem including history', and his own epic, *The Cantos*, embraces many chronicles. Renaissance Italy joins ancient China, together with the early years of the United States, and the story of money interlaces these and other histories like the 'gold thread in the pattern'.[1] But *The Cantos* are themselves included in the history they include, for they record the way that Pound read Europe and the way that Europe, in revenge, read Pound. His poem tells the history of its author, an author who becomes a history in the interminable process of his own inscription. Poem and poet weave each other's destinies. Caged at Pisa in 1945, Pound gazes through the legs of a guard, knowing at last that history is enframed by power, and the historian imprisoned in the systems that he scrutinises:

a sinistra la Torre
seen thru a pair of breeches (LXXIV 431)[2]

Pound believes that the 'usurocracy' has been unwriting history for centuries, and that our knowledge of the past is marred by 'OMISSIONS of the most vital facts'.[3] By usury, Pound means excessive interest rates, but he capitalises on the word itself until it implicates all forms of exorbitance. He works this doctrine out in his aesthetics before he uses it to back his fascism in the thirties, and *The Cantos* stage the confrontation of his psychic and political economies. While the anti-Semitism of the times gave content to the form of Pound's obsession, the holocaust itself was the obsessive ritual where Europe purged itself of Jews. It is the ingenuity of this obsession that Pound's work reveals, the rigour of its blindness to itself. For his discriminations crumble every time he sets them up : and his writing stutters on its own delusions, unable to progress or to retreat. This essay investigates his blindness with the perspicuity of his own idiom, as if obsession could observe its own finesse.

'History' can either mean the past as it happened or the past as it is reconstructed by historians, but Pound prefers to disavow this difference. In Canto IV, the swallows cry, ' 'Tis. 'Tis. 'Ytis!' (14): and the poem as a whole asserts 'It is' of each historic fact that it incorporates. While he cuts and pastes his documents, Pound conserves their idiom, for the lessons of history can only be induced from a sufficient 'phalanx of particulars' (LXXIV 441). History itself must speak from the pages of *The Cantos*, unencumbered by the judgements of the author. However, it is through citation that the text conceals the most imperious of authors: 'lord of his work and master of utterance' (LXXIX 442). There is no innocent history, no matter what the swallows say; and there is no voice more monologic than the poet's when he rattles off the interest rates. Pound uses history tendentiously, and the facts that he amasses in *The Cantos* constitute a kind of legal dossier against usury. He believes that history is a spiral rather than an evolution, in which the same errors teach the same lessons, and a few ideograms patiently repeat themselves through time. 'We do NOT know the past in chronological sequence', he declares. 'It may be convenient to lay it out anaesthetized on the table with dates pasted on here and there, but what we know we know by ripples and spirals eddying out from us and from our own time.'[4] Here, Pound envisions history as a vortex, where the past whirls around the present with a kind of centrifugal energy. He insists that 'A man does not know his own ADDRESS (in time) until he knows where his own time and milieu stand *in relation to* other times and conditions' (*GK* 83). Without addresses, men and letters err through time as Odysseus meandered through enchanted seas. An address implies a proper place, a boundary, and a destination; but it is paradoxical that Pound insists upon a fixed abode in the same breath that he asserts the relativity of history. If a man can only know his place '*in relation to*' other places and conditions, the pattern must be new at every moment, and there can be no private property in time.

The rulers Pound redeems from history are often those who forge roads or cut canals that speed the circulation of commodities and news (XXII 101).[5] Canto XXXI, for instance, praises the canal as a 'channel of correspondence' and a 'water communication' (153, 156), because it articulates one region to another and encourages the trade of words as well as money. These canals retrace the text's topography, for they engrave the landscape with the channels that *The Cantos* forge through history. The poem superposes 'luminous details', plucked out of the flux of history, and the poet's art lies in the silences that canalise the text, suturing one era to another.[6] Pound described this technique as the ideogrammic method (*SP* 239), and he derived it from the work of Ernest Fenollosa, which he began to edit in 1913. According to Fenollosa, the Chinese written character juxtaposes images that fuse into concepts in the reader's mind. Pound argues by analogy that juxtaposing *histories* should shock the reader into recognition of the moral that unites them. 'All truth is the transference of power', wrote Fenollosa; and for Pound, each Chinese ideogram forms a kind of 'switchboard' in which meaning circulates like electricity.[7] In *The Cantos*, he drives the 'lines of force' through history which enable past and present to converge in an economy of power.[8]

'Money is an articulation', wrote Pound in 1951.

> Prosody is an articulation of the sound of a poem.
> Money an arti / of / say NAtional money is articulation of
> total purchasing power of the nation.[9]

The word 'articulation' puns on suturing and speech, suggesting that the very power of enunciation depends on the 'canals' that cut through speech. Pound identifies the channels with the force that furrows them, for power *is* its current and its currency, and only operates when it is cashed in words or notes or coins. While money is the means by which the nation speaks its power, it is through prosody that poems budget their expenditure of sound. All economies depend upon the 'power to issue' (CXI 782), whether they issue forth in wisdom, banknotes, poetry, or progeny, the rhythmical purgations of the flesh or the 'holy mystery of fecundity'.[10] To purify the flow of one economy will rectify the rhythm of the others, for one diversifying power courses through them all, sluicing out impurities through sheer velocity.[11]

History is also an articulation, and therefore it aspires to the condition of a poem. The 'repeat in history' corresponds to the refrain in song; the 'subject rhyme' to rhyme in poetry.[12] But history also has a 'melopoeic' and a 'phanopoeic', that is, a rhythmic and a figural dimension (*LE* 25–6). 'Run your eye along the margin of history', Pound urges, 'and you will observe great waves, sweeping movements and triumphs which fall when their ideology petrifies.' 'Ideas petrify', he adds for emphasis (*GK* 52). Pound regards rhythm as the 'fundamental drive' in music, and *The Cantos* strive to rescue the rhythm of history, its waves and movements, from the anaesthetic of chronology and the petrification of ideas.[13] Time must not be treated like the evening etherised upon a table: it is through rhythm that history purges its canals of the 'clog' or 'blockage' Pound calls hell.

While rhythm is 'a form cut into TIME', the image is time's pigment.[14] Pound contrasts the *idea* which petrifies history to the *image* in which history is stored. 'Tradition inheres . . . in the images of the gods, and gets lost in dogmatic definitions', he argues. 'History is recorded in monuments, and *that* is why they get destroyed.'[15] Images and monuments transport the past into the present, and thus make history possible at all: for history is not the past as such, but the force that sweeps the past into the present, 'in ripples and spirals eddying out from us and from our own time'. Pound insists that tradition *inheres* in images, and it is in these living forms that the *power* of the past survives. The image is history incarnate.

If ideas inhibit history's rhythms, they also threaten to erase its images. The same sorcery that petrifies history 'putrefies' its monuments and symbols. 'The power of putrefaction aims at the obfuscation of history', Pound rages:

> it seeks to destroy not one but every religion, by destroying the symbols, by leading off into theoretical argument. Theological disputes take the place of contemplation. Disputation destroys faith, and interest in theology eventually goes out of fashion. . . . Suspect anyone who destroys an image, or wants to suppress a page of history. (*SP* 317; see also 306)

Ideas deny the poetry of history, imposing theory in the place of phanopoeia, melopoeia. The 'petrification of putrefaction' (XV 64): this is how the Hell Cantos execrate the power that effaces history. And hell is just another name for Usura.

In Canto XIII, Kung remembers:

> A day when historians left blanks in their writings,
> I mean for things they didn't know,
> But that time seems to be passing. (XIII 60)

The blanks in history are not truth itself, but these historians affirm the truth, for they know they do not know it. They figure truth as absence. *The Cantos* try to bring the blank back into history; but they must cancel cautiously, because the blank that stands for truth has been supplanted by another blank that stands for usury. 'The one history we have NOT on the news-stands is the history of Usura', Pound fulminates. 'All this is still blank in our histories' (*GK* 115). It is usury that supplements the living image with inert ideas, and entrammels history with theory. What tops it all is that *Usura has no history*. By vandalising images and rhythms, it threatens to engulf the rest of time into its own amnesia. At once erased and erasing, usury designates a suicidal mechanism whereby history would obliterate itself. To defeat Usura, *The Cantos*, paradoxically, must blank the blank, erase erasure.

Though Pound's crusade against usury did not reach full frenzy till the thirties, he had already diagnosed paralysis in history. In *Guide to Kulchur* (1938), he claims that he has not deflected a hair's breadth from his lists of beautiful objects, 'made in my head and held before I ever thought of usury as a murrain and a marasmus' (109). He discovered 'blobbiness' and 'mess' in music and in painting long before he knew that they were caused by the degree of tolerance a culture showed to usury (*GK* 109; *I* 198). *Antheil and the Treatise on Harmony* (1927) reveals the strange aesthetic that will bring him to believe that usury deranges rhythm and defaces images. It is this aesthetic which will make him risk his life and lose his freedom, to drive the 'barb of time' into the clog of usury.

II 'THE YELLYMENT OF TIME'

'The element most grossly omitted from treatises on harmony up to the present is the element of TIME.' So Pound launches his promotion of Antheil.

> The early students of harmony were so accustomed to think of music as something with a strong lateral or horizontal motion that they never imagined any one, ANY ONE could be stupid enough to think of it as static; it never entered their heads that people would make music like steam ascending from a morass. (*A* 9. 11)

Pound believes that the deepest life of music lies in measure rather than harmonics. Measure has the nobler pedigree, for it originates in 'the age-lasting rhythms of the craft, cloth-clapping, weaving, spinning, milking, reaping' (*A* 88). These crafts still move to nature's rhythm, rather than the dead tick of the metronome. Pound implies that rhythm has escaped miscegenation, so that the stamp of the original survives. Elsewhere, he argues that rhythm is the only aspect of a poet's work which is 'uncounterfeiting' and 'uncounterfeitable' (*LE* 9).[16] Though one may steal the poet's words, it is impossible to forge the inkless signature that he inscribes in time. On both the personal and racial levels, rhythm testifies to parentage and origin.

In the twelfth century, however, steam began to ooze from the morass, and to settle over poetry and music, where it has thickened through the centuries (*A* 11). This steam disfigures rhythm. Wagner, for example, 'produced a sort of pea soup, and ... Debussy distilled it into a heavy mist, which the post-Debussians have desiccated into a diaphanous dust cloud' (*A* 40). All these gases rose out of the chord, and have asphyxiated rhythm since the Middle Ages. Chords are spatial. Only the gross omission of the element of time enabled them to seep out of the swamp where they belong. Space congeals music, and Pound compares the study of the chord to examining 'the circulation of the blood from corpses exclusively' (*A* 23). Like Bergson, he believes that everything went wrong when space usurped the seat of time.[17]

In music, 'slushy chords' betray that space has ousted time; in painting, colour is the stigma of its usurpation. 'Chords are like colour', Pound declares, and he uses the same metaphors of obfuscation and incontinence to denounce them both as spatial 'heresies' (*A* 18, 19, 40, 48, 62). Like Blake, he censures colour in favour of the line, which he regards as a form of rhythm (*A* 33). Through the line, the plastic arts dispel the fumes of space, for the line pays tribute to the element of time. 'The line is unbounded', writes Pound in his Introduction to *Sonnets and Ballate of Guido Cavalcanti* (1912): 'it marks the passage of a force, it continues beyond the frame . . . all our ideas of beauty of line are in some way connected with our ideas of swiftness and easy power of motion. . . .'[18] Like the canal, the line provides a path for energies to flow, while colours tend to block the arteries of power. Pound even measures colours in terms of their duration and their frequency, to acquit them of their spatiality: for it is only when the painter slights the 'razor edge' of time that he permits his pigments to besmirch the line (*A* 148). He admires Wyndham Lewis's parsimony with colour, and suspects that he should leave his lines alone:

> I don't see why he should paint pictures, his gift as I see it is so much in invention, it is so much a matter of almost speech in form, that I myself would probably keep him at drawings if I had any control over him.
>
> He h££££ himself is very apt not to finish or to fill in the colour of his drawings. I feel this is a real indication that the job is finished, that the creation is finished when he has drawinn in his figure, or indicated a few tones.[19]

Pound identifies the line with 'speech in form' because he sees both speech and line as arts of time. It is only with the supplement of space that both degenerate.

'Clogs are spatial', Pound states in a letter to Zukofsky of 1936 (which he dates 'anno XIV' in recognition of the fascist calendar). He is speaking of the clog of usury : and it is through such metaphors as these that his early and *aesthetic* allergy to space creeps into his later economics. In fact, 'usury' comes to mean the magic that perverts time into space. 'You will have to pry up at least ONE eyelid to the changed status of Ez', he warns Zukofsky, for he has now discovered that 'monetary reform occurs in TIME'. This is the same 'YELLYment of TIME' which 'inheres in etc/music etc.' If time can overcome the ravages of space, power flows and money moves like music. 'Whereas clogs (as the German railway signs tells us, are SPATIAL. raumlich).'[20] Space produces clogs and constipation on the one hand, incontinence and foetor on the other. And these are the two sides of usury.

Usury rose from the morass at the same time that space polluted rhythm and the line. By '1200/ or after 1221', at the latest, 'it ALL went to rot. . . .'[21] Space erases time from music with the same miasmal mist with which usury erases history. Both rely upon a fatal trope which Pound calls 'satanic transubstantiation' :

> Only spoken poetry and unwritten music are composed without any material basis, nor do they become 'materialised'.
>
> The usurers, in their obscene and pitch-dark century, created this satanic transubstantiation, their Black Mass of money, and in so doing deceived Brooks Adams himself, who was fighting for the peasant and humanity against the monopolists.
>
> '. . . . money alone is capable of being transmuted immediately into any form of activity.' – This is the idiom of the black myth! (*SP* 307)

Because spoken poetry and unwritten music unfold in time, they cannot be corrupted into space, or sink into materiality. The same majestic rhythm that articulates their movement should also regulate the flow of cash.[22] Pound agrees with Major Douglas that money should be treated as a ticket, because tickets are 'timed', and the 'timing of budgets' is crucial to economic rhythm.[23] Instead, money has declined into a fetish. It hoards power, when it should merely mark the passage of a force, and trace a path for power. In their obscene and pitch-dark century, the usurers spatialised money, and ever since it petrifies and putrefies.

Writing hoards the energies of music and the spoken phrase in the same way that the bankers hoard the powers of production. As soon as writing intervenes, poetry and music undergo satanic transubstantiation, for they stagnate in space when they should lilt in time. The more Pound worries about usury, the more telegraphically he writes : it is as if he feared that words might be fetishised like money if the reader were to linger too tenderly upon their substance :

> in
> discourse
> what matters is
> to get it across e poi basta (LXXIX 486)

In Pound's 'world of moving energies', writing must transport thought with the 'greatest possible despatch', to mimic speech in its electric grace.[24] However, he urges speed in dread of petrifaction, and in the fear that writing, in so far as it is spatial, must always bear the incremental 'ooze' of usury. For Pound's satanic transubstantiation means that writing is the usury of speech.

III 'THIS COIL OF GERYON'

In every sphere of culture, usury obliterates the mark of time. It destroys the rhythms of the craft, where the music of poetry originates, rusting the chisel, blunting the needle, gnawing the thread in the loom. In painting, the line grows thick, and colours clog its moving energies. In music, the chord befouls time. In language, the sudden incandescence of the spoken word succumbs to the 'palsy' and the usury of writing (XLV 229–30). 'All things that are are lights', quotes Pound, endorsing Scotus Erigena (LXXIV 429) : but all these lights are quenched in Usura's Black Mass.[25] Silently, invisibly, it takes possession of the world of light, and substitutes the dazzle of its deathly gold. 'Pecuniolatry' supplants the contemplation of the mysteries (*SP* 348). Satanic transubstantiation mocks the incarnation of a god or of a thought, while the fetish is the demoniac double of the image. With its gross materialisations, the Black Mass mocks art and travesties enfleshment.

These doubles ooze into all economies. 'Ooze' itself is usury's parodic supplement to Pound's Heraclitean principle of flow. 'Properly understood capital is liquid', urges Pound : but usury mocks liquidity with sludge.[26] Even the rhythms of the flesh pervert themselves, and the human frame turns upside-down and back to front :

> Standing bare-bum,
> Faces smeared on their rumps,
> wide eye on flat buttock,
> Bush hanging for beard.
> Addressing crowds through their arse-holes,
> Addressing the multitudes in the ooze . . . (XIV 61)

In defiance of Pound's principle of 'clear demarcation', the anus takes the place of mouth and genitals at once, and substitutes its ooze for speech and sperm. Usury has seized 'Control of the outlets' (CIV 738): be they the outlets of the market, the organs of the news, or the very orifices of the human body. In his Postscript to Remy de Gourmont's *Natural Philosophy of Love* (1921), Pound concocts an extraordinary theory that the world began in a cosmic ejaculation, and that the same spermatic power still circulates through art and nature, dispensing incarnation as it moves. The brain itself is a clot of genital fluid, eager to enflesh a second cosmos.[27] But usury derides this spermatic thrust – 'phallic and ambrosial' – and substitutes the anus's perverse fecundity: 'a continual bum-belch / distributing its productions' (XV 65).[28]

This bum-belch is a non-origin, which parodies the very notion of a source. To purify the currencies of words or flesh or finance, it is necessary to return to sources, be they the classics, time, the mint, the phallus, or the sun. But usury is money 'created out of nothing', as Pound quotes wrathfully from Paterson, the founder of the Bank of England.[29] It corresponds to the attempt, in discourse, 'to lift zero by its own bootstraps' (*GK* 78). Having no origin, it also has no destination, and thus defies the very principle of teleology in history. Wherever usury's influence has spread, foul aftergrowths engorge their origins. Following Dante, Pound damns the sodomites and the usurers to the same circle of his inferno, because both seek wealth or pleasure 'without regard to production' (XLV 230n.). 'By great wisdom sodomy and usury were seen coupled together', for both are the enemies of history, defying fruitfulness (*I* 233; *SP* 265). *The Cantos* mourn the '*coitu inluminatio*' which has surrendered to these usurious excesses (LXXIV 435). In a proper economy, ' "any note will be paid" ': 'the deposits', Pound repeats, 'will be satisfied' (LXXXVI 564; XXXVIII 190). But neither sodomy nor the 'buggaring bank' is ever satisfied, nor cashed into the pulchritude of nature (LXXVII 468). Instead, they fester in the sty of the between. Teeming in darkness, they create an excremental universe, exuberant as the spermatozoic one they imitate.

Pound vilifies betweenness more than any other crime of usury, because it undermines the telos of his economics. 'Entering all things', usury *defers.* It comes between the stonecutter and the stone; 'between the young bride and her bride-groom':[30]

between the usurer and any man who
wants to do a good job
(perenne)
without regard to production –
a charge
for the use of money or credit. (LXXXVII 569)

This passage suggests that any form of interest interrupts production, breeding difference and delay where union should occur. However, even interest has a base in nature before it grossens into usury: for nothing can come of nothing, no matter what the wretched Paterson might say. 'INTEREST', Pound declares, 'is due teleologically to the increase in domestic animals and plants'; and it therefore guarantees both reference and history.[31] He insists that money should 'represent something . . . such, namely AS rams and ewes'.[32] But usury inflates the sign out of all proportion to the signified. Now money represents its own unnatural fecundity, obliterating the distinctions between animal and vegetable and mineral (see *SP* 341, 346, 349):

> The idea of Interest existed before the invention of metal coin.
> And there is MUCH more justification for collecting interest on a loan of seed, on a loan of she-goats and buck-goats, than on a loan of non-breeding, non-breedable metal. (*RS* 176–7; see also *SP* 318)

Money is 'the middle term', a sign that mediates *between* the vendor, the consumer, and the goods, just as language mediates between the speaker and the world (*SP* 342; LXXXVII 574). Both begin 'in the middle' (LXXVII 464); but usury paralyses speech and money, impeding distribution and bloating the between. Under Usura, the medium signifies itself alone, and fattens on its own tautology, indifferent to the destiny of meaning. 'Money is now the NOTHING you get for SOMETHING before you can get ANYTHING,' writes Frederick Soddy, an economist whom Pound admired despite his name.[33] By destroying demarcations between flesh and metal, the living and the dead, usury undermines the very means of representation. For money which is created out of nothing remains invisible: there is no need for credit slips at all. Soon, the power of the nation rots away because there is no currency to represent it. Pound's economic mentor, Silvio Gesell, argues that the 'coined money of a nation is a drop in the ocean of uncoined money', and Major Douglas also thinks that 'real purchasing power is not represented by figures anywhere, but can be materialised by those in possession of the secret of the process, as and when required'.[34] To represent this power is to let it forth to purge the clogs from the economy; but usury proscribes representation, so that the banks emasculate the powers of production.

Pound endorses Major Douglas's argument that '*under the present system* there are never enough credit slips to deal with the product; to distribute the product; to conjugate any of the necessary verbs of a sane economics and a decent and agreeable life'.[35] This metaphor suggests that Usura descends on language, too, depriving 'verbs' of definition and exactitude. Indeed, Pound believes that economic mess is both the cause and the result of 'muddling and muddying terminology' (*GK* 31). Clear definition unblocks the economy, cleaning the canals of communication and exchange. When word and world disband, under the influence of usury, the economies of language, history, finance, and the flesh can no longer articulate themselves. Pound fumes:

> MESSES of cliche supplied by Iouce and the restuvum to maintain the iggurance spewed out by the OOzevelt Anschauung.
> AND the OOze was possible because writers did not keep the language clean.[36]

Is it usury that defiles definition? Or did the writers unleash usury's marasmus when they failed to purify the dialect of the tribe? Whether the ooze originates in money or in language now becomes impossible to tell, for both succumb to hell's black alchemy. The sewers take the place of the canals. The 'infamy which controls English and U.S. finance', Pound declares, 'has made printing a midden, a filth, a mere smear . . .' (*GK* 184). Money seethes in the 'usurers' dunghill'; while language, which was once the 'Jade stream' or 'rushing crystal', degenerates into the 'piles of books' that fester in the 'great scabrous arse-hole' of the Hell Cantos.[37] 'Gold bugs against ANY order', the usurocracy inscribes the currencies of finance, word and flesh alike with its excremental signature, its 'smear' (LXXXVII 572).

It is through the smear that usury disseminates itself through history, and it betrays itself wherever monuments and records are destroyed. The word 'smear' conveys the calumny of usury, in addition to its filth and its erasures. If the world was created by an ejaculation, hell's bum-belch is busy decreating it by blotting out its history. 'My generation was brought up ham ignorant of economics', Pound frets in a radio broadcast. 'History was taught with OMISSIONS of the most vital facts. Every page our generation read was overshadowed by usury' (*RS* 339). It is by 'destroying the symbols' that Usura spreads her empire of forgetfulness, and she even keeps herself under erasure. An 'octopus', she disappears behind her ink.[38] For it is in the 'ugly print marks' of the written page that she at once impresses and deletes her signature (*CSP* 49). Pound argues that the 'press' erases history, by which he seems to mean the newspapers, but he could also mean the printing-press itself: 'The press, your press, is a machine for destroying the memory, the public memory. For effacing, for washing out the memory of yesterday and the day before yesterday' (*RS* 339).

However, there are secrets of light as well as secrets of the darkness, and Pound is hard put to distinguish usury's deletions from the Dionysian mysteries of Eleusis, which he regards as the hidden inspiration of the West. 'Secret history is at least twofold', he writes:

> One part consists in the secret corruption, the personal lusts, avarices, etc. that scoundrels keep hidden, another part is the 'plus', the constructive urges, a *secretum* because it passes unnoticed or because no human effort can force it on public attention.

A handful of men like Avicenna, Scotus Erigena, Grosseteste, Dante and Cavalcanti preserved Greek joy through the centuries of darkness.[39] They constitute the 'plus part', the 'conspiracy of intelligence' which Pound believes to have 'outlasted the hash of the political map' (*GK* 264, 263).

> Dionisio et Eleutherio
> Dionisio et Eleutherio
> "the brace of 'em
> that Calvin never blacked out (XCV 647)

According to Pound, the 'mysteries are self-defended, the mysteries *can* not be revealed' (*GK* 145). But usury creates a pseudo-mystery, an Ersatz reticence, as self-defended as the genuine article. In the same way, the blanks in history that stand for secret truth surrender to the blank that stands for usury.

This blank cannot be kept at bay, but threatens to engorge the world into the nothing out of which it was created. More than a blank, it is a black hole, lodged:

> in hell's bog, in the slough of Vienna, in
> the midden of Europe in the black hole of all
> mental vileness, in the privy that stank Franz Josef
> in Metternich's merdery in the absolute rottenness.
> among embastardised cross-breeds . . . (*L* 245)

Here, Pound makes Vienna the capital of hell because the 'Jewish science' flourished in its slough. (Perhaps he dimly sensed how the 'kikiatry racket' would have interpreted his own psychic economy, in which the sphincter is equated with the usurer.[40]) As the refuge of the Jews of 'middle' Europe, Vienna is a 'midden', for it stinks of usury's betweenness; and a contagion of the signifier turns 'middle', 'midden', 'mud', and 'muddle' into synonyms for one another in Pound's idiom. The Jews not only practise usury, but they refuse to represent or even name their god. Their taboo against the graven image instigates the drive to undefine, erase, unname, unrepresent that Pound execrates in usury. 'Without gods, something is lacking', he states, laconically (*GK* 126). And it is from this lack that usury creates its anti-cosmos out of nothing.

'The Semitic', Pound declares, 'is excess. The Semitic is against any scale of values' (*I* 125). The Jews destroy the tools of representation: 'with usura', the line grows thick, and categories seep through one another's boundaries. The term 'Semitic' comes to *mean* erasure in Pound's writing, and particularly the erasure of history: 'Time blacked out with the rubber' (VII 25). But he does not restrict the epithet to Jews. Protestantism is nothing more than 'jewdianity . . . renewed jewdianity, reJEWed whichianity';[41] and both these religions conspire 'semiticly to obliterate values, to efface grades and graduations' (*GK* 185). If Canto C proclaims that usury is 'beyond race and against race' (798), this is because the Semitic must at last obliterate *itself* by rotting boundaries and embastardising breeds.

IV 'NAME 'EM, DON'T BULLSHIT ME'[42]

Of all usury's assaults on definition, the last and consummate is the erasure of the proper name. Identity dissolves into the slime. Pound despairs of anyone 'whom the ooze cannot blacken', for 'the stench of the profit motive has covered their names' (XCVI 662). No name is proof against the smear. Moreover, the law of libel forces Pound himself to collude in the destruction of the name, for all the Semites he would name sneak through *The Cantos* under pseudonyms. 'That ass Nataanovitch', for instance:

> Or some better known -ovitch
> whose name we must respect because of the
> law of libel (XXXV 172)

Pound attacks the law of libel in the *Guide to Kulchur*: 'The purpose of law is to eliminate crime not to incubate it and cause it to pullulate' (186). This law flouts Pound's first principle of poetry and economics: 'to call things by their right names – in the market' (XXXIV 168; cf.

SP 333). While the act of definition purges the economy, withdrawing names from circulation only helps to breed the crimes they name. Like interest, they pullulate in darkness.

Unnamed and unnaming, smearing names with their semitic ooze, the Jews defy the very principle of definition. They uncreate the universe that the Australian demigod Wanjina creates by naming it in Canto LXXIV :

> and Rouse found they spoke of Elias
> in telling the tales of Odysseus   ΟΥ ΤΙΣ
>   ΟΥ ΤΙΣ
> "I am noman, my name is noman"
> But Wanjina is, shall we say, Ouan Jin
> or the man with an education
> and whose mouth was removed by his father
>   because he made too many *things*
> whereby cluttered the bushman's baggage
> *vide* the expedition of Frobenius's pupils about 1938
>   to Auss'ralia
> Ouan Jin spoke and thereby created the named
>   thereby making clutter (LXXIV 426–7)

Wanjina named the world, and thereby brought it into being; but his father, like an incarnation of the law of libel, removed his mouth and his capacity to name. As if to sympathise with this unlucky onomast, the poem stammers on Odysseus, and his name declines into its alias, Elias. From Odysseus to ΟΥ ΤΙΣ to no man, the poet traces his own odyssey to anonymity; for Pound has donned Odysseus as his persona from the very outset of the text. W. D. Rouse figures here because he travelled the itinerary of *The Odyssey*, and discovered that the Greek islanders still told Odysseus's stories under the name of the Jewish prophet Elias.[43] By identifying with Odysseus, Pound implicates himself with Elias, and therefore with the race responsible for all 'historic black-out' (LXXXVIII 595). Better noman than Elias : better to be unnamed and unmanned than to be named after the prophet and the profit-motive. Yet the ooze, the smear betrays itself in every pseudonym, from Mauberley to noman, in which Pound tries to hide his name : Bastien von Helmholtz, Hermann Karl George Jesus Maria, John Hall, Walter Villerant, B. H. Dias, William Atheling, M. D. Adkins, T.J.V., J.L., B.L., Hiram James, Abel Saunders, A. Watson, Alfred Venison.[44] In his typescripts, Pound uses the £-sign to blot his errors out, thus turning his own signature into a roving cancellation. And indeed, it is in the act of self-erasure that he gives his name most unmistakably away.

He discloses it, for instance, in his reading of *Ulysses*, where he disapproves of Bloom's cloacal pleasures, hinting: 'I don't arsk you to erase . . .'[45] It is the arse that Pound would like to arsk Joyce to erase, but the arse invades the very letters of the word 'erase'. And we have seen, the arse provides the ooze that usury erases history with. Joyce spotted another word secreted in the letters of erase: in *Finnegans Wake*, he spells Ezra with an 's', making it an anagram of both 'erase' and 'arse' – and also hinting at a pun on usura.[46] Moreover, Joyce unites Odysseus with the wandering Jew in the character of Leopold Bloom, and Pound was well aware of this when he effaced his own name in the name of Homer's hero. In *Guide to Kulchur*, he acknowledges his 'nomadic' temperament, and adds that 'it is not for me to rebuke brother Semite for a similar disposition' (*GK* 243). By Pound's own logic, to be polyglot is to put oneself beyond race and against race, as embastardised as fraud or as a Jew. Yet *The Cantos* prolong his wanderings through space and time, and make him master of 'a hundred tongues', like Geryon, the queen of fraud, in Canto LI (251). What is more, the text itself falls foul of usury's between, and pullulates when it should circulate, unable to conclude or to cohere. It seems that there is more than a fraternal bond between the poet and the race – the non-race – that he abominates.[47] Could it be that Ezra the wanderer, Ezra the prophet, and, indeed, Ezra the Pound, is the Semitic incarnate? And if, as *The Cantos* say, 'there is / no end to the journey' (LXX 477), how could Ez defeat ooze, or Ezra erase usura?

In Pound's hell, the anus has displaced the mouth, and therefore writing has supplanted speech, for the letter is the ooze that issues from the baser orifice. It is to stop the spread of ooze that Wanjina, the creator, must be silenced. How his mouth could be removed is something of a mystery, since the mouth already hollows out a void: one might as well erase Esra. His father would have had to seal it shut, and semiticly obliterate its cleft, so that Wanjina gains the only face in hell that cannot smear. However, his broken name, Ouan Jin, transliterates a Chinese ideogram meaning 'man of letters', 'literary gent'. This pun suggests that Wanjina stands for the voicelessness of writing, which unfaces and unnames its own creator. Blank, mutilated, the 'man of letters' represents the work of Thanatos in language: the text's relentless drive to disfigure and obliterate itself.

In the first Canto, Tiresias foretells that Odysseus will lose all his companions. In the *Pisan Cantos*, this curse comes true:

but I will come out of this knowing no one
neither they me (LXXXII 526)

'This' may mean the cage at Pisa, where the Americans incarcerated Pound; but it may also mean the prison of the text itself, and the compulsion to erase erasure. Neither will they know me, Pound mourns – because his name itself has now become the blank in history.

V 'WE WHO HAVE PASSED OVER LETHE'

'The celestial and earthly process can be defined in single phrase: its actions and its creations have no duality. (The arrow hath not two points)', Pound declares.[48] The powers of darkness do not amount to the antithesis of light, for he denies erasure the *prestige* of a negation. He abhors the dialectic, because the Semitic is 'schizophrenic essentially', and the labour of the negative must therefore bear the stain of usury (*I* 140). Rather than a dialectic, history consists of a single principle of light, which darkness merely counterfeits without dissevering. But it is because Pound rejects duality that *The Cantos* sink under the darkness they are striving to obliterate. Usury and history ooze through the partitions that he draws between them. A rhetorical contagion infects time with space, rhythm with chords, line with colour, speech with writing, until it is impossible to purify the truths of history from their mockeries. For instance, the 'gold thread in the pattern' represents 'the sun's cord unspotted' – 'light tensile immaculata' – the filament of light which flickers faintly through the centuries of darkness (CXVI 797; LXXIV 429). But gold is the colour of usury as well; and the gold thread represents the vein of death that usury has woven through the tissue of the text, poisoning the images of time.

Pound urges a return to 'Sagetrieb, or the oral tradition' (LXXXIX 597), where the past regenerates itself perpetually.[49] He would sign his name in speech, in rhythm, on the air, rather than in any medium corrupted by the usury of writing. But his names are both compounded in all that *The Cantos* denounce. Pound himself is the infected currency; and Ezra is the other face of the same coin, the face that belches into hell. In the end, the blank of Ezra subsumes the blank of truth, for the text is truly created out of nothing – out of the ruins of the excremental pound.

NOTES

1 Ezra Pound, *Literary Essays*, ed. T. S. Eliot (London: Faber, 1954), p. 86: henceforth *LE*; Ezra Pound, *The Cantos* (New York: New Directions, 1975), Canto CXVI, p. 797. All references to *The Cantos* are to this edition, and will be designated in the text by the number of the Canto in Roman numerals followed by the page number.

2 The reference is to Dante's *Paradiso*, 8, 2. Because of his fascist broadcasts for Rome Radio, Pound was imprisoned in 1945 on a charge of treason at the U.S. Army Detention Training Centre (D.T.C.) near Pisa, where he drafted *The Pisan Cantos*. For about three weeks he was kept in a cage measuring six by six and a half feet.

3 *Ezra Pound Speaking: Radio Speeches of World War II*, ed. Leonard J. Doob (Westport, Connecticut and London: Greenwood, 1978), p. 339. Henceforth cited as *RS*.

4 Pound, *Guide to Kulchur* (London: Faber, 1938; rpr. London: Peter Owen, 1952),p. 60. Henceforth *GK*.

5 I owe this insight to Tom Furniss.

6 Pound, *Selected Prose, 1909–1965*, ed. William Cookson (London: Faber, 1973), p. 21. Henceforth *SP*.

7 *The Chinese Written Character as a Medium for Poetry*, ed. Ezra Pound (1936; rpr. San Francisco: City Lights, 1968), p. 11; *SP* 22–3; Pound, *ABC of Reading* (London: Routledge, 1934; rpr. London: Faber, 1951), p. 22.

8 Fenollosa, *Chinese Written Character*, p. 12.

9 Letter to Agresti, TS (5 July, 1951), Pound Archive, Beinecke Library, Yale.

10 'Heaven AND earth / nothing cd / be more idiotic than a religion which has put corsets on the holy mystery of fecundity. In fact Xtianity is one of the worst hoaxes.' Pound, letter to Agresti, TS (August, 1949), Pound Archive. See also Pound, *Impact: Essays on Ignorance and the Decline of American Civilization*, ed. Noel Stock (Chicago: Henry Regnery, 1960), p. 94. Henceforth *I*.

11 As in the 'Project for a Scientific Psychology', where Freud maps out a similar economy of power, it is impossible to abstract form from force, or trace from tracing. See Freud, 'Project for a Scientific Psychology', in *The Origins of Psychoanalysis* (New York: Basic Books, 1954), pp. 349–455; see also Jacques Derrida, 'Freud and the Scene of Writing', in *Writing and Difference*, trans. Alan Bass (London and Henley: Routledge, 1978), pp. 196–231.

12 See Pound, *Selected Letters*, ed. D. D. Paige (1950; rpr. New York: New Directions, 1971), p. 210. Henceforth *SL*.

13 Pound, *Antheil and the Treatise on Harmony* (Chicago: Pascal Covici, 1927; rpr. New York: Da Capo Press, 1968), p. 48. Henceforth *A*.

14 See Pound, *ABC of Reading*, p. 198.

15 Pound, *A Visiting Card*, Money Pamphlets by £, no. 4 (London: Peter Russell, 1952), p. 18; rpr. in *SP* 322.

16 See Donald Davie, *Ezra Pound: The Poet as Sculptor* (New York: Oxford, 1964), for discussions of Pound's 'quotation' of metres.

17 *The Cantos* treat all ages as if they were contemporaneous, and thus suggest that history is a kind of chord: but Pound would urge that human time unfolds 'in contrapunto' (LXXIV 431: see Pound, *The Spirit of Romance* (London: Dent, (1910)), p. vi.) In counterpoint, each melodic line remains intact, unstained by the harmonics of the other – even though they move in unison.

18 Introd. to *Sonnets and Ballate of Guido Cavalcanti* (London: Stephen Swift, 1912), p. 11.

19 Letter to Quinn, TS (13 July, 1916), in Quinn Collection, New York Public Library.

20 Letter to Zukofsky, TS (March? 1936), Pound Archive.

21 Letter to Boris de Rachewiltz, TS (31 May? 1954), Pound Archive.

22 Pound, *Gold and Work*, Money Pamphlets by £, no. 2 (London: Peter Russell, 1951), p. 12; rpr. in *SP* 346.

23 See *I* 91–2; and *The Douglas Manual*, ed. Philip Mairet (London: Stanley Nott, 1934), p. 13; *SP* 291; XCIX 706: 'You forget the timing of budgets / That is to say you probably don't even know that / Officials exist in time.'

24 See Pound, 'Cavalcanti: Medievalism' (1934) in *Make it New* (New Haven: Yale University Press, 1935), p. 351; *LE* 50. Cf. *SP* 313.

25 See Walter B. Michaels, 'Pound and Erigena', *Paideuma*, 1 (1972), 37–54.

26 Pound, *Social Credit*, p. 14.

27 See Pound, Postscript to Rémy de Gourmont, *The Natural Philosophy of Love* (London Casanova Society, 1926), pp. 179, 169, 174; rpr. in *Pavannes and Divagations* (Norfolk: New Directions, 1958), pp. 203–14.

28 See Pound, 'Hugh Selwyn Mauberley', Pt 1, III, line 6, in *Collected Shorter Poems* (London: Faber, 1968), p. 206. Henceforth *CSP*.

29 XLV 233; LXXIV 468; see also *SP* 290, 308, 338; and Christopher Hollis, *The Two Nations* (London: Routledge, 1935), Ch. 3.

30 XLV 230; Addendum for C 798.

31 Quoted from Alexander del Mar, *The Science of Money* (London: George Bell, 1885), p. 101, in Pound, letter to Maverick, 9 September, 1957, Pound Archive.

32 *'Ezra Pound Speaking': Radio Speeches of World War II*, ed. Leonard W. Doob (Westport, Connecticut and London: Greenwood, 1978), p. 176. Henceforth cited as *RS*. See also *SP* 347.

33 Frederick Soddy, *The Role of Money* (1934), in Montgomery Butchart, ed., *Money* (London: Stanley Nott, 1945), p. 268.

34 Silvio Gesell, *The Natural Economic Order*, trans. Philip Pye (1929; London: Peter Owen, 1958), p. 185; *Douglas Manual*, p. 34. See Del Mar, *The Science of Money*, p. 13; and Pound, *ABC of Economics* (London: Faber, 1933), p. 47; rpr. in *SP* 237. See also Earl Davis, *Vision Fugitive: Ezra Pound and Economics* (Lawrence, Kansas and London: University of Kansas Press, 1968), for discussions of Pound's economic sources.

35 Pound, *ABC of Economics*, p. 33.
36 Letter to Sister Bernetta Quinn, TS (1954), Pound Archive.
37 LXXVIII 481; CXII 784; IV 15; XIV 63; XV 64.
38 See XXIX 145: 'She is submarine, she is an octopus, she is / A biological process.' Here Pound is describing 'woman', but the images of femininity, usury, and excrement are implicated in his visions of economic chaos.
39 See Leon Surette, *A Light from Eleusis: A Study of Ezra Pound's Cantos* (Oxford: Clarendon, 1979).
40 Pound, letter to Sister Bernetta Quinn, TS (5 August, 1954), Pound Archive.
41 Letter to Boris de Rachewilz, TS (1 August, 1954, in Berg Collection, New York Public Library).
42 See LXXIV 430; LXXVII 473.
43 See Guy Davenport, 'Pound and Frobenius', in *Motive and Method in The Cantos of Ezra Pound*, ed. Lewis Leary (New York and London: Columbia University Press, 1961), pp. 49–52.
44 See Noel Stock, *The Life of Ezra Pound* (London: Routledge, 1970), pp. 44, 151, 163, 203, 209, 210, 212, 226, 229, 234–5, 246, 329, 330, 443.
45 *Pound/Joyce: The Letters of Ezra Pound to James Joyce, with Pound's Essays on Joyce*, ed. Forrest Read (London: Faber, 1966), p. 157.
46 James Joyce, *Finnegans Wake* (1939; rpr. New York: Viking, 1967), p. 116.
47 See my 'Floating the Pound: The Circulation of the Subject of *The Cantos*', *Oxford Literary Review*, no. 3 (1979), 26; see also Daniel Pearlman, 'Ezra Pound: America's Wandering Jew', *Paideuma*, 9 (1980), 461–81.
48 Pound, *Confucius: The Great Digest and the Unwobbling Pivot* (1952; London: Peter Owen, 1968), p. 183; *SP* 306.
49 Sagetrieb is a word coined by Pound, literally meaning 'say-drive', or as David Gordon argues, 'Pass on the tradition'. See also LXXXV 557 and Carroll Terrell, *A Companion to the Cantos of Ezra Pound*, Vol. II (Berkeley and London: University of California Press, 1984), p. 479.

The phonograph in Africa: international phonocentrism from Stanley to Sarnoff

WILLIAM PIETZ

I

I begin with an epigraph, a preface, and a question.

My epigraph is taken from an early draft of this article. It reads: Any schoolchild knows that on the map-flattened surface of the earth the continent of Africa looks like a great, heart-shaped elephant's ear, a territorial organ that silently listens and always remembers.

My preface is this: I would like to examine the case for a *non-deconstructive* post-structuralism for historiography particularly interested in the problem of modern history and capitalism. Specifically, I wish to consider the argument of Deleuze and Guattari in their two-volume work on *Capitalism and Schizophrenia*[1] that the social and linguistic order of capitalism is not an order of the signifier and that, therefore, the general deconstructionist critique of the phonocentrism of 'western' society is particularly inapplicable to modern, capitalist society. If it is true that a phonocentric subjectivity still holds an important place in societies dominated by capital, it is an essentially displaced phonocentrism, a phonocentrism reinscribed in the language machines proper to capitalism, such as the phonograph. The recording surface of the phonograph is not a recording surface inscribed with signifiers the way speech is inscribed in phonic writing and vice versa; rather it is inscribed with singular material points or lines which can be *decoded* but which do not *represent* what they record. The phonograph reproduces speech without itself speaking; its lines and bands are silent, without intention or subjectivity, and can support a micro-regime of phonocentrism without themselves participating in phonocentrism – rather the way large universities today can support humanities programs without having the questions and issues these departments generate disturb the technical training and research which is the real business of these institutions.

Hence a question: What happens when the non-signifying phonograph which reinscribes a regime of phonocentrism within itself is placed in the non-capitalist geography of Africa, that territorial ear that listens and records in a massive silence which is not at all the silence of the phonograph?

My interest in considering this specific issue, and with the question of 'post-structuralist history' in general, is twofold. First, it is a truism that historiography, at least since Ranke, has defined and legitimated itself among the human sciences in terms of its approach to the written document and the specificity of this object (the document, as opposed to the material artifact of the archaeologist, the participant observation of the ethnographer, and the empirically gathered data of the sociologist). Such post-structuralist approaches as Deleuze and Guattari's 'schizo-analysis' seem to me to add a new and useful dimension to the study of the historical document.[2] Second, there can be no doubt that twentieth-century historiography has been importantly shaped by structuralism : both the structuralist history resulting from the rise of economic and demographic social history, with its view of historical change in terms of the 'conjuncture' of the variable cycles of structured systems (annual harvest, business cycles, trends of all sorts); and by theories of the structure of historical experience as such (and hence of all history) based on a philosophical understanding of the essential historicity of the human condition. This latter refers not only to German hermeneutic philosophy and the sort of cultural history it generates; but it also refers to Sartrean and later Lacanian–Althusserian attempts to reintegrate biography and historiography by using such notions as the 'project' (which identify the act of signification necessary to make meaning possible with the originary temporalising act synthesising the threefold structure of human historicity necessary to make experience possible) to mediate between the psychoanalysis of individuals and their lived experience and desires, and Marxist analysis of objective history;[3] and finally it refers to Lévi-Strauss's structuralist view of history with its stress on history's essentially encoded nature as chronology.[4] The impact of these various 'structuralisms' of temporal conjunctures, codes, and conditions on social and cultural history has evoked, on the social scientific side of historiography, the *Annales* view of 'total history' as a hierarchy of multiple temporalities dominated by structures whose 'velocity' is that of the nearly changeless *longue durée*[5] (objective structures to which correspond the 'everyday life' and subjective *mentalité* of the 'common man') and, on the humanist side, a turn to narratology by historical theorists[6] where they locate the act of synthesising historical multiplicities into meaningful wholes, the essential meta-historical act of individuals who thereby define their own personal and ethical relation to the historical context in which they are situated (this applies equally to historical actors and to historians). The key question, then, for structuralist or 'post-structuralist' history has to do with understanding how the connections between the different types (or 'strata') of structures operating in history are made, and how such transversal connections influence the development and change of structures. Neither the principles of coincidence and conjuncture between multiplicities of objective structures nor those of meta-historical synthetic narratives grounded in the unchanging constitutions or aporia of the human condition appear adequate answers to the renewed question of *mediations* or *connections* between the structures of history.

One of the most suggestive responses to this question from those writers commonly called 'post-structuralist' – Barthes, Foucault, Derrida, etc. – is the notion of 'schizo-analysis' developed by a radical psychiatrist and political activist, Felix Guattari,[7] and a philosopher with a particular interest in the history of philosophy, Gilles Deleuze.[8] The argument I wish to make in considering the question of the phonograph in Africa – the question of the encounter between capitalist linguistics and a non-capitalistically encoded territory or culture – is that the schizo-analytic model is a useful one for studying the history of consciousness and its transformation within specific historical–social contexts. (It is, however, not useful insofar as it claims to provide a total historical or political analysis: for this one would need a post-structural *institutional* history, and this has not yet been developed.)

In *Anti-Oedipus*, Deleuze and Guattari criticise one of the most powerful notions regarding the history of consciousness developed by a post-structuralist thinker: Derrida's conception of phonocentrism. In chapter six of his 1967 work *Speech and Phenomena* Derrida, basing himself on Saussurian structuralist semiotics, criticised the Western philosophical tradition for grounding itself on an objective illusion made possible by the unique temporal structure of one particular signifying medium: the voice. 'What constitutes the originality of speech, what distinguishes it from every other element of signification, is that its substance seems to be purely temporal.'[9] Because of this peculiar transparency, the voice permits a fundamental blindness to the originary temporalising semiosis, which Derrida termed '*différance*' because it differentiated (and thereby established) a present from a past and a future just as a phoneme achieves a unitary status only through its difference from the other phonemes constituting the basic sounds of a given language. The voice permits both a specific experience of the self and a particular relation to the world. One's self can be experienced as being immediately present to oneself only through the act of 'hearing oneself speak', for speaking allows one the experience of objectifying oneself without seeming to pass from subjective interiority to the external world : 'the subject can hear or speak to himself and be affected by the signifier he produces, without passing through an external detour, the world, the sphere of what is not "his own" '.[10] This permits a peculiar logocentric ego which appears to possess itself autonomously within a pure, immediate present, an ego whose experience of self is based on the repression of difference and otherness. At the same time the pure self-effacement of spoken sound from its own status as an objective body or external existence toward its experience as pure meaning, pure ideality (the self-effacement of signifier into signified), permits an experience of worldly objects as pure intelligible and manipulable presence : 'the determination of being as presence constitute[s] the epoch of speech as *technical* mastery of objective being'.[11] Derrida, at least in his earlier work, seems to view this peculiar metaphysic of being as grounding Western culture since the Greeks up to today. Deleuze and Guattari would argue, on the contrary, that capitalism has fundamentally transformed the experience of being, of desire, of self, and of language.

This leads to one of three characteristics which, I believe, distinguish schizo-analysis from other post-structuralist approaches to history. Deleuze and Guattari criticise Derrida's general deconstructive theory of language and writing for failing to recognise the radical transformation of language within capitalism; the supposedly universal logic of the supplement, of *différance*, allows Derrida (in 'Plato's Pharmacy' and elsewhere in his early work) to place 'capital' in the line of phallogocentric Western metaphysical forms along with 'sun', 'the Good', 'the Father', 'the Signifier' and so on.[12] Deleuze and Guattari argue in *Anti-Oedipus* that the type of language proper to capitalism has nothing to do with signifiers, transcendental or otherwise, but rather with information flows and data processing in which it is not necessary to know what a message means in order to know what it indicates you should do :

> the capitalist use of language is different in nature; it is realized or becomes concrete within the field of immanence peculiar to capitalism itself, with the appearance of technical means of expression that correspond to the generalized decoding of flows . . . Language no longer

signifies something that must be believed, it indicates rather what is going to be done, something that the shrewd or the competent are able to decode, to half understand.[13]

'Writing', Deleuze and Guattari write, 'has never been capitalism's thing. Capitalism is profoundly illiterate.'[14] The language in capitalism is pragmatic and axiomatic rather than semiological and encoded. This results in a radical displacement of phonocentrism.

Schizo-analysis is also characterised by its criticism of semiology for being limited to the study of codes and code structures. Deleuze and Guattari argue that language and semiotic systems within capitalism are not concerned with signifying codes but with decoded flows: these are material flows able to reproduce at an instant the image or simulacrum of something without expressing its meaning or significance:

These figures do not derive from a signifier nor are they even signs as minimal elements of the signifier; they are nonsigns, or rather non-signifying signs, points-signs, having several dimensions, flows-breaks or schizzes that form images through coming together in a whole . . . Three million points per second transmitted by television, only a few of which are retained. Electric language does not go by way of the voice or writing; data processing does without them both.[15]

These are the sorts of language flows set in motion by capitalism, which is itself the conjunction of all flows at the specific point of conjunction between the monetary flow of abstract (decoded) exchange value and the deterritorialised flow of abstract labour.

This notion of flows as distinct from codes necessarily raises another problem completely outside the realm of semiology: what Deleuze and Guattari call 'territorialisation', that is, the initial encoding of material flows of all kinds, and the subsequent problem of deterritorialisation and decoding of material flows that is the essence of capitalism (which must then reterritorialise the flows in the form of abstract wealth), but which Deleuze and Guattari argue is also the essence of that purely intensive desire that refuses all reterritorialisation, which they call schizophrenia.

Finally, the three-level schizo-analytic model of (1) the primitive territorialisation of coded flows (which they call the inscription of the body of the earth), (2) the overcoding of territories by metalanguages (which they call the inscription on the body of the deposit), and (3) the deterritorialisation and decoding of flows by capitalism onto the body of money, is explicitly proposed as a theory of universal history. This theory of world history, which identifies as basic modes (1) segmentary, territorial savage societies (characterised as the regime of cruelty), (2) overcoding despotic states (the regime of terror), and (3) the decoding, deterritorialising capitalist state (the regime of cynicism), has the merit of refocusing political thinking in terms of a global theory of History as colonialism, subordinating the East–West axis to the North–South axis. It is perhaps in this emphasis on global colonialism, along with the insistence on theory rather than a series of discursive analytical apparatuses, that the micro-politics of Deleuze and Guattari can be distinguished from that of Foucault.

In short, the post-structuralist historical project of schizo-analysis can be distinguished from deconstruction, semiology, and knowledge–power discourse analysis, first, by its insistence on capitalism and the supersession of capitalism as the principal historical and theoretical problem, and, second, by its specific arguments concerning (1) the nature of language, (2) the question of territorialisation (what at one point they speak of as a 'geo-graphism'[16] – Deleuze insists that he and Guattari always speak as geographers), and (3) the theory of the global colonial situation of all micropolitics. This last argument is most evident in the first volume of *Capitalism and Schizophrenia* when the Oedipus of psychoanalysis is identified as a specific form of colonialism, 'our intimate colonial education'.[17]

II

'The Phonograph in Africa' is the title of a newspaper article that appeared in the *New York Times* in 1885. It reports that two travellers planned to cross Africa with the recently invented phonograph to collect specimens of Central African languages. The writer goes on to fancy a deeper desire beneath the scientific one of the travelling linguists:

> Not only would the native Kings have an unbounded respect for the proprietors of such a wonderful fetich, but they could be induced or entrapped into making remarks in the presence of the phonograph which could afterward be reproduced with excellent effect. For example, no African would venture to disobey the voice of his King ordering him to 'bring the white men food', and the fact that the voice issued from the phonograph instead of the King's own lips would add, if anything, additional force to the order. With the help of such an instrument Central African travel would be made as easy as travelling in civilized lands.[18]

Beyond the possibility of this micro-migratory exploitation enabled by the phonographic capture of the King's voice within the linear continental crossing of the linguists, the author imagines the use of the machine as an instrument of imperial domination through an ecclesiastical overcoding of the territorial political apparatus of the native Kings:

> The travellers could describe the phonograph as a new and improved portable god, and call upon the native Kings to obey it. A god capable of speaking, and even of carrying on a conversation, in the presence of swarms of hearers could be something entirely new in Central Africa, where the local gods are constructed of billets of wood, and are hopelessly dumb. There is not a central African who would dare refuse to obey the phonograph god.[19]

What is to be made of such a text as this? 1885 is the year the European scramble to colonise Africa began in earnest, the year Bismarck, sitting in Berlin and playing a purely European balance-of-power game, carved up a map of Africa into zones of European power. American papers at the time were full of reports of European power politics and colonial adventurism. But beyond this political context, the report of two scientists venturing into savage Africa with the latest in communications technology set off in the journalist a public fantasy (that is, a fantasy a writer could know the audience addressed would recognise and appreciate) of a very specific sort determined by the commonplace narrativity already invested in such objects as Africa, the phonograph, the fetish, the King's voice, and so on. The fantasy concerns the capture of the social power embodied in the ruler's voice in simple societies by modern men of science via their new communications machine. It is thus a fantasy of a new politics of language. Language is not viewed here as primarily an instrument for the communication of messages and meanings, but rather as an instrument of political power, power to command economic and social behaviour. As the text says, language here is important as a 'force' capable of controlling the behaviour of others and the circulation of goods, rather than as a signifying medium. The fantasy is that the 'proprietors' of the phonograph can capture that savage power of 'the voice of the King', thereby giving the travellers control over economic resources and social relations without themselves becoming resident barbarians. That is, it is a fantasy about the capacity of modern language technology to acquire the power of the 'fetish' of primitives and despots without the need to participate in the forms of subjectivity imagined to be proper to pre-civilised 'fetishism'. This is the wish fulfilled by the fantasy of the phonograph in Africa: the historical fact of the phonograph becomes the social fantasy (an aesthetic fact, if you like) of 'the phonograph god'. It is the fantasy of inscribing 'Africa' itself within 'the phonograph', a techno-colonial dream in which the true referent of 'Africa' for this *New York Times* article is, of course, America (an America still reinventing an image of itself after the shattering of the Civil War and the more recent influx of new immigrants : the 1880s and 1890s were precisely the years when the basic popular images were forged through which Americans still identify themselves as American, both to themselves and to others; anti-ethnic 'deterritorialising' images of modern machine technology (Henry Adams's dynamo) were central to this new cultural ideology).

'The Phonograph in Africa' is not the sort of text that usually receives either literary or historical attention. I would like to propose that a post-structuralist, and more specifically a schizo-analytic approach to historical texts such as this can help illuminate a plane of historical reality not otherwise open to theoretically-grounded analysis. This is the plane of social desire, of desire invested in the social field forming part of that schizophrenic delirium which Deleuze and Guattari claim 'is the general matrix of every unconscious social investment'.[20]

The most outrageous and accurate argument in their two-volume work on *Capitalism and Schizophrenia* characterises the relation between History and sexual desire in the following way :

> It is the function of the libido to invest the social field in unconscious forms, thereby hallucinating all history, reproducing in delirium entire civilizations, races, and continents, and intensely 'feeling' the becoming of the world.[21]

Their name for this intensive libidinal body that registers all History in the form of singular desires of varying degrees of intensity is 'the body without organs', a phrase taken from the delirious writing of Artaud. 'The body without organs' is both that surface where desire is inscribed in a purely quantitative way, and a slippery plateau where the structures and machines of desire slide around, couple, and connect as partial objects in novel molecular chains of desire ('desiring machines').

But if History is inscribed in desire, it is no less true that desire is inscribed on the surfaces of History. And it is the schizo-analytic project to study that social delirium which constitutes the investment of desire in History.

For civilised states north of the Sahara desert, 'Western' or 'Oriental' alike, the continent of Africa has always been a geography of excessive delirium. Prior to the European colonisation of the

Americas, Africa was the great source of gold, that infinitely desirable substance; and the inaccessibility to non-Africans of the forest-hidden gold mines held an immense fascination, as did the countless stories of the monstrous races of people who populated this strange land: races of people without heads, whose eyes and mouths were in their shoulders and breasts; peoples with the faces of dogs or with other animal organs or with permanently mutilated organs; races composed entirely of women, who reproduced by bathing in a sacred lake and bore only girl children – there even seemed to be grotesque exchanges between human organs and the land itself. The twelfth-century Arabic historian Al-Zuhri speaks of the people of Amima, 'the poorest of the Janawa', who:

> also have the magic stone, which is a stone shaped like a human being in whole or in part, as in the shape of a hand or a leg or heart; but stones of complete form are found [i.e. full bodies without organs]. Anyone who acquires a complete stone can bewitch with it kings and *amirs* and all mankind. It is too well known to need description.[22]

In the terminology of Deleuze and Guattari, Africa has throughout History been the geographical (or 'territorialised') delirium of a body without organs, an immense unorganised body over which organs wander and make novel connections with each other.

Another common social delirium invested in Africa – and it would be a mistake to call it merely a 'literary tradition' which happened also to become a millenium-long pseudo-historical belief – concerns the so-called 'silent trade' in African gold. We find accounts of the silent trade in Herodotus, in the earliest Arabic historians, and in the accounts of the first Europeans who voyaged to black Africa in the fifteenth century. It is in these latter texts that the African gold producers with whom non-Africans traded began to be described as members of those monstrous races which had always been known to populate the African continent. The silent trade was a procedure in which civilised merchants exchanged their goods for the gold of a secretive savage race of gold diggers without employing any spoken language whatsoever and indeed without even seeing the other. At a given site, the story goes, merchants would leave their bundles of goods in a clearing and go away; when they returned the next day a quantity of gold would be found lying beside each bundle of commodities. If the amount of gold was acceptable to the traders, they would take it, and presumably the unseen gold diggers would take the goods in exchange; if the amount of gold was insufficient the merchants would leave it and return the next day to see how much additional gold had been left. Eventually the bargaining succeeded in an act of exchange, or else the merchants or the gold diggers withdrew their offerings in fatigue or disgust, thereby ending the negotiation. As I stated, it would be wrong to dismiss this as merely a pseudo-historical literary tradition; it is, on the contrary, the expression of an authentic social delirium expressing the incapacity of language and established social codes to articulate or contain cross-cultural value judgements and transactions, and perhaps also expressing the mysterious capacity of gold to increase in amount from day to day in situations of commodity exchange. The essential *silence* of cross-cultural commodity exchange, which admittedly has its own pragmatic language of signs and contractual obligations (which for the seventeenth-century mind will begin to seem to be the natural code of human transaction, prior to society and linguistic conventions), clearly exists and functions (without *meaning*) outside the order of phonocentric writing and signification central to earlier states. In his article on the silent trade, P. F. de Moraes Farias claims that it was the Venetian trader Cadamosto, who sailed to black Africa in 1455 under Portuguese charter probably funded by venture capital from Lisbon or Genoa, and whose account was the authoritative text on black Africa for sixteenth-century Europe, who introduced 'the theme of the monstrosity or deformity of the black gold diggers' involved in the silent trade: they were most often characterised as dog-faced people, with the fangs and tails of dogs. P. F. de Moraes Farias notes that this version of the silent trade story emerged 'at the very time when the end of the Middle Ages seem to herald the dismissal of all monsters from European books and maps'.[23] Deterritorialised from the European map, they were reinscribed, not only in the psychogeography of Africa, but into a situation where goods were exchanged for quantities of the absolutely desirable and valuable inanimate substance, gold.

There also appears in Cadamosto's text the first example of another common type of narrative concerning exchanges between the anthropomorphic and the non-anthropomorphic, this time concerning European technological appliances. Cadamosto reports with amusement that the Africans assumed his ship must have eyes, since how else could it have navigated its way across the horizonless seas?[24] This is the beginning of a tradition in colonial texts and popular Western culture in which the primitiveness of the primitive was characterised as a propensity to anthropomorphise technical machines and inanimate nature. All sorts of colonial technology – sailing ships, guns, gunpowder, navigation and surveying instruments – were invested with a highly characteristic narrativity, so that in both literary and historical accounts they prove the crucial narrative elements distinguishing the sane, rational men of civilisation from terror-driven, fetish-worshipping, anthropomorphising savages. The investment of desire and narrativity in the new communications machines that began to appear in the late nineteenth century, such as is evident in 'The Phonograph in Africa' article, is thus in many ways a continuation of a centuries-old colonial discourse characterising the savage's experience of civilisation through an anthropomorphic apprehension of its technology.

Capitalist desire is essentially the desire for the liberation, control, and direction of flows of all sorts; it is the subversion of all concrete cultural and territorial codes. There is not only a linguistic desire specific to it, but equally a geographic desire which in this essay I identify with the proper name of 'Stanley'. Henry M. Stanley's *The Congo and the Founding of its Free State: A Story of Work and Exploration* appeared the same year as 'The Phonograph in Africa'. The book is essentially a celebration of that Congo – simultaneously, at least in conception, the private property of King Leopold II of Belgium and a completely unrestricted free trade zone for all capitalist powers – which Bismarck created formally by drawing European lines over a map of Africa in Berlin. In the following passage Stanley describes a steamship ascending the Congo passing the 'Fetish Rock':

> At 10.30 we were passing within a few hundred yards of the rock called Fetish (bewitched), a low and isolated hilly headland, topped with large masses of granite, cliffy in its river front, having in its outlines something of the appearance of a huge monumental stone . . .
>
> In the old sailing days, I am told by the pilot, few cared to approach the neighbourhood of the Fetish Rock. Whether from sheer bewitchment, or the eccentricities of the ever-boiling flood, tradition becomes piquant when reciting the odd adventures that have befallen the helpless ships; how they were suddenly sheered off their course and curvetted round and round with lazy see-saw motions of prow and stern, and were swung far off after the dance, with distracted sails and slack ropes and braces, while the pale sailors gazed upon one another blankly, and finally swore 'the d——l had done it'. I myself tell the pilot that I believe all this, 'for, my friend, it was a wicked time altogether, for then white men believed that to buy and sell their black brothers was a work sanctioned by God'.
>
> Steamers, however, pay no heed to the contemptible whirlpools, though they are noisy, and we proceed upward without a flaw in our course, having now deep water under our keels. Looking round for

wonders, we are shown a feature on the crest of a tall hill on the northern shore, said to be the Lightning Stone, by natives known as the Ma-Taddi Nazzi, and sometimes as Limbu Li Nzambi, the finger of God. It is merely the core of the mountain rock, revealed ages ago by the washing away of the soil from the smooth dome-like summit, and today it stands, not a poor resemblance to a lighthouse, or some monumental structure.[25]

The passage begins with an implicit distinction between primitive and civilised modes of linguistically apprehending landscape. On the one hand, a magical act of naming ('the rock called Fetish') which transforms the earth into a territorialised field of supernatural investment; on the other, precise quantitative temporal and spatial observation ('10.30', 'a few hundred yards') and objective description of an inanimate landscape ('a low and isolated hilly headland . . .') that is able to distinguish between physical reality and figurative appearance ('having in its outlines something of the appearance of . . .'). Indeed the ideological allegory of this anecdote concerns the way the scientifically enlightened capitalist mind also gains ironic mastery over figurative language and hence not only frees itself from superstition but can free the unenlightened from superstition by revaluing their narratives.

Stanley is being told a story by his African pilot of 'the old sailing days' when sail-driven ships on the river avoided the waters around the Fetish Rock 'Whether from sheer bewitchment, or the eccentricities of the ever-boiling flood'. This humorous rhetorical alternative explanation is a standard figure of colonial discourse; but in this long sentence the disruption of grammar becomes the very disruption of the ship's straight line of travel by the turbulence around the Fetish Rock. Indeed the expected grammatical referent of the initial clause containing the rhetorical alternatives is the subject of the sentence, 'tradition', which is precisely the alleged origin of the pilot's narrative of the 'odd adventures' around the Fetish Rock that befall, not the human agents, but their anthropomorphised vehicles ('helpless ships'). The helplessness of the human sailors consists of their inability to control their ship, to hold it in its straight course up river. The movement of the ship becomes random and repetitious, makes no progress at all, when it enters the 'neighbourhood' of the Fetish Rock's erratic flows. (Erratic flows, or erotic flows, if one considers this on the level of a male trying to navigate his 'ship' on a straight course up river past the turbulent waters of the clitoris and female sexuality – if there is an equivalent on the overcoded human body to the historical–geographical delirium of Africa as a body without organs, it is surely the clitoris.) The ship loses its power of movement, the men lose their capacity for purposive directional activity : after a cuttingly sharp deviation ('sheered off their course') into a rotating and repetitious movement in place ('curvetted round and round with lazy see-saw motions of prow and stern'), after this 'dance', the sailors find themselves displaced 'far off' their course. The little ship, still anthropomorphised, is dazed and deflated ('with distracted sails and slack ropes and braces'), and the loss of objective motive power of the ship determines the similar state in the subjectivity of the 'pale sailors'. Both ship-object and sailor-subjects are entranced and directionless. The sailors share a state of impotence and incomprehension, of the loss of all power of decision and action. Hence – and here is the alleged origin of superstitious explanations – they turn to verbal action and irrational religion : 'and finally swore "the d——l had done it" '. That superstition here is coded as primarily a linguistic fixation, the result of a displacement from reality to language, is indicated by Stanley in the sailors' superstitious fear of pronouncing the magically powerful name of the devil.

It is at this point that Stanley, white possessor of the new motive power of the steamship, intervenes in the black pilot's narrative and revalues the superstitious interpretation to serve an enlightened end. Stanley's declaration of belief is at once a lie and a higher truth; it is able to break through into a communal apostrophe ('my friend'), a verbal act restoring the lost communication and group purpose signified by the sailing-ship's sailors' blank gazes. Stanley, the man of technology and commerce, successfully negotiates the text of religious superstition (and what lies beneath it) and of history in the same gesture, revaluing the illusory causality of the devil into a justification for condemning the slavery created by an earlier phase of capitalism and for assuming the complete break between past and present commercial relations between white Europeans and black Africans. (What is presented as a historical break with the unenlightened European past actually referred to and legitimated the usurpation of contemporary Portuguese colonialism by Belgium and its backers through the creation of the Congo Free State.)

Having sailed through these dangerous discursive waters of figurative revaluation, Stanley is now the ironic master of the anthropomorphising power at the root of superstition : 'Steamers, however, pay no heed to the contemptible whirlpools, though they are noisy, and we proceed upward without a flaw in our course, having now deep water under our keels'. The lower parts of the ship are now safe from violent mutilation from sharp rocks and shallows below ('deep water under our keels'), and a perfectionist's ('without a flaw') linear purposeful movement is restored. Desire is the desire for a straight line of movement along a flow. Stanley and the pilot, safe in the steamer with its completely self-contained power of movement, can now take the aesthetic pleasure of tourists in the 'wonders' of the figured landscape, free from danger of falling into literalist superstition. Anthropomorphising naming and magical animistic causality are revealed as grounded in nothing more than 'resemblance'. The rock, which to superstitious primitives is 'the Lightning Stone' and 'the finger of God', is in fact merely 'the core of the mountain rock, revealed ages ago by the washing away of the soil from the smooth dome-like summit', which bears a 'resemblance' to 'a lighthouse, or some monumental structure'. The civilised figurative perception sees, not the transformation of landscape into the organs of a divine body, 'the finger of God', but into the semblance of a human artifice – 'a lighthouse' – constructed to ensure safe navigation on a linear course along a flow free from 'flaw' and 'turbulence'.

The steamer here, like the railroad, guns, surveying instruments, and other emblems of European technology, are endowed in Stanley's text with a narrativity which anchors the ideology of scientific enlightenment in the text as simple, material fact. Technical machines are presented as the best way of guaranteeing the safe opening and maintenance of 'flawless' (i.e., incapable of deviance) linear routes into an interior and its resources. This is of course congenial to that ideology of free trade and mercantilist capitalism championed by Stanley. Although written as well for a general popular audience, *The Congo and the Founding of its Free State* is specifically an appeal to English merchants to invest in the development of trade routes into the interior of Africa. The preface of the book is a simple argument for private capital investment in building African railroads: Stanley calculates the rate of exploitation per mile per population density along the coast, and, assuming an equal rate of exploitation for the interior, argues that steamers now render river banks no different than sea coasts. Moreover, the amount of investment to build those most desirable and reliably non-deviant of routes – railroads – would be minimal compared to the potential profits, Stanley argues. Such enterprises would also be a civilising mission, making the Dark Continent's 'roadless regions fatal to all good-doing' accessible to 'the humanities'.[26]

The interior is populated by two sorts of savages, those amenable to commerce, and those not. The problem is 'the road is rendered unsafe for the more amiable people in the interior by the turbulent and rapacious petty chiefs who dwell along the route'.[27] This problem of opening the dark African interior to science, prosperity and civilisation called forth two non-military policies: the use of steamers and ideally railroads to secure permanent, reliable routes for the flow of commodities from the interior to the coast, and the establishment through treaties of trade stations to produce the initial flow of resources from a point of origin in the interior.

The colonisation of Africa can thus be conceived on a schizoanalytic model, with the Dark Continent itself as a body without organs. The colonial policy of mercantile capital sought to cut partial objects (organ-machines) into the African body in the form of trade stations, steamers, railroads, and ports. A trade station is an organ machine established to cut into and channel a flow (of palm oil, of palm kernels, of ivory, of ground nuts, etc.). These flows would in turn be interrupted by metropolitan organ-machines: a soap factory cuts into a flow of palm oil, a margarine manufacturer cuts into a flow of palm kernels, etc. The establishment of a station-machine is thus an initial cathexis, an investment. The colonial–capitalist anxiety is to multiply and preserve the organ-machines and their flows. It is precisely in relation to this anxiety that the colonial delirium of superstitious fetish worshippers appears as a political reality. Fetishism was understood to manifest itself as the paranoid resistance of 'native Kings' to the establishment of Capital's organ-machines, and as the setting up of anti-production machines along the channels of commodity flows. An example recently studied by D. J. E. Maier[28] is that of the Dente Bosomfo, the priest of a rural shrine and oracle of 'the Fetish Dente' that was located in a cave above the Volta river to the east of Asante. From the 1870s to 1894 the fetish priest of the Dente shrine was the centre of the Bron Confederation, an alliance made possible by the traditional authority of the Dente fetish to sanction oaths. Installed along the Volta at the intersection of several trade and tax-gathering routes, the Dente Bosomfo drained off wealth through tolls, tribute, and fees for advice from the oracle. British and French officials wrote with dismay of 'this rogue of a fetish priest' and of Asante delegations travelling to the shrine 'to put themselves under the fetish'.[29]

III

That capitalist geographic desire which shaped social perception and political judgement in the late nineteenth century has a corresponding linguistic desire : a desire also for flows, for a monopolisation of the maximum number and density of all lines of linguistic flow. I am going beyond the historical period on which I have focused to find a proper name for this desire : 'David Sarnoff'. While the discursive and juridical forms proper to capitalist geographical desire were developed in the nineteenth century (very often developed and then generalised from cases concerning rights over riparian property and the potential utility of water flows),[30] the equivalent forms proper to capitalist linguistic desire were only forged in the second quarter of the twentieth century as laws for the new broadcasting communications technologies and ideologies such as cybernetics, information theory, systems theory, etc., were developed. It was Sarnoff, an exemplary capitalist, who grasped the true importance of the new communications technology as an immigrant boy in New York City in the first years of the twentieth century, when Marconi first introduced his wireless telegraphy. And it was General Sarnoff who, as chairman of RCA, invested huge amounts of capital in the research necessary to develop television, and who founded NBC, the first broadcast network. Sarnoff had envisaged television already in the early 1920s, and he is justly regarded as 'the father of television'. It was also Sarnoff who bought up the Victor phonograph company and made its logo RCA's : the little dog listening to 'His Master's Voice' emanating from a phonograph (essentially the same trope as that found in the 1885 'Phonograph in Africa' article). Finally, it was also Sarnoff who, as one of the pioneers of the cold war, invented the phrase 'Voice of America' and conceived the cold war project of addressing the entire 'undeveloped' world with a flood of technologically-mediated information and anti-communist ideology.

In this project, free market ideology is less important than the need to maximise flows of information colonising the linguistic channels of the globe. Indeed the phonograph and the other new machine communications technologies – especially the electronic broadcast technologies – discovered a vast new intentional space, as yet unterritorialised, which capitalism colonised with as much eagerness and anxiety as it colonised the geographical world (even the economically unimportant continent of Africa).

1877 prophecy: 'Terrors of the Telephone' *New York Daily Graphic* (from Eric Barrow, *Tube of Plenty: The Evolution of American Television*. New York: Oxford University Press, 1975).

While the institutionalised social forms appropriate to capitalist linguistic desire may have appeared only in the twentieth century, expressions of this desire can be found concurrent with the first public appearance of new communications technologies. There is a newspaper cartoon of 1877 which perfectly expresses the project of Sarnoff; entitled 'Terrors of the Telephone', it is a response to Alexander Graham Bell's display of the telephone at the Philadelphia Centennial Exposition the previous year. The cartoon depicts an overwrought, frock-coated orator shouting into the speaking tube of a crude telephone, whose countless tangled wires send his single voice to receivers installed among groups of listeners throughout the world; root-like lines carry the voice of the perspiring, wild-haired orator to London, Dublin, Berlin, San Francisco, Cairo, Hong Kong, Sydney, Lima – the Fiji Islands are prominent – and a host of other geographical names. Everywhere we see relaxed, seated groups of listeners smiling in gentle amusement or pleased approval, except for one tableau in an unnamed territory where a wild savage listens in terrified awe, while at the edge of the frame we see the fleeing feet of his equally terrified social group. The easy joke of the cartoon at the expense of the superstitious primitive who experiences religious terror at an anthropomorphically behaving technological apparatus (an inanimate object that speaks), is at odds with the truly disturbing figure at the centre of the picture. Clearly, after all, it was the tribal savage who alone 'got' the message.

What message? What is the orator saying? It doesn't matter. There is no real message except the all-consuming passion and labour to fill up all possible lines and routes within the new non-territorial space of technological communications. This new, non-geographical social space cannot be encoded in the sense of territorialisation, a fixed social meaning invested in some place or thing or relation. It can only be occupied as a channel or reservoir through its filling with an ongoing decoded flow. Meaning is irrelevant or even counter-productive when the goal is to fill up the body of communication with maximal information flows and data banks; signifiers and meaning systems could only impede the efficiency and performance of the production, channelling, and interruption of flows. And indeed, in the cartoon, the voice is only important as such a decoded flow able to fill up the body of communication. The flow of the telephonic orator's voice does indeed occupy the phonocentric attention of the members of civilised states and sedentary societies; only the pre-literate savages respond to the novel truth at work here.

Their response is perhaps the only possible one: to pursue a line of group flight which takes them altogether outside the frame of representation.

I have tried to demonstrate the usefulness of certain notions developed in Deleuze and Guattari's schizo-analysis for illuminating the history of capitalist society and for showing the connection between historically specific forms of desire and subjectivity, and historically specific concepts and principles that guided and legitimated the restructuring of social and institutional arrangements. This is the context of the question of post-structuralist history which faces the problem of understanding the historical relations between different historical structures. I have tried to argue for the importance of a text-oriented approach to the history of consciousness for studying the connections between forms of cultural experience of the self and desire and objective discursive and juridical forms.

But the historical method proposed by Deleuze and Guattari is also conceived by them as having a direct political significance. 'History', they write, 'is always written from a sedentary point of view, and in the name of a unitary State apparatus; or at least a possible one, even when written about nomads. What we lack is a nomadology, the opposite of a history.'[31] Such writing would not follow the 'segmentary' encoding lines which bring regions under laws and the State but rather the 'lines of flight' which seek to escape the segments:

> The segments stem from binary machines, which are necessarily very diverse. Binary machines of social classes, sexes (men/women), ages (child/adult), races (black/white), sectors (public/private), and subjectivizations (ours/not ours) . . . The segments imply power set-ups . . . Each power set-up is a code-territory complex . . . By discovering this segmentation and this heterogeneity of modern power, Foucault was able to break with the hollow abstractions of the State and of 'the law', and to rethink all the givens of political analysis. Not that the State apparatus has no meaning: it has a very particular function, insofar as it overcodes all segments, simultaneously both those it takes for itself at a particular moment and those it leaves outside itself. Or rather the State apparatus is a concrete arrangement that puts a society's overcoding machine into effect.[32]

The State is conceived as an 'overcoding machine' able to establish secondary coded territories whose stability saves capitalism from its own decoding, territorialising process. ('There is no universal capitalism, no capitalism in itself; capitalism is at the cross-roads of all kinds of formations.'[33]) Deleuze and Guattari, therefore, seek a writing and a politics which will undo the State, thereby allowing capitalism to supersede itself through its own dynamic into a new society of politically acephalic group arrangements of a post-capitalist 'nomadic' society: 'nomadic and rhizomatic writing, a writing that embraces a war machine and lines of flight, and abandons strata, segmentations, sedentarity, and the State'.[34] Like capitalism, nomadism is above all a process of deterritorialisation and decoding, but it is one which resists recuperation through the overcoding of the State.

As a practice of writing cultural criticism, it seems to me that Deleuze and Guattari's 'micro-politics of desire' is a real contribution; but they proposed it as a *politics*. Guattari writes:

> I do not think it absurd to base a revolutionary politics on semiotic and analytical exercises that have broken with the dominant semiology; in other words, on ways of using the spoken and written word, pictures, gestures, groups and so on, that would direct along very different lines the relationship between the flux of signs and all the deterritorialized fluxes. In point of fact, it is getting caught up in the net of interpretive semiologies that the masses fail to realize the true springs of their power – that is their real control over industrial, technological, scientific, economic and social semiotics – and become bogged down in the phantasies of the dominant reality, and in the modes of subjectivation and repression of desire imposed upon them by the bourgeoisie.[35]

Deleuze and Guattari seriously propose schizo-analysis and micro-politics, not as a mode of historical analysis and cultural criticism, but as the privileged mode of political analysis, as a program – I use the American spelling here for, if it is hard on our side of the Atlantic to see how Foucault's views differ significantly from traditional pluralism, it is doubly hard to distinguish a micro-politics of desire, if it is more than infantile leftism, from the newly revived libertarianism of the American right. Both would stress a historical meta-narrative of desire; if the difference is that libertarians would use a liberationist code of individual desires and property rights, while Deleuze and Guattari would use a liberationist code of group desires and rights to desire incommensurable with the bourgeois property code, then the schizo-analyst will have to return to the non-nomadic problem of constructing a code on the basis of which rights can be claimed.

NOTES

1 The first volume, *L'Anti-Oedipe* (Paris: Editions de Minuit), appeared in 1972 and has been translated into English as *Anti-*

Oedipus: Capitalism and Schizophrenia, tr. Robert Hurley, Mark Seem, and Helen R. Lane (New York: Random House, 1977). The second volume, *Mille Plateaux* (Paris: Editions de Minuit) appeared in 1980; the introduction, 'Rhizome', has been translated in Gilles Deleuze and Felix Guattari, *On the Line*, tr. John Johnston (New York: Semiotexte, 1983), pp. 1–65.

2 Although he would probably loathe the label 'post-structuralist', Carlo Ginzburg's approach to sixteenth-century inquisition documents in *The Cheese and the Worms: The Cosmos of a Sixteenth-Century Miller*, tr. John and Anne Tedeschi (New York: Penguin, 1982), is surely an examplary instance of such a novel approach to historical texts.

3 For instance, Sartre remarks: 'Man defines himself by his project. This material being perpetually goes beyond the condition which is made for him; he reveals and determines his situation by transcending it in order to objectify himself – by work, action, or gesture . . . Man is, for himself and for others, a signifying being, since one can never understand the slightest of his gestures without going beyond the pure present and explaining it by the future' (*Search for a Method*, tr. Hazel E. Barnes (New York: Random House, 1963), pp. 150, 152). This conception is obviously grounded in the connection between language and temporality for 'fundamental ontology' developed by Heidegger in his 1927 work *Sein und Zeit*.

4 In *The Savage Mind* (Chicago: University of Chicago Press, 1966), Lévi-Strauss writes: 'History does not therefore escape the common obligation of all knowledge, to employ a code to analyse its object, even (and especially) if a continuous reality is attributed to that object. The distinctive features of historical knowledge are due not to the absence of a code, which is illusory, but to its particular nature: the code consists in a chronology' (p. 258).

5 See not only Fernand Braudel's classic essay 'History and the Social Sciences: The *Longue Durée*' (tr. Sarah Matthews, *On History* (Chicago: University of Chicago Press, 1980), pp. 25–54) but also his more recent chapter on 'Divisions of Space and Time in Europe' in *The Perspective of the World* (French title, *Le Temps du Monde*: this is the third volume of his *Civilization and Capitalism, 15th–18th Century*), tr. Sian Reynolds (New York: Harper and Row, 1984), pp. 21–44.

6 See Hayden White, *Metahistory: The Historical Imagination in Nineteenth-Century Europe* (Baltimore: Johns Hopkins University Press, 1973) and Paul Ricoeur, *Time and Narrative*, tr. Kathleen McLaughlin and David Palmer (Chicago: University of Chicago Press, 1984).

7 Guattari began as a Lacanian analyst whose political engagements led him both into political activism and into radical approaches to psychiatry itself (at the famous La Borde psychiatric clinic). Some of his essays have been translated in Felix Guattari, *Molecular Revolution: Psychiatry and Politics*, tr. Rosemary Sheed (New York: Penguin, 1984).

8 After writing notable studies on Hume, Spinoza, Nietzsche, Bergson and other philosophers, Gilles Deleuze elaborated his own philosophical position in 1968 in *Différance et répétition* (see the revised second edition: Paris: Presses Universitaires de France, 1972). The same year (1968) his thinking on language and aesthetics (he had already written an influential book on Proust) appeared in *Logique du sens* (Paris: Editions de Minuit); he has since gone on to write books on the painter Francis Bacon and on cinema.
9 Jacques Derrida, *Speech and Phenomena*, tr. David B. Allison (Evanston: Northwestern University Press, 1973), p. 83.
10 *Speech and Phenomena*, p. 78.
11 Ibid., p. 74.
12 Jacques Derrida, *Dissemination*, tr. Barbara Johnson (Chicago: University of Chicago Press, 1981), p. 168.
13 *Anti-Oedipus*, p. 250.
14 Ibid., p. 240.
15 Ibid., p. 241.
16 Ibid., p. 188.
17 Ibid., p. 170.
18 'The Phonograph in Africa', *New York Times*, 19 January, 1885, p. 4.
19 'Phonograph', p. 4.
20 *Anti-Oedipus*, p. 277.
21 Ibid., p. 98.
22 N. Levtzion and J. F. P. Hopkins, *Corpus of early Arabic sources for West African History*, tr. J. F. P. Hopkins (Cambridge University Press, 1981), p. 100.
23 P. F. de Moraes Farias, 'Silent Trade: Myth and Historical Evidence', *History in Africa* I (1974), p. 13.
24 Alvise da Cadamosto, *The Voyages of Cadamosto*, tr. G. R. Crone (London: Hakluyt Society, 1967), p. 50 – where Cadamosto reports that the blacks 'were also struck with admiration by the construction of our ship, and by her equipment – mast, sails, rigging, and anchors. They were of the opinion that the port holes of the ship were really eyes.'
25 Henry M. Stanley, *The Congo and the Founding of its Free State: A Story of Work and Exploration* (London: Sampson Low, Marston, Searle, and Rivington, 1885), vol. I, p. 89–90.
26 *Congo*, p. 24.
27 Ibid., p. 30.
28 D. J. E. Maier, 'The Dente Orocale, the Bron Confederation, and Asante: Religion and the Politics of Secession', *Journal of African History*, 22 (1981), p. 229–43.
29 'The Dente Oracle', pp. 230 and 234. The Dente Bosomfo was executed by the Germans in 1894.
30 See, for an example from American legal history, the chapter on 'The Transformation of the Conception of Property' in Morton J. Horwitz, *The Transformation of American Law 1780–1860* (Cambridge, Mass.: Harvard University Press, 1977), pp. 31–62. While

property rights were reconceptualised from principles of natural use and prior appropriation to more utilitarian principles of reasonable, proportional use and valuable, maximal use in water cases, material flows of all sorts and the potential for vesting of property rights in them were reconceived according to the potential utility of these flows as inputs for productive organ-machines; hence property rights in flows such as the flow of sunlight which could not be so cut into came to be viewed as 'imaginary' and nugatory (see, for example, the 1838 New York City case of *Parker v. Foote*). Such judgements about real versus imaginary values of material objects and flows were of course being made by European colonisers in Africa at the same time.

31 'Rhizome', p. 53.

32 Gilles Deleuze, 'Politics' in *On the Line*, pp. 78–9.

33 'Rhizome', p. 45.

34 Ibid., p. 54.

35 'Towards a Micro-politics of Desire' in *Molecular Revolution*, p. 106.

Notes on the contributors
(as at 1987)

DEREK ATTRIDGE is Professor of English Studies at the University of Strathclyde. His publications include books on the history and theory of English metrics and essays on James Joyce and literary theory. He co-edited *Post-structuralist Joyce: Essays from the French* (1984), and his *Peculiar Language: Literature as Difference from the Renaissance to James Joyce* is forthcoming.

TONY BENNETT is Associate Professor in the School of Humanities at Griffith University. His interests lie mainly in contemporary literary and cultural theory, and his publications include *Formalism and Marxism* (1979) and, with Janet Woollacott, *Bond and Beyond: The Political Career of a Popular Hero* (1986). He has also co-edited several anthologies in the areas of cultural and media studies.

GEOFF BENNINGTON is Lecturer in French at the University of Sussex, and an editor of the *Oxford Literary Review*. He is the author of *Sententiousness and the Novel, Laying Down the Law in Eighteenth-Century French Fiction* (1986), and has translated work by Lyotard and Derrida.

MARK COUSINS is Senior Lecturer in Social Sciences at Thames Polytechnic. He is the author, with Athar Hussain, of *Michel Foucault* (1984).

JONATHAN CULLER is Professor of English at Cornell University, and Director of the Society for the Humanities there. He is the author of several books, including *Structuralist Poetics: Structuralism, Linguistics, and the Study of Literature* (1975); *Saussure* (1976); *The Pursuit of Signs: Semiotics, Literature, Deconstruction* (1981); *On Deconstruction: Theory and Criticism after Structuralism* (1982); and *Barthes* (1983).

MAUD ELLMANN is Lecturer in English at Southampton University. Her publications include essays on modern literature and literary theory. She will shortly be publishing a book on modernism entitled *The Poetics of Impersonality.*

RODOLPHE GASCHÉ is Professor of Comparative Literature at the State University of New York at Buffalo. His publications include *Die hybride Wissenschaft* (1973), *System und Metaphorik in der Philosophie von Georges Bataille* (1978), and *The Tain of the Mirror: Derrida and the Philosophy of Reflection* (1986). A new book, *Rethinking Relation: On Heidegger, Derrida, and de Man*, is nearing completion.

MARIAN HOBSON is a Fellow of Trinity College, Cambridge; she is a founder and editor of *Paragraph*, and the author of *The Object of Art: The Theory of Illusion in Eighteenth-Century France* (1982) and essays on Denis Diderot and French critical theory.

JEAN-FRANÇOIS LYOTARD is Professor of Philosophy at the University of Paris VIII-Vincennes at Saint-Denis, and the President of the Assemblée collégiale of the Collège international de philosophie. He is the author of numerous books, including *Discours, figure* (1971); *Economie libidinale* (1974); *Instructions païennes* (1977); *La Condition postmoderne: rapport sur le savoir* (1979); and *Le Différend* (1983).

MARY NYQUIST is a Fellow of New College at the University of Toronto, where she co-ordinates the Women's Studies Programme; she is cross-appointed to the Department of English and to the Literary Studies Programme. The author of articles on feminist theory, Wallace Stevens and Milton, she is currently co-editing *Re-Membering Milton: New Essays on the Texts and Traditions*, and has a book on Milton forthcoming.

WILLIAM PIETZ is currently Assistant Professor of History and Humanities at Pitzer College, Claremont, California. He has written on the history of the idea of fetishism and the impact of colonialism on European intellectual history.

GAYATRI CHAKRAVORTRY SPIVAK is Mellon Professor of English at the University of Pittsburgh. She has published widely in feminism, deconstruction, Marxist literary theory, and the critique of imperialism, as well as translating the work of Jacques Derrida. Her new book, *Master Discourse, Native Informant*, will be published by Columbia University Press.

Ann Wordsworth teaches at St Hugh's College, Oxford, and is an editor of the *Oxford Literary Review*. She has published in the areas of contemporary critical theory and nineteenth-century poetry.

Robert Young is Lecturer in English at Southampton University, and an editor of the *Oxford Literary Review*. His publications include *Untying the Text: A Post-Structuralist Reader* (1981) and *Sexual Difference* (1986). A new book on politics in contemporary literary theory will be published by Methuen in 1987.

Index